virgin film
GEORGE LUCAS

virgin film

GEORGE LUCAS

Jim Smith

For my Dad,
who caught me when I fell

First published in Great Britain in 2003
by Virgin Books Ltd
Thames Wharf Studios
Rainville Road
London
W6 9HA

Copyright © Jim Smith 2003

The right of Jim Smith to be identified as the Author of this Work has been asserted
by him in accordance with the Copyright, Designs and Patents Act, 1988.

A catalogue record for this book is available from the British Library.

ISBN 0 7535 0755 2

Typeset by TW Typesetting, Plymouth, Devon
Printed and bound in Great Britain by Mackays of Chatham PLC

Contents

Acknowledgements

Kirstie Addis (my editor, without whom), Neil Corry (at *Film Review*), Mark Clapham ('Sheer hell for two months'), James Clive Matthews ('So, anyway, John Wayne's niece . . .'), Melanie Davies, Jane Dunton ('Strategically placed rips'), Gary Gillat (at *Starburst*), Stephen Lavington (Read Through Ninja), Lawrence Miles ('Have they ever met you?'), Jonny (de Burgh) Miller, Sarah McAllister, Johnny Minkley ('Awesome'), Lance Parkin ('I am Curious [Ewok]'), Eddie Robson ('That's why I wasn't listening'), Jim Sangster ('You will believe'), Louisa Smith, Matt Symonds (for pouring scorn at exactly the right moments) and Harris Watson ('If you wanna talk auteur theory then . . .').

The staff at the BFI library and screening rooms, the British Library and the University of London Libraries and GOSH! comics.

Introduction

George Lucas is the most successful independent moviemaker who has ever lived. To the public at large he is primarily known for his *Star Wars* film series, and for having created the character of Indiana Jones.

The two most important words in that first sentence above are 'independent' and 'moviemaker'. In an environment where calculated studio product consciously and unconsciously apes Lucas every year it is often hard to remember that the man himself has spent a lifetime deliberately forswearing the Hollywood elite. Equally, in a world in which a vague misunderstanding of some form of auteur theory (say, Sarris's) quietly underpins most discussion of film, it's easy to use the fact Lucas has only directed five theatrical feature films as an excuse to overlook his creative contribution to American film; to dismiss him as a mere technician, a fund-supplier or – that hated, assumed to be non-creative role – a producer.

The retort to that must be that George Lucas isn't just a director, or a producer, or a writer/director/executive producer. He's an icon, a mogul, an economic and social force and – uniquely amongst living film directors – a one-man *brand*. Like or dislike his work (and few could honestly reject his technical accomplishments), it's hard to deny that it has had a huge impact – the nature and consequences of that impact are more open to discussion, and will be discussed further later.

He remains one of the greatest technical innovators the cinema has ever seen – a pioneer in, amongst many other things, sound systems, digital projection and the development of CGI. Many of his characters have – either accidentally or on purpose – sunk deep into the pop-cultural landscape of western civilisation. Some have gone further in their description of Lucas's cultural impact. Fellow filmmaker Kevin Smith – whose attitude to Lucas is not atypical of his generation – has been quoted more than once as saying, 'I don't care who you are . . . Luke fucking Skywalker . . . is one of our modern-day Greek myths'.

George Lucas is a great technician and a talented storyteller whose gift lies in making the remarkable nor merely accessible, not merely popular, but *enormously* popular. It is this very

1

populism that has often caused him to be overlooked by those who can't bring themselves to see complexity and import in anything successful; people who seem to have forgotten the idiosyncratic triumphs of his early career and overlook his defiantly independent status.

As noted above Lucas is more than simply a film director, and a book on him which restricted itself to his directorial work – even if one incorporated his substantial body of student films (made while attending the University of Southern California, now arguably the most famous film school in the world) – would be adopting a needlessly dogmatic approach to a career that has embraced so many more projects. This book therefore devotes full chapters to the Star Wars sequels *The Empire Strikes Back* (aka Episode V) and *Return of the Jedi* (aka Episode VI) which Lucas co-wrote and executive produced but of which he was not the credited director, the *Indiana Jones* films, and *Willow*. Also afforded coverage in the main part of the book are the sequel to Lucas's *American Graffiti*, *More American Graffiti* (BWL Norton, 1979), the two Ewok TV movies of the 1980s, 1994's *Radioland Murders* (directed by Mel Smith) and the 1990s *Young Indiana Jones* TV series over which Lucas kept tight creative control as executive producer (as well as co-writing and supervising the editing of many episodes). These are all productions which Lucas created and wrote the story outlines for; he also contributed significantly to them during the production process as, to use *Willow* director Ron Howard's phrase, 'a creative producer'.

A final section includes a list and brief discussion of films and television series that Lucas has been personally involved in, albeit on a smaller scale – usually as a producer, an adviser or an additional pair of eyes in the editing suite (those who know Lucas personally insist that it is ultimately film editing rather than producing, writing or directing that remains his first love in terms of filmmaking). These projects include Paul Schraeder's controversial *Mishima*, Haskell Wexler's anti-Reaganite *Latino* (1985) and The Rolling Stones' *Gimme Shelter* (1970), as well as the *Star Wars – Droids* cartoon series, Wilfred Huyuck's critically disastrous *Howard the Duck* adaptation and other ephemera.

The majority of these chapters begin with a list of relevant writing/acting/production credits for the film in question, with the remainder of the chapter broken down into categories. Not all of the categories will be used in every chapter – indeed the advantage of utilising this format is that it's elastic. Most of the headings (listed below) are self-explanatory.

Title of the Film (Year)

Distributor
Production Company
Screenplay by
Story by
Cinematography by
Production Designer
Producer(s)
Executive Producer
Music by
Edited by
Directed by

PRINCIPAL CAST: These cast listings aren't complete. They often don't include extras, background actors or (sometimes) minor characters. The clue is in the word 'principal'.

TAGLINE:

SUMMARY:

TRAILER:

SCREENPLAY:

CASTING:

PRODUCTION:

ALTERNATIVE VERSIONS: Lucas often produces alternative versions of his films; he has re-edited *Star Wars* on an almost annual basis since its original release. This process has sometimes had press and public attention drawn to it (such as during the twentieth anniversary re-release of *Star Wars*) while on other occasions it has slipped by unnoticed. Here I'll note some of the major variations in the released versions of his films.

CUT SCENES: Find out what didn't make it into the final cut.

QUOTES: For a man constantly accused of being unable to write dialogue (Harrison Ford is repeatedly quoted as having once told Lucas, 'You can write this shit, but you can't say it') Lucas has come up with more than a few iconic one-liners in his time. The truth is that sometimes Lucas's dialogue makes you shudder, but sometimes it makes you sing. This section is for noting down the best, worst and the most memorable of what the actors say.

MUSICAL NOTES: A great fan of silent cinema, Lucas sets much store by a musical score and the talents of John Williams in particular. This category is for discussion of the films' musical elements.

RECURRING CONCERNS: Recurring ideas, images and motifs are signs of a creator working from a personal philosophical, moral and intellectual palate. That said, they can also be indicators of a reluctance to deviate from old – or utilise new – subject matters and beliefs. This category is for looking at concepts that recur across Lucas's work, both frequently and infrequently. As the man himself once said, 'The underlying issues, the psychological motives are the same . . . in all my movies: personal responsibility and friendship, the importance of living a compassionate life as opposed to a . . . selfish life.'

VISUAL INTERESTS: Visual elements of Lucas's films which deserve explanation or exploration for filmmaking, textual or thematic purposes.

FORWARDS/BACKWARDS: Sequels, prequels, in-jokes. Lucas often returns to the world of a film more than once, and this category is particularly useful for noting how an earlier or later film alters perception of the one under discussion.

EXTERNAL REFERENCES: In-jokes, quotations, references to ideas and/or people outside the internal fiction of the particular film.

RELEASE: Details of the film's release, often including box office numbers and public reactions.

CRITICISM: Critical comments from multiple countries, both contemporary with the film's release and afterwards. This section will often also contain my own qualitative judgement on the film in question.

AWARDS: The awards that were proffered, and those that were received. The tale of how George Lucas has never won an Oscar for himself despite owning a company that has accepted more technical Academy Awards than any other.

AFTERLIFE: Lucas has more than once tested technology in a minor film before using it in a larger project. See which films have been his guinea pigs here.

TRIVIA: Those interesting, niggly facts that won't fit into any other category no matter how hard you try.

TITLE TATTLE: What's in a name? Many of Lucas's films have variant titles or interesting sources.

EXPERT WITNESS: Enlightening comments from crew or cast members intimately involved in the film.

LUCAS ON [THE TITLE OF THE FILM]: Some words from the man himself on the topic under discussion.

Notes on Nomenclature:
For ease of reference the first-shot, second-set *Star Wars* trilogy (Episodes IV–VI: *A New Hope, The Empire Strikes Back, Return of the Jedi*) will often be referred to as the Imperial trilogy, and the second-shot, first-set trilogy (Episodes I–III: *The Phantom Menace, Attack of the Clones*, the as yet untitled third instalment) as the Republic trilogy. These aren't terms used by Lucas or Lucasfilm, but are here to avoid confusion and/or discussion about what constitutes the 'first' *Star Wars* trilogy. Equally, the 1977 film is usually referred to as *Star Wars* in these pages rather than *A New Hope* (because that's what *everybody* calls it –

5

always have and always will) and the overall project is the *Star Wars* sequence or project or series.

Some pages have on-page footnotes giving details of the careers of Lucas's friends and contemporaries who are mentioned in passing. The notations for quotes are included at the end of the book, before the index.

Before USC

This is not a biography. Neither is it a tell-all about one of America's richest men. It's a career guide, a work of film criticism and a book about Lucas as a filmmaker, a charting of a career in film and the effects of those films on the world into which they were released. Nevertheless it's best to begin a progression through someone's life where they did, and the following brief personal information may prove useful when moving through the film-specific chapters ahead.

George Walton Lucas Junior was born in Modesto, California in May 1943. His family owned a stationery and office furniture store, and later moved into walnut farming. An unexceptional student at his local High School, his main interest as a teenager was automobiles. He cruised the streets of Modesto, refitted and rebuilt cars and worked in various technical capacities for race-car teams.

Just weeks before his high-school graduation George Jr survived a car crash that statistically he really shouldn't have done. The edition of local paper the *Modesto Bee* for the following week printed a photograph of a lump of twisted metal, unrecognisable as his car, above the incredulous caption 'George W Lucas Jr survived this crash'. For three days his life was in the balance; for three months afterwards he was in and out of hospital on a regular basis.

In countless interviews since then Lucas has made it clear that this near-death experience at such a young age caused him to reassess his life. Before his accident he liked to grease his hair, hang out with a crowd his father disapproved of and race his imported Fiat at high speeds on public roads. Afterwards he become more contemplative and less inclined to take risks. He enrolled at Modesto Junior College to study (amongst other things) social sciences, anthropology and comparative religion.

As a child Lucas admits to having been more influenced by television – available in the home with a minimum of effort – than the cinema, but once at college his interest in movies grew exponentially. Film became for him, by his own admission, 'an addiction', and his enthusiasm was all-embracing enough for him to seek out and attend screenings of films by underground filmmakers like Scott Bartlett, Bruce Connor and Jordan Berlson.

Encouraged by cameraman Haskell Wexler,[1] he decided to apply to the University of Southern California's Film School, to try to learn how to become a filmmaker himself. His father disapproved, but George Jr applied anyway. When he succeeded in his application George Sr was even more disapproving. He virtually banned his son from accepting his place, but George Jr went anyway. Industry legend has it that as George Jr left his father's house after an argument about his chosen career he coolly informed the elder Lucas that not only would he make a success of film school, he would be a millionaire at 30. Lucas arrived at USC in time for the Fall Semester of 1964, and made his first film as part of the college's '448 (animation)' course the next calendar (albeit the same academic) year, quickly establishing himself as one of his year's exceptional students; when his parents attended a screening of one of his shorts at the college they were surprised by the obvious respect their son inspired from staff and students alike.

In 1973, Lucas's second theatrical feature, *American Graffiti*, would net him personally $7 million. He was 29.

---

[1] Haskell Wexler, director of photography, winner of two Oscars and three further nominations. Films include *In the Heat of the Night* (Norman Jewison, 1967), *The Thomas Crown Affair* (Norman Jewison, 1968), *The Conversation* (Francis Ford Coppola, 1973), *Bound for Glory* (Hal Ashby, 1976), *Mulholland Falls* (Lee Tamahouri, 1996); director *Medium Cool* (1969); writer/director *Latino* (1985).

Look at Life (1965)

(1 minute)

a short film by George Lucas

SUMMARY: A rapid, black and white photomontage of images cut from *Life* magazine issues published in 1965. Rather than simply cutting from one image to another, the camera pans across images, and zooms onto aspects of them. Movement is suggested by cutting between very similar images shot from different angles, and the inclusion of blurred photographs. Images include scantily clad women, dead civilians, couples kissing, children, puppies and scenes of people fleeing. There are also portrait shots of former Vice President (1953–1961) Richard Nixon, President Lyndon Baines Johnson, Dr Martin Luther King, pictures of a missile and a shot of a small child dressed in a Ku Klux Klan uniform.

PRODUCTION: Shot on black and white 16mm, *Look at Life* was made using an Oxberry animation camera as a first-year examination assignment for the 448 (animation) course at the University of Southern California.

QUOTES:
Voice-over: 'Hate not the oppressor for hate comes before strife and love covers all sins.'

The film also contains many caption cards cut from the magazine. These range from the frivolous ('Help Stamp Out Runny Noses') to the contemplative ('Anyone for survival' – without a question mark) and the straightforwardly simple – 'Love'.

MUSICAL NOTES: Initially the film is accompanied by mournful, clanging guitar chords, which are rapidly replaced by rhythmic tribal noises.

CRITICISM: Speedy but never rushed, *Look at Life* picks through the recent events of the day both dynamically and with distance. Its juxtaposed images and sounds prefigure *THX-1138* (which Lucas called 'a cubist film') insofar as that juxtaposition is meant to create in a viewer a sense of the experience the filmmaker is representing beyond the simple sum of the picture and sound.

Look at Life is a compelling snapshot of how a moment in time appeared to an individual.

Herbie (1965)

(3 minutes)

These moments of reflection have been brought to you by Paul Golding & George Lucas.

SUMMARY: Three minutes of reflections of light off various pieces of a stationary car. Shot at night, on black and white 16mm. Special attention is paid to the spherical reflections that come off hubcaps; this is all set to jazz music by Herbie Hancock.

QUOTES:
Voice-over: 'What can I do for ya? Not like sittin at home I can tell ya.'

VISUAL INTERESTS: Lucas is – as a director – often drawn to compositions involving circles and curves. This is the earliest (and perhaps the most obvious) example of that.

Freiheit (1966)

(3 minutes)

A film by LUCAS

PRINCIPAL CAST: Randall Kleiser (*Boy*), Christopher Lewis (*Soldier*)

SUMMARY: A bespectacled young man is seen running away from the sounds of an artillery battle; as he attempts to cross a border – meant to represent that between East and West Germany – he is shot dead by an equally young-looking uniformed soldier. As he dies graphically on the floor, the soundtrack swells with voices intoning platitudes about the value of freedom and the need to make sacrifices in order to secure it. The effect seems intended to verge on the condemnatory and ironic.

CASTING: The young man is played by Randall Kleiser. Kleiser later became an noted filmmaker himself, directing box office smashes such as *Grease* (1978) and children's pictures like Disney's *Flight of the Navigator* (1985) and the Paul Reubens vehicle *Big Top Pee-wee* (1988). Kleiser was also a film student at USC, and he and Lucas shared a house during college.

In the role of the murderous soldier is Christopher Lewis, son of movie star Loretta Young and her producer husband Tom Lewis. The younger Lewis was a USC classmate of Lucas and Kleiser.

TITLE TATTLE: The title means 'freedom' in German.

1:42.08 to Qualify (1966)

(5 minutes)

Written and Directed by George Lucas
Camera: Emmett Alston, Bob Steadman
Second Unit: Paul Rayton, Gary Young
Sound: George Hubbard.
Editing: George Lucas, Mike Padilla, George Hubbard, Alan Gadney

PRINCIPAL CAST: Peter Brook (*Driver*)

SUMMARY: A yellow sports car, bearing the identifying number 3, is driven by a racing driver making multiple laps of a racing circuit. During one lap he nearly loses control of the vehicle.

PRODUCTION: Lucas's final undergraduate film, shot in colour by a crew of fourteen.

RECURRING CONCERNS: Cars, speed and racing are common occurrences in Lucas's later films. Asked at one point if he had always intended to be a filmmaker Lucas replied, 'As a boy [I] never thought about making movies – never in a million years. I wanted to be a racing driver.'

VISUAL INTERESTS: Hugely ambitious for a student film, *1:42.08 to Qualify* features shots taken using a camera mounted in Lucas's friend Edward Johnson's plane.

EXTERNAL REFERENCES: Lucas has admitted the influence of Jean-Claude Labrecque's documentary short *60 Cycles*, a visual record of the *Tour de St Laurent* made for the National Film Board of Canada. The film was shown at USC, and Lucas reportedly watched it repeatedly, even borrowing a print for private study.

TITLE TATTLE: Also referred to as *1:42.08: A Man and His Car*.

anyone lived in a pretty (how) town (1967)

(6 minutes)

Screenplay by Paul Golding & George Lucas, from the poem
by e e cummings
Photography: Rick Robertson
Unit Manager: Elvira Csondor
Music Score: Lynton B Eckhart
Editing: Paul Golding
Assistant Director: Bob Konikow
Directed by George Lucas

PRINCIPAL CAST: John Strawbridge (*Photographer*), Nancy Yates (*Girl with sewing machine*), Lance Larson (*Man*)

SUMMARY: A hat-wearing photographer working with an antique box camera moves around a small town reducing each individual he comes across to a static, sepia image by photographing them. As he takes their picture they disappear.

PRODUCTION: Having – like all young men of his age – been drafted to Vietnam, and decided to serve as a mobile unit cameraman, Lucas failed his standard medical for entry into the US armed forces. The army discovered that he had diabetes – something he himself was unaware of at the time – and rated him 4F, unfit for military service. Lucas found himself at a loss for what to do; it was too late to enrol back at USC as a postgraduate student for the 1966/67 academic year, but Lucas found that the college was sufficiently impressed with him and his abilities to offer him a staff position. He would teach a night-school refresher course for Navy and Marine corps cameramen who were, ironically, returning from exactly the kind of tour of duty he'd been turned away from. After a year in this job he returned to the University's student rolls as a postgraduate student, but continued to teach the course. His first assignment as a post-grad was also his first in Techniscope – a process whereby the full width but only half the height of the frame of 35mm film is used. Blown up to full size in developing, the technique gives a widescreen image, albeit a low-quality one with a visual grain of 16mm. The film is based upon the poem of the same name by e e cummings.

MUSICAL NOTES: The film, which has no dialogue, is accompanied at all times by what sounds like a tune played by a music box, overlaid with some woodwind noises to give an added 'organic' feel.

The Emperor (1967)

(24 minutes)

Written by George Lucas, Bob Hudson, Rick Robertson,
Paul Golding, John Milius, Gary Rockland
Director of Photography: Rick Robertson
Sound: Paul Golding
Editing: Paul Golding & Rick Robertson
Directed by George Lucas

PRINCIPAL CAST: Walter Murch, Bruce Green, John Milius, Ivan Kruglak, Gary Rockland, John Strawbridge (*Boys*), Randy Day, Leslie Godfrey, Camille Franck, Kathi Carmack (*Girls*)

SUMMARY: DJ Bob Hudson, a regular on the KBLA radio station which serves Hollywood suburb Burbank, has christened himself 'The Emperor'. He makes a triumphant tour of the streets in the back of a Rolls-Royce, continually watched by adoring fans.

PRODUCTION: Lucas initially wanted to make a documentary about Wolfman Jack, his favourite DJ, but Wolfman (real name

Robert Weston Smith) had so successfully managed his anonymity that this proved impossible (see **American Graffiti**). Lucas's film, shot in Techniscope, mixes newly shot footage with stock pieces of crowds and helicopter shots of cities. USC students Walter Murch[1] and Matthew Robbins,[2] on vacation in England, had apparently discovered an abandoned Rolls-Royce, which they then devoted considerable time and energy to renovating. It is this vehicle that Hudson travels in.

QUOTES:
'Get off the freeway, peasant! The Emperor is coming!'

RECURRING CONCERNS: The almost hypnotic power of middle-aged DJs over adolescent Americans forms part of *American Graffiti*. A middle-aged man proclaiming himself 'the Emperor' is integral to both *Star Wars* trilogies.

VISUAL INTERESTS: The credits for the film are shown at exactly the midpoint of the film rather than at the beginning or end, and include practically every student at USC – even those who didn't contribute directly to the film are credited as 'student advisers'. These credits are rolled over a close-up of an unkempt, slovenly Hudson looking anything but imperial.

TRIVIA: Marcia Griffin, Lucas's then girlfriend and later his wife, assisted him with the editing of this film. A supremely talented film editor, she cut (amongst other things) the original version of *Star Wars, Alice Doesn't Live Here Anymore* (Martin Scorsese, 1974) and *New York, New York* (Martin Scorsese, 1977) They had met whilst co-editing a documentary (see **Other Projects**).

---

[1] Walter Murch, USC, 'sound montages' and co-writer *THX-1138* (George Lucas, 1971), editor and 'sound montage & re-recording' *The Conversation* (Francis Ford Coppola, 1974), co-writer and director *Return to Oz* (1985), editor *The Godfather Part II* (Francis Ford Coppola, 1974), *The Godfather Part III* (Francis Ford Coppola, 1990) and *The English Patient* (Anthony Minghella, 1996), for which he won an Oscar.
[2] Matthew Robbins, USC, co-writer *The Sugarland Express* (Steven Spielberg, 1974), *Mimic* (Guillermo Del Toro, 1997); co-writer and director *Corvette Summer* (1978), *Dragonslayer* (1981) and *Batteries Not Included* (1987).

THX 1138 4EB (1967)

(15 minutes)

A film by George Lucas
Photography: FE 'Zip' Zimmerman
Sound: Daniel Tueth
Editing: Dan Natchsheim
Written and Directed by George Lucas

PRINCIPAL CAST: Dan Natchsheim (*1138*), Joy Carmichael (*7117*), David Munson (*2222*), Marvin Bennett (*0480*), Ralph Steel (*9021*)

SUMMARY: In a dystopian future a man identified as THX 1138 tries to escape a grey, uniform world, fleeing down a series of corridors. He is watched through surveillance systems by blank-faced individuals who are being watched in turn.

PRODUCTION: Inspired by Jean-Luc Godard's *Alphaville* (1965), a science-fiction film that used no special props and only contemporary locations to suggest a dystopian future world, Lucas set about making his final postgraduate film. Ably assisted by a crew composed of the Navy cameramen he had been teaching in his capacity as a postgraduate lecturer, he took twelve weeks to shoot a fifteen-minute film concerning THX, a citizen of a sinister labyrinthine society who goes on the run. Lucas was unable to acquire a proper camera dolly with which to shoot the film; for many scenes the cameraman sat on a trolley which was being pulled along by another member of the crew.

QUOTES:
Voice-over: 'This is authority. You will stop where you are.'

Voice-over: 'You are in violation of mercy act one five eight two six eight six six seven.'

MUSICAL NOTES: The music that opens the picture sounds very like the refrain from The Yardbirds' 'Still I'm So Sad'.

RELEASE: *THX 1138 4EB* was part of a package of USC films shown at the Fairfax Theatre, Hollywood, for an invited audience

Lucas and Coppola

Lucas and Coppola first met when Lucas, as an intern at Warners, began observing the production of the Coppola-directed *Finian's Rainbow*. Virtually the only two people on the lot under 50, they became friends and worked together on a number of occasions. When Coppola set up American Zoetrope studios the first time Lucas was named as his vice president, and assisted in the development of the company's slate of projects.

Like all longtime creative/personal relationships Lucas and Coppola's seems to have had its ups and downs, including a very public spat after the release of their joint project *Tucker: The Man and His Dream*. Nevertheless the two seem to have remained close. Coppola appears on *The Phantom Menace* DVD to discuss film editing with Lucas, and the two men appear together on the *American Graffiti* DVD to talk about the making of that film. A BBC Omnibus documentary from 1999 shows the two men talking amicably and at length at Skywalker ranch in that year. Lucas and Coppola have often inspired each other to do their best work (on *Graffiti* and *Apocalypse Now*, for example) and the possibility of their future collaboration on some project should be keenly anticipated by anyone with a genuine love for American film.

that included producer/director/special effects innovator George Pal – *The War of the Worlds* (1953), *Destination Moon* (1950), *The Time Machine* (1960) – and legendary German filmmaker Fritz Lang. Lang had directed many remarkable films in Germany, such as *Metropolis* (1926), *M* (1931) and *The Testament of Dr Mabuse* (1932) – all of which have a claim to being the best film ever made – before fleeing Nazi persecution in 1934. A less notable Hollywood career followed. Lang was convinced that *THX* was by far the best film in the selection, and delighted in gently mocking anyone who thought otherwise during discussions after the screening.

AWARDS: *THX 1138 4EB* was exhibited at the Third International Student Film Festival in 1968, where it took first prize.

AFTERLIFE: In an effort to avoid confusion, this film was subtitled *Electronic Labyrinth* after the production of the feature-length version *THX-1138* in 1971.

6.18.67 (1967)

(10 minutes)

Written, photographed, edited and directed by George Lucas

PRODUCTION: Carl Foreman was a Hollywood screenwriter turned producer who had been blacklisted as a Communist during the McCarthyite witch hunts of the early 1950s. He had contributed to the screenplay of *High Noon* (Fred Zinneman, 1952) and had latterly produced *Born Free* (James Hill, 1966). In 1967 Foreman was working on *Mackenna's Gold*, a film for director J Lee Thompson (best known for *Cape Fear* [1961] and later to direct two of the *Planet of the Apes* sequels). The studio, Columbia – keen to attract a younger audience to the film – offered to fund a number of student documentaries about the making of the film. Two of the students were to come from USC. Although opinion differs on whether he was first, second or third choice for the assignment, Lucas got the job. Shot in Page, Arizona, the project was being supervised by the legendary title designer Saul Bass, with whom Lucas had already worked (see **Other Projects**). Each student was given a vehicle, equipment and a weekly spending allowance of $200, most of which – by all accounts – the frugally natured Lucas managed to save.

SUMMARY: Lucas's documentary eschews the normal process of 'making of' shorts. There are no interviews with participants in the production; instead the film consists of long shots of the production being made and footage of the landscape. This gives a distant, ethereal, almost patronising view of the production as something small and insignificant in an awesome landscape.

RELEASE: *6.18.67* was shown at the Third National Student Film Festival, where its exhibition received an 'Honourable Mention'.
   In April 1971 TV channel LA PBS 28 made and showed a documentary entitled 'George Lucas: Maker of Films', a one-hour documentary about the young director, which included the whole of both *THX 1138 4EB* and *6.18.67* as well as a lengthy interview.

TITLE TATTLE: The title is merely the date of the last day of shooting – 18 June 1967.

filmmaker (1968)

(64 minutes)

SUMMARY: A documentary about the making of Francis Ford Coppola's film *The Rain People*, which starred Robert Duvall, James Caan and Shirley Knight. The documentary covers the entire filmmaking process from early rehearsals with the actors to the actual shooting. Lucas follows the crew of the low-budget feature as they indulge in the kind of 'guerrilla filmmaking' favoured by what would become known as New Hollywood (when shooting low-budget films filmmakers of the Coppola generation liked to move fast, shooting on real locations – often without the permission of the relevant authorities – and doing as few takes as possible). The crew travel in domestic cars rather than the vans favoured by larger-scale productions. There is a feeling of genuine spontaneity to the filmmaking process Lucas depicts; at one point Coppola rewrites his own screenplay to take account of the production's discovery of a local carnival in one of the towns they visit.

As the title suggests Coppola himself is the focus, although Caan and Duvall are also fairly visible throughout. The picture offers a rare glimpse of Coppola *sans* beard. Although bearded at the opening of the film, halfway through his facial hair disappears, and a voice-over by Lucas explains that, in order to avoid incensing locals in towns they visited Coppola decreed that the entire cast and crew be clean-shaven and short-haired.

PRODUCTION: Lucas, armed with a 16mm camera and a Nagra tape recorder, suggested to Coppola that he could make a documentary film covering the picture's production. Charmed by the idea, Coppola used $12,000 of the feature's publicity budget to fund it.

QUOTES:
Coppola, shouting during a telephone conversation in which he foresees the death of Old Hollywood: 'The system will fall by its own weight. It can't fail to!'

THX-1138 (1971)

(86 minutes)

Warner Bros
An American Zoetrope Production
Lucas Film
Screenplay by George Lucas and Walter Murch
Story by George Lucas
Directors of Photography: Dave Myers and Albert Kihn
Art Director: Michael Haller
Producer: Lawrence Sturhahn
Executive Producer: Francis Ford Coppola
Music by Lalo Schifrin
Sound Montages: Walter Murch
Film Editor: George Lucas
Directed by George Lucas

PRINCIPAL CAST: Robert Duvall (*THX 1138*), Donald Pleasance (*SEN 5241*), Don Pedro (*Colley SRT*), Maggie McOmie (*LUH 3417*), Ian Wolfe (*PTO*), Marshall Efron (*TWA*), Sid Haig (*NCH*), John Pearce (*DWY*), Irene Forrest (*IMM*), Gary Alan Marsh (*CAM*), John Seaton (*OUE*), Eugene I Stillman (*JOT*), Raymond J Walsh (*TRG*), Mark Lawhead (*Shell Dweller in Prison*), Robert Feero (*Chrome Robot*), Johnny Weissmuller Jr (*Chrome Robot*), Claudette Bessing (*ELC*), Susan Baldwin (*Police Control Officer*), James Wheaton (*OMM*), Henry Jacobs (*Mark 8 Student*), Bill Love (*Mark 8 Instructor*), Doc Scortt (*Monk*), Gary Austin (*Man in Yellow*), Scott L Menges (*Child*), Toby L Stearns (*Child*), Paul K Haje (*Trial Prosecutor*), Ralph Chesse (*Trial Proctor*), Dion M Chesse (*Trial Defender*), Bruce Chesse (*Trial Pontifex*), Mello Alexandria (*Hologram Dancer*), Barbara J Artis (*Hologram Dancer*), Morris D Erby (*Hologram Newscaster*), Willie C Barnes (*Hologram Comedian*), Richard Quinnell (*Hologram Straight-Man*), Jean M Durand (*Listener*), Scott Beach (*Announcer*), Neva Beach (*Announcer*), Terrence McGovern (*Announcer*), Julie Payne (*Announcer*), James Cranna (*Announcer*), Ruth Silveira (*Announcer*), Bruce Mackey (*Announcer*), David Ogden Steers (*Announcer*), Bart Patton (*Announcer*)

TAGLINES: 'Visit the Future Where Love is the Ultimate Crime!'

'The Future is Here.'

'Visit the Future Where Escape is the Ultimate Crime!'

SUMMARY: In an anonymous grey city, where human identity is reduced to numbers and letters, and resistance kept in line with sedatives, a man known as THX 1138 inadvertently takes the wrong medication and begins to rebel. His crimes, which include having sex (with his roommate LUH 3417) and failing to take his medications, see him committed to an endless white void, where he is beaten regularly. Escaping in the company of another prisoner – ironically one THX reported to the authorities himself – THX crosses a white expanse where distances are incalculable, only to escape back into the city. Stealing a police car he outraces police motorcyclists, who are eventually called back from chasing him because their pursuit is judged by management to be too costly; then, after climbing up a long ladder, he emerges onto a rocky, desolate world where the sun is setting on vistas containing no signs of life except for a solitary bird.

TRAILER: There's no trailer (or at least no extant trailer) for the feature itself, but the film actually opens with a forty-five second trailer for 'Tragedy on Saturn', the second episode of *Buck Rogers* (1940). With its repeated protestations that Buck is an 'ordinary, normal human being' and its promises of 'turning the clock forward' for a look into 'the wonderful world of the future', the effect is, considering the film that follows, brutally ironic. One subtle aspect of this trailer that appears to have gone without comment is that the vocal track has been edited so that the voice-over talks of 'the twentieth century' rather than 'the twenty-fifth', as it does on the original print. Once this subtlety is discovered it renders the piece even more disconcerting, suggesting – as it does – that the feature that follows is a portrait of the present rather than a projection of the future (see **LUCAS ON THX-1138**).

SCREENPLAY: *THX-1138* is an expansion of Lucas's prize-winning 1967 short *THX 1138 4EB*. The idea of transforming the fifteen-minute filmic experiment into a full feature was first suggested to Lucas by – of all people – Carl Foreman (see **6.18.67**), who admired the short and felt that a full-length script would be of interest to his contacts at Columbia. Urged on by Francis Ford Coppola Lucas wrote a first-draft script for the full-length version. Upon reading it Coppola advised Lucas to hire a writer to redraft it, and to read the complete works of Shakespeare to improve his own sense of the dramatic. A writer was duly found, supposedly an experienced playwright with some small movie experience, but Lucas intensely disliked his draft and rejected it immediately. The writer's identity has never been officially disclosed.

Instead of hiring another writer Lucas decided to write it himself, collaborating with Walter Murch (see **The Emperor**) on another draft.

CASTING: The most experienced of the main players was Donald Pleasance, who had previously appeared as the luckless Syme in a British television production of Orwell's *Nineteen Eighty-Four* (Rudolph Cartier, 1954), a role that in plot function is roughly analogous to SEN's in *THX*. A far more versatile and subtle actor than his reputation would suggest, Pleasance was memorable (though not actually very good) as James Bond's nemesis Ernst Stavro Blofeld in the spectacular *You Only Live Twice* (Lewis Gilbert, 1967). He ended his career making bad horror films, including several of the *Halloween* series. For THX he claimed to have drawn on his experiences in a German prisoner-of-war camp during World War Two (Pleasance was a Lancaster bomber gunner shot down and listed as missing in action). 'One doesn't get over that sort of thing completely', he commented. 'Further confinement, even in the make-believe sense of a film, brought it all back to me.' Robert Duvall, portraying the film's eponymous lead, had yet to acquire the prominence and respect in Hollywood that he would later assume. He had appeared in Coppola's *The Rain People* (see **filmmaker**), during the production of which he met Lucas for the first time. He would later work for Coppola again on the first two *Godfather* films (for the first of which he was nominated for an Oscar) and *Apocalypse Now*. He appeared alongside Pleasance for a second time in *The Eagle Has Landed* (John Sturges, 1976). The late 90s saw him write, direct and star in *The Apostle*, a $5 million picture which – in the absence of support from a studio – he funded out of his personal wealth.

It was difficult for the production to hire enough extras who were willing to shave their heads for the duration of filming;

eventually someone hit on the idea of contacting Synanon and the Delancey Street Foundation, two drug rehabilitation clinics where attendees were expected to shave their heads to show their commitment to the programme. Many patients of the two clinics accepted Lucas's offer of working as paid extras to fill out the crowd scenes. They were paid $30 each for shaving their heads, over and above their normal extras fees. Check Dederich, the founder of Synanon, was philosophical about the offer; 'Nobody's hair is worth $30', he commented when asked.

PRODUCTION: *THX* quickly became used for Coppola's empire-building. It would be the first film in a ten-picture deal he offered Warner Bros: ten films, each costing under a million dollars, which they would pay for and his American Zoetrope company would supply. All he wanted initially was $300,000 to develop the screenplays, referred to collectively as the 'multipicpac'. Amongst the other titles on Coppola's list of ten were a script of his own (later made as *The Conversation)* and a Vietnam War film, *Apocalypse Now*, which had John Milius and George Lucas attached as writer and director respectively.

After protracted negotiations and a reading of Lucas and Murch's draft of *THX*, Warners offered to lend to (as opposed to invest *in*) Zoetrope $350,000 to make *THX*. Despite the fact that it was a far smaller deal than he'd hoped for, Coppola agreed. Lucas was to be paid $15,000 for writing and directing the picture. Although Coppola grandly announced location shooting in Japan for the picture (Lucas had suggested it was a good way to achieve a look alien to American audiences), it was never feasible within the budget. Instead Lucas shot much of the film in the tunnels of San Francisco's Bay Area Rapid Transit System – the city's new underground which was currently under construction. Other sequences were shot in Marin County Civic Center in San Rafael, a cold and impersonal building designed by Frank Lloyd Wright, and still more at the Lawrence Livermore Atomic Energy Authority building in San Francisco. Wary of costs, Lucas shot scenes with two cameras simultaneously in order to give himself maximum coverage from minimum takes. Both cameras were handheld, and had 1,000-metre telephoto lenses. Lucas was shooting in Techniscope, which was far from ideal (see **anyone lived in a pretty (how) town**), but it was the only system available on the budget. Once shooting was over, Lucas cut the film at home, House Mill in the valley, while Murch, sitting alongside him, cut the sound.

On the day of the first screening for Warners management (including Jerry Weintraub and Ted Ashley) Coppola and Lucas – shrewd enough to know in advance that the executives would hate it – arranged for Walter Murch, Caleb Deschanel[1] and Matthew Robbins to wait outside the theatre until the executives began to emerge, and then to rush into the projection room, state they were from the editing department of the studio and then steal the (only) workprint of the picture from the screening room, so that the studio would not be able to recut without Lucas's consent and involvement.

Despite this they were later unable to stop the studio's head of editing, Rudy Fehr, removing – on Ted Ashley's instructions – four minutes from a film he perceived as overlong. It is unknown what was lost and from where. This infuriated Lucas, who has since repeatedly described the process as being 'like watching someone cutting the fingers off of his child' although it was nothing compared to what he would experience on his next feature (see **American Graffiti**). Lucas felt he had been treated thoughtlessly – worse, arbitrarily – by Ashley, and refused to speak to him for over a decade (see **Raiders of the Lost Ark**).

ALTERNATIVE VERSIONS: Although never put into action it was the considered opinion of studio executives that the addition of 'some monsters' to the first reel of *THX* would strengthen the picture and increase its commercial impact. The monsters in question were the bearded dwarfs visible in later scenes. One studio man told Lucas to 'put the freaks up front' and the comment quickly became a derisory catchphrase used by the New Hollywood crowd to describe a corporate way of doing things.

CUT SCENES: The screenplay's shooting draft had sequences where LUH is beaten to death on television – a fate that befalls many who question the state. Lucas elected not to shoot these scenes at all, instead preferring to allow the character to disappear with the audience remaining as unaware of her fate as THX does

---

[1] Caleb Deschanel, USC, director of photography *More American Graffiti* (BWL Norton, 1979), *The Right Stuff* (Philip Kaufman, 1983), *The Natural* (Barry Levinson, 1984), the latter two of which he was Oscar-nominated for. Director of *The Escape Artist* (1982) and *Twin Peaks* (episodes 6, 15 and 19).

(all he, and the audience, ever discover is that her number has been re-assigned to an embryo growing in a tank, a clear indication that she somehow no longer exists).

QUOTES:

Voice-over: 'For more enjoyment and greater efficiency, consumption is being standardized. We're sorry.'

Voice-over: 'If you feel you are not properly sedated, call 348 844 immediately. Failure to do so may result in prosecution for criminal drug evasion.'

Television: 'Terrible, wonderful, terrible, wonderful.'

MUSICAL NOTES: The music playing during the end credits is the first movement from Johann Sebastian Bach's *St. Matthew Passion.*

RECURRING CONCERNS: Lucas the filmmaker's career-long obsession with visuals involving circular shapes is very visible here. There are frequent shots of bubbles, circular corridors, wheels, bald heads and medical tablets. Most of the corridors are long and curved and the furniture is uniformly rounded. All combine to reinforce the idea of a society that infantilises its citizens.

LUH's initial maternal response to THX's obvious distress (vomiting, unconsciousness, distraction) transfers into erotic attachment; the same process occurs across *The Phantom Menace* and *Attack of the Clones* with the relationship between Anakin Skywalker and Padmé Amidala.

Cars – for the first hour of the film they lurk menacingly in the background; they are the only things which move at speed and none of the characters observed has access to one. Moreover, no one is ever seen getting in or out of a car, thus reinforcing the distant, wonderful image of these machines. It is only when THX actually gets hold of an automobile that his liberation becomes even remotely possible. Cars are, as often in Lucas's work, a symbol/method of escape (see **Star Wars, American Graffiti** et al).

The nameless administration refuses to do something worthwhile (capture THX) because it has now cost more than it should; operations cease despite the amount of money already spent and the fact that THX is within their grasp. An effective, if none-too-subtle dig at the approaches to funding of major Hollywood studios.

VISUAL INTERESTS: The sterility of the setting produces some amazing moments; when LUH first tentatively puts THX's hand to her face the audience is suddenly aware of the fact that this is physical human contact, the first seen in the film. The imagined warmth of skin against skin compared to the coldness around them is somehow profoundly shocking. This is compounded by the almost pornographic urgency of THX and LUH's movements after this moment, something itself undercut and made painful by how long it takes the drugged would-be lovers to remember (or is it discover?) how to kiss another.

As in *Star Wars* the sun symbolises imminent freedom: it is the first thing THX sees as he emerges from underground; it is the last thing Luke Skywalker sees the day before he finally gains his wish to escape Tatooine for good. Equally in *American Graffiti* it is only after dawn that Curt truly knows that he has to leave his hometown.

Asked if his film was science fiction, Lucas responded that it was a 'documentary fantasy'. One of the things *THX* shares with all of Lucas's directorial features is its commitment to constructing a world which it then allows its audience a glimpse of. Unlike in the films of – for example – Coppola, the camera is not somehow a character in its own right, creating mood through its movements. Rather it is a lurking, anterior presence, artfully placed in the middle of the action. Things happen *around* it, not to it or with it. Lucas's unobtrusive directorial style combines with the distinct yet somehow incomplete settings, and the casual attitude of the characters to their peculiar surroundings, to suggest that these events, however outlandish, are really happening somewhere. That this is *normal*. Contrary to popular belief there is a typical Lucas shot: a large object in one of the corners of the foreground is our focus whilst details slide past deep in the picture in the other three quarters of the screen. Here it is employed to great effect during the walks through the white void, and more subtly when THX is in the confessional booth or watching the screen in his room.

THX is the first, and to date last, time that Lucas has married his interest in abstraction to a feature-length narrative; as a result it is – especially once THX acquires a car – disjointed in narrative terms. '*THX* was designed for the camera,' Lucas later said, explaining that, 'some of the dramatic was sacrificed in favour of the camera,' resulting in a rush of images and ideas that didn't quite seem to work as a story on first viewing. His next picture was to take a more traditional narrative approach, but in this case the film is not to be taken entirely literally – it has been described by its writer/director as 'a cubist film' in which the visuals, sounds and story elements were different, albeit simultaneous, views of the same issue which combine to make a point; the argument is only convincing if you feel the film makes a point that is worth making (see **LUCAS ON THX-1138**).

Near the very beginning of the film the police report to Control that they have found something they don't understand and destroyed it – cut to a shot of an insect. This is the perfect example, in microcosm, of the attitude of the society the film is presenting to all that it cannot comprehend.

EXTERNAL REFERENCES: At several points characters intone the question 'Are you now or have you ever been . . .?', the totemic enquiry of inappropriate delving into someone's life. Tellingly, in this context it stops after 'been . . .', rendering it an all-purpose general enquiry/invasion of privacy. It's used (with varying suffixes) in, amongst other things, Anthony Burgess's 1964 novel *A Clockwork Orange*, and Stanley Kubrick's 1974 film of the novel. It's a question asked of people who are about to be committed to British Prisons and is included in the Official Secrets Act and various declarations of allegiance worldwide. In an American context it is mostly associated with Senator Joseph McCarthy's virulently anti-Communist House UnAmerican Activities Committee (HUAC) hearings of the early 1950s – and Eric Bentley's play (1972) about the same for which the phrase is also the title.

RELEASE: *THX-1138* opened at Loew's State II, Hollywood on 11 March 1971, and was then expanded to other cinemas in the Loew's Cine Theaters chain. A week later *Variety* noted disappointedly that it was not doing well financially (it took in total, according to several reputable sources, around $5,000). Before long it was consigned to the bottom half of drive-in movie theatre double bills, and it only made a profit when Warner Bros sold the television rights as part of a larger package.

At the behest of Francois Truffaut the 1971 Cannes Film Festival contained a section entitled *Quinzaine de Realisateurs* (Fortnight of Directors). This was outside the festival's competition, and the pictures within it did not therefore have to comply with the usual Cannes stipulation that any picture screened could not yet have opened in its country of origin. *THX-1138* was chosen by the festival's organisers to be a part of this. The audience's reaction was so positive that an impromptu press conference was organised to allow the writer/director to discuss his work. Unfortunately, no one could find the young director, as he wasn't staying at any of the festival's usual hotels; for whilst Lucas and his wife Marcia *were* attending the festival, lack of funds had made them approach it in an unorthodox manner. They were backpacking, staying at campsites and visiting Formula One tracks between screenings. They didn't even have tickets for the festival and had had to sneak into the premiere screening of Lucas's own film.

CRITICISM: Reviews were generally favourable towards this abstract, sinister film, especially as it was the work of a new director. 'A psychedelic science fiction horror story' noted *Variety* approvingly, '. . . an Orwellian *Alice in Wonderland*' which was '. . . photographed superbly'. In the *New York Times* Roger Greenspun expressed 'many reservations' about the content but found his concerns outweighed by his 'admiration for a technical virtuosity [that] achieves exceptional emotional intensity'. A few days later one of the same paper's other reviewers also praised the picture, citing it as one of a number of recent films that gave him hope for the future of innovative American cinema, he called it 'Beautiful, guilt ridden [and] visually hypnotic . . . a stunning montage of light, colour and sound effects that create their own emotional impact'. Once the film was finally released in Britain *Sight and Sound* got in on the act, claiming Lucas's film had 'an intensity reminiscent of Beckett' and was '. . . stunningly impressive to look at', its sterile interiors being 'a bleached vacuum where the only colour is the flesh of face and hands'.

THX is bewitchingly shot and subtly edited, and Lucas's contention that it's a parable demonstrating a metaphorical view of then contemporary LA has to be given some consideration. It is also a distressing film to watch, painful and human exactly because of – not in spite of – the lack of emotions displayed by the protagonists.

TRIVIA: A novelisation of the film's screenplay was written by Ben Bova and released to coincide with the film's premiere. It bore the cover hype 'As chillingly prophetic as *1984*' but sold poorly. Reprinted with a new cover after the success of *Star Wars* it did rather better, thanks to the prominent placing of Lucas's name and other credits on the cover.

EXPERT WITNESS: 'We spent weeks underground, in tunnels around San Francisco and Oakland. That alone has quite an effect on you. Everyone in the picture had his or her head shaved and wore the same kind of white coverall, reducing everyone to a common denominator. The impact of all this was terrific. You felt like a cow in a herd and you could see where a kind of apathy would settle over everyone if they had to live like that.' Actor Robert Duvall (*THX-1138*).

LUCAS ON THX-1138: (Describing the film as a 'cubist' portrait of Los Angeles) '[the movie's protagonist] comes off drugs and discovers he's . . . living in a cage . . . with the door open . . . we are all living in cages and the doors are wide open and all we have to do is walk out.'

American Graffiti (1973)

(108 minutes)

A Lucasfilm/Coppola Co-Production
Written by George Lucas and Willard Huyck & Gloria Katz
Art Director: Dennis Clark
Visual Consultant: Haskell Wexler
Co-Produced by Gary Kurtz
Produced by Francis Ford Coppola
Sound Montage and Re-recording: Walter Murch
Film Editors: Verna Fields and Marcia Lucas
Directed by George Lucas

PRINCIPAL CAST: Richard Dreyfuss (*Curt Henderson*), Ronny Howard (*Steve Bolander*), Paul Le Mat (*John Milner*), Charlie Martin Smith (*Terry 'The Toad' Fields*), Cindy Williams (*Laurie Henderson*), Candy Clark (*Debbie Dunham*), Mackenzie Phillips (*Carol*), Wolfman Jack (*Disc Jockey*), Bo Hopkins (*Joe Young*),

Manuel Padilla Jr (*Carlos*), Beau Gentry (*Ants*), Harrison Ford (*Bob Falfa*), Jim Bohan (*Officer Holstein*), Jana Bellan (*Budda, Car Hop at Mel's Drive-in*), Deby Celiz (*Wendy*), Lynne Marie Stewart (*Bobbie Tucker*), Terry McGovern (*Mr Bill Wolfe*), Kathy Quinlan (*Peg, Girl at Dance*), Tim Crowley (*Eddie, Boy at Dance*), Scott Beach (*Mr Gordon*), John Brent (*Car Salesman*), Gordon Analla (*Bozo*), John Bracci (*Station Attendant*), Jody Carlson (*Girl in Studebaker*), Del Close (*Man at Bar [Guy]*), Charles Dorsett (*Man at Accident*), Stephen Knox (*Kid at Accident*), Joe Miksak (*Man at Liquor Store*), George Meyer (*Bum at Liquor Store*), James Cranna (*Liquor Store Thief*), Johnny Weissmuller Jr (*Badass #1*), William Niven (*Clerk at Liquor Store*), Al Nalbandian (*Hank Anderson*), Bob Pasaak (*Dale*), Chris Pray (*Al*), Susan Richardson (*Judy*), Fred Ross (*Ferber*), Jan Dunn (*Old Woman*), Charlie Murphy (*Old Man*), Ed Greenberg (*Kip Pullman*), Lisa Herman (*Girl in Dodge*), Irving Israel (*Mr Kroot*), Kay Ann Kemper (*Jane, Girl at Dance*), Caprice Schmidt (*Announcer at Dance*), Joe Spano (*Vic*), Debralee Scott (*Falfa's Girl*), Ron Vincent (*Jeff*), Donna Wehr (*Car Hop*), Cam Whitman (*Balloon Girl*), Jan Wilson (*Girl at Dance*), Suzanne Somers (*Blonde in T-Bird*)

TAGLINE: Where were you in '62?

SUMMARY: 1962 – a single night in the life of four young Americans: John Milner, the coolest kid on the block, the drag racer everyone wants to beat; Terry 'The Toad' Fields, the town joke; and Steve Bolander and Curt Henderson, two boys with ambition and college places, both of whom are meant to be leaving town the next day. Steve breaks up with his long-time girlfriend Laurie (Curt's sister), Toad finds love, and Curt, whilst following the girl of his dreams, accidentally falls in with local gang the Pharaohs. Milner finds himself saddled with having to look after a precocious twelve-year-old girl even as Bob Falfa, a cowboy in a white Chevy, challenges his supremacy on the roads. John races Falfa, and beats him, but knows that his nerve has somehow gone. Steve and Laurie make up and he promises to stay with her and not go to college; Curt, after a meeting with the mysterious, legendary DJ Wolfman Jack, realises that if he doesn't leave his hometown now he never will. He flies away to college the next morning, leaving his friends behind. As his plane rises the audience discovers the eventual fates of Curt and his buddies. Milner dies in a car crash in December 1964; Terry is reported missing in action in An Loc, Vietnam in 1965; Steve marries Laurie and never leaves Modesto; Curt dodges the Vietnam draft and becomes 'a writer living in Canada'.

TRAILER: Universal might not have liked the film (see **RELEASE**) but the trailer put together to promote it is far better than most of the era. It begins with a shot of a high-school yearbook which opens to reveal caricatures of all of the main players. The film's tagline is repeated over and over again by a man doing an impersonation of Wolfman Jack whilst voices ask questions – 'What's that?' 'It's a movie!' A montage of clips follows which give a good idea of the picture's style, thanks to the rock'n'roll backing it.

SCREENPLAY: Pushed by Francis Ford Coppola into writing and directing something more 'warm and fuzzy' than the cold, distressing *THX-1138*, Lucas turned to an idea he'd been considering for some time. He was growing increasingly aware that the world in which he had grown up, the 'innocent' 50s of the Eisenhower era, was long gone; and he was being drawn to the idea of a film which would portray a single, vital night in the life of a group of West Coast American teenagers during this bygone era. It would be semi-autobiographical, concentrating on cruising with automobiles – something he now understood to be 'a uniquely American mating ritual' – and portraying that vanished world with a mixture of honesty and mythmaking. He later told William Friedkin[1] it would be an American version of Fellini's *I Vitelloni* (1953) – a film he greatly admired, and one also concerned with bright young men trapped in the small town of their birth.

With an appreciation for the subtleties of his subject matter he chose to set the picture not at the height of the 50s, but rather at a point when much of the world outside Southern California had already begun to move on to something else entirely – 1962. For Lucas the film was about documenting the end of an era as well as his own experiences; he was to explore a point in American

---

[1] William Friedkin, director *The French Connection* (1971), *The Exorcist* (1973), *Sorcerer* (1977), *To Live and Die in LA* (1985), etc.

history that he felt represented 'the loss of innocence' as honestly as possible.

Writing the screenplay for *THX* had convinced Lucas that he never wanted to write another screenplay as long as he lived; in order to get the script written he therefore went to husband-and-wife writing team Willard Huyck and Gloria Katz. The Huycks had attended USC with him, and he knew them well. Moreover, Willard had grown up in the San Fernando Valley and intimately understood the cruising culture that Lucas wanted to portray.

The three writers worked together at first, discussing the characters, their world and the issues, and working through Lucas's notes and outline to create something more tangible that could be shown to a studio. Lucas then went off to find some funding for the picture, a quest which, after some effort, began to yield real results. The Lucases' trip to Cannes (see **THX-1138**) brought them into contact with David Picker, who had recently become head of United Artists. Picker had family connections going way back into old Hollywood and was – indeed is – a pivotal figure in the history of Eon's James Bond film series. Picker liked Lucas, liked *THX* and liked the idea for *Graffiti*. He advanced him $10,000 for a screenplay. A delighted Lucas called the Huycks only to discover that they were no longer available. They were working to a tight deadline on what would eventually become *Messiah of Evil* (Willard Huyck, 1974).

Casting around for someone else to write the script, he alighted on USC alumnus Richard Walter, who had become a successful screenwriter since college. Walter initially attempted to persuade producer Gary Kurtz to abandon the West Coast idea of the story, and to set the film in New York City. Kurtz demurred, and Walter went away and prepared a West Coast-set draft which he delivered to Lucas upon George's return from Europe. The script deviated heavily from Lucas's conception for the film and the director instantly knew that it wasn't right. It was drawn from Walter's experiences, not Lucas's outline. It was set in Modesto, but philosophically it really dealt with an East Coast urban adolescence, not a West Coast open-state one. Moreover, the tone, for Lucas, was simply wrong. Drag racing had become playing chicken; there was a sex scene; Steven and Laurie eloped at the end. Walter did a second draft which – whilst Lucas felt it was an improvement on the previous one – still wasn't what was required. Walter was paid off and Lucas sat down and wrote his own screenplay in three weeks. Writing to classic rock'n'roll records, he structured it so that each scene was evocative in tone or mood of a particular hit. Once the screenplay was finished he took it to United Artists. They hated it.

After nearly a year casting around for other opportunities for finance, Lucas eventually got some interest from Ned Tanen at Universal. Tanen was then in charge of Universal's Youth Division, a small subsection of the company which financed low-budget films made by young talent. The unit was in the process of closing down, written off as a short, unsuccessful experiment. Tanen liked the idea for *Graffiti* – he has grown up in California himself and had some understanding of the cruising culture it was trying to portray. He took it to the board, which approved the picture at a budget of $600,000. This was to include all the rights and permissions for the many classic rock'n'roll records that the screenplay specified would be used to underscore key moments. Universal's contract also gave them first refusal on two other Lucas-originated projects, one a murder mystery set in the golden age of wireless (see **Radioland Murders**) and the other an as-yet-untitled science fiction epic. Although they didn't know it at the time, *Graffiti* would become the last film made under the youth unit's auspices.

The Universal board felt very strongly that *American Graffiti* needed a name to sell it. The question was how to attach a bankable name to a film about teenagers. Thirty years later teen actors capable of opening a movie would number around a dozen, but in 1972 the notion was ridiculous. It was suggested to Lucas that the name needn't be that of an actor, a respected filmmaker who could nominally act as a producer would do just as well. Coppola, who had just finished shooting *The Godfather*, and who had won an Oscar for his screenplay for *Patton* (Franklin Schaffner, 1969), would be an acceptable name. Coppola duly signed on as producer, and got a $25,000 fee and 25% of the studio's share of the box office (the same percentage as Lucas himself and $5,000 more than the writer/director's flat fee of $20,000) for his trouble. Kurtz accepted a demotion (in title if not in fact) to co-producer. With Coppola now involved Lucas was able to extract a further $150,000 from Universal, but in order to do so he would have to concede several rights granted to him under the original contract. Foremost amongst these was his right to final cut of the movie, a concession he would later regret.

With the movie on the verge of being made Lucas felt he had time to address what he felt were the deficiencies of his own screenplay and so he returned to the Huycks, who knew the characters, and asked them to do a quick pre-production rewrite. In particular he asked them to pay attention to the Steve and Laurie story. This was based far less on his own experiences than the other plot strands and he had had the most difficulty making it work. The Huycks, now available, were happy to return to the project, and it was their rewrite that Lucas's small crew began shooting in the last week of June 1972.

CASTING: Fred Roos – who had worked on *The Godfather* for Coppola – was hired as the film's casting director. He held 'open auditions' or 'cattle calls' in order to acquire much of the picture's young cast. He saw thousands of teenagers, many of whom had no previous acting experience, and whittled these numbers down to the mere hundreds that Lucas would interview himself. The interviews took place in an office they'd acquired on the Universal lot and lasted on average less than five minutes.

Those who'd passed the interviews were asked back to do readings and screen tests (shot on video), and those who made it through that stage were asked back again to do further auditions shot by Haskell Wexler on 16mm film. In these tests the young actors were put together in groups and told to improvise around concepts for scenes. Lucas, Coppola and Roos put complementary contenders in together – they were casting the groups, not the individuals – and then went away and studied the footage.

Richard Dreyfuss was someone Roos had seen and admired, someone he felt deserved a major role in a motion picture and whom he'd frequently brought in to casting calls for directors because he was absolutely convinced of the young man's 'enormous talent'. Dreyfuss had had one line in *The Graduate* (Mike Nichols, 1967) and had worked in the theatre, but his upward career trajectory was interrupted by two years of military service during which – having pleaded conscientious objections – he worked in a US military hospital. Having passed all the requisite tests (a process he's since described as 'readings, readings, more readings'), Dreyfuss was delighted to be offered the choice of two roles: Steve or Curt. He immediately accepted Curt, feeling it to be by far the more interesting role.

Cast as Steve was Ronny (later Ron) Howard, who had been a TV child star as Little Opie in *The Andy Griffith Show* and was by 1972 – at the ripe old age of eighteen – featuring in *The Smith Family*. Roos had worked for Andy Griffith and knew and liked Howard. It was felt that his TV work precluded him being thought of for movie roles, and Ross resolved to change that.

Boxer Paul Le Mat met Lucas early on, and remembers being asked if – as a boxer – he really could act. Le Mat replied in the affirmative, somewhat puzzled. Lucas was impressed with the longhaired, moustached Le Mat, who he felt understood the character of John Milner intuitively; he knew without being told that a cool guy carried a packet of cigarettes twisted into the sleeve of his T-shirt, for example.

Weeks later Le Mat was hitchhiking through LA and was picked up by a car driven by a man he vaguely recognised. Willard Huyck reintroduced himself to the actor and asked excitedly if he'd been contacted by Lucas yet. Le Mat said no, but knew instantly that the part was his.

Already a working actor, Charlie (later Charles) Martin Smith was spotted by Lucas on the Universal lot, and asked to audition for the role the writer/director felt was perhaps the hardest of the four main principals to play, that of Terry 'The Toad' Fields.

Harrison Ford had been an actor in small films and television but was, by 1972, working as a carpenter. He'd done some household work for Roos, who felt that Ford was ideal for the movie's Bob Falfa. Roos asked him to put the carpentry on hold to play the character, and Ford agreed despite the fact that he would make less money per week on *Graffiti* than he was doing woodwork.

The female leads went through the same process as the male. Cindy Williams auditioned with Ron Howard, and their initial screen test – immaculate except for the scripts clasped by their sides – still exists. Asked to play Laurie on the strength of this, Williams was reluctant, feeling it to be the least interesting of the female characters for an actress. She was persuaded to accept after Coppola called her and convinced her that the movie was going to be a huge popular success.

Candy Clark was a model suggested to Roos by old friend Jack Nicholson, and MacKenzie Philips, twelve years old during casting, was spotted fronting a high-school band at the Troubador. The daughter of 'Poppa' John Philips from *The Mommas and the Poppas*, she had no acting ambitions of any kind, and despite screen-testing with the other actors she had forgotten all about Lucasfilm's approach when she got the call telling her she'd been cast.

Kathy (later Kathleen) Quinlan, cast in the relatively minor role of Peg, was found by Roos whilst he was looking for extras; one high school known for supplying good young background actors was Mount Temple Pilots in Red County, California, and Quinlan came with a strong recommendation from her former drama teacher. She would later feature in *Airport 77* (Jerry Jameson, 1977) and garner an Academy Award nomination for the Ron Howard-directed *Apollo 13* (1997).

Robert Weston Smith (known professionally as Wolfman Jack) had been Lucas's favourite DJ growing up, and for a while had successfully managed his anonymity to such an extent that no one knew his real name, age or ethnic background (in *American Graffiti* Carol complains that her mother won't let her listen to the Wolfman's show 'because he's a negro' – just one of the subtle criticisms Lucas's film throws at its setting) and wild reports and urban myths circulated about where he broadcast from and how (again, in the film Carol believes he's based in a plane which never lands). By 1972 this was no longer the case, but enough mystery still surrounded Smith for him to be announced purely as 'Wolfman Jack' on the film's opening and closing credits. Aside from his in-camera cameo Wolfman would also record a few new dialogue tracks to be dropped into the film to represent his show. These were specific things required by the script (such as the dedication from Curt to the girl in the white Thunderbird), and for the most part Lucas and Murch used recordings of genuine Wolfman shows from the 60s in the film.

PRODUCTION: Lucas had asked his friend (and by then Academy Award winner for *Who's Afraid of Virginia Woolf?*) Haskell Wexler to be his director of photography, but – despite a personal liking for Lucas – he'd refused. Now directing and writing his own scripts, he didn't want to be someone else's cameraman; he did however agree to help shoot the cast's screen tests (see **CASTING**). Later problems would lead to Wexler becoming involved in the film anyway (see **VISUAL INTERESTS**).

As with *THX* Lucas shot the film with two cameras simultaneously, an Arriflex and an Éclair, in order to give himself more coverage and thus more flexibility in the editing suite. He was also shooting in 35mm Techniscope, as he had for *anyone lived in a pretty (how) town*. The downside of the technique was that it reduced the picture quality, giving the film the appearance of 16mm rather than 35mm. In this instance it was a sacrifice Lucas was prepared to make. The grainy effect would add a documentary realism suitable for the film.

The first working day of night shooting (9 p.m. to 5 a.m.) was undertaken in San Rafael, the next town along from Lucas's hometown of Modesto, and problems presented themselves almost immediately. The mounts required to fit the cameras to the sides of cars for the travelling shots proved more difficult to handle than anticipated, and half a day's shooting was lost immediately. On the afternoon of the next day Lucas was called and told that his licence to shoot in San Rafael had been revoked because of complaints from residents, an action that could have finished his movie – and his career – then and there. Gary Kurtz bargained with the town authorities, asking for a few more days whilst they found somewhere else. In the meantime Lucas drove to the nearby town of Petaluma and begged to be allowed to shoot there instead. Town officials agreed.

The entire cast and crew were required to be on location for the whole 27-day shoot, which led to those actors who were not working a particular night – but who were nevertheless required to be available and therefore to sleep days – indulging in a series of legendary parties.

One evening, horseplay led to Richard Dreyfuss being thrown into the hotel's swimming pool, where he cut his head on the bottom. Despite the best efforts of Cindy Williams – using her own foundation as the film had no make-up budget – his black eye is visible in close-ups in a few scenes (for example when Joe asks Curt to join the Pharaohs).

The film was shot more or less in sequence; Lucas gambled that if his overworked cast looked worn-out in later scenes, it could be excused on the artistic grounds that their characters had been up all night. Lucas shot most scenes several times regardless of time constraints, and many of the cast and crew got the feeling that he was waiting for something to go wrong with each set-up, for the element of the random that would add to the documentary naturalism he was looking for. Thus the take when Terry nearly crashes his Vespa (a result not of forward planning, but of Charlie Martin Smith's inexperience with scooters) was the one he used. Equally, another take where Smith nearly failed to catch a bottle thrown at him was judged far more suitable than the many where he'd caught it perfectly, and various takes of actors mumbling lines were preferred to those in which they'd rattled through the shooting with stage-like precision.

The one location outside Petaluma they used was the round diner, Mel's, that was to become one of the film's most enduring visual symbols. This was in downtown San Francisco, and the built-up area around it restricted the camera angles available to Lucas and Wexler; if they'd shot facing away from the diner it would have been painfully obvious that this was an urban environment the actors were in (see **ALTERNATIVE VERSIONS**).

At the wrap party Lucas showed the exhausted cast and crew a montage of scenes from the picture. Over the applause at the end industry legend has it that Harrison Ford could be heard shouting 'This is a fucking hit!' at the top of his voice.

Despite Ford's enthusiasm, the production's troubles were far from over – Universal assigned Verna Fields[1] to the production as editor, despite Lucas's insistence that his wife Marcia cut it. In the end the three of them worked together cutting it at Coppola's Mill Valley facilities. It had been a hard shoot, but the most difficult period of the film's gestation was still to come (see **RELEASE**).

ALTERNATIVE VERSIONS: Before release the studio removed two and a half minutes from the picture. These were: Steve shouting at one of his former teachers; Bob Falfa (Harrison Ford) singing the Richard Rodgers and Oscar Hammerstein II song 'Some Enchanted Evening' and a surreal moment where Terry is accosted by a salesman whose patter is so intense and quick-fire that Terry can't explain that he's only pulled up to check the damage to his vehicle and doesn't want either to buy or sell a car. Lucas distrusted Universal's motivation for the trimming, believing the alterations to be completely arbitrary and the entire affair a deliberate, entirely cynical display of their power over

---

[1] Verna Fields, editor *Targets* (Peter Bogdanovich, 1967), *What's Up Doc?* (Peter Bogdanovich, 1972) and *Jaws* (Steven Spielberg, 1975), for which she won an Oscar.

him. After the film became a success – and before the 1978 rerelease – Lucas reinserted the deleted sequences. His preferred cut is the version available on DVD.

The DVD version also contains one digital addition: in the original theatrical release, during the first scene in front of Mel's Drive-In buildings are visible behind the restaurant. On the DVD edition an empty sky at dusk has been added into the shot in place of the buildings. The original shot is featured for comparison in 'The Making of American Graffiti', a documentary featured on the same DVD release.

The 1978 rerelease was remixed for Dolby Stereo, a system unavailable when the picture was originally mixed; given the complex sound design achieved by Murch the remix is entirely to the film's benefit.

It has been suggested that the theatrical release listed the date of John Milner's death as June (not December) 1964, and that the 1978 rerelease was altered to say December in deference to the structure of the movie's sequel (see **More American Graffiti**). However this is not the case. A glance at the shooting script shows that Milner's death was always intended to occur in December 1964.

CUT SCENES: Early on in planning Lucas wanted to open the film with a shot of the Suzanne Somers character (the nameless 'Blonde in T-Bird') driving through a deserted drive-in cinema. She would be transparent, indicating what the finished film already hints at: that the dream girl Curt is chasing is phantasmagoric, an idea rather than a real person (this scripted element is hinted at in the finished film by the way every person Curt meets on his quest has a different explanation of who she is, and by Curt's sudden vision of the white Thunderbird leaving town right at the very end). The scene was never shot.

QUOTES:
Steve: 'You just can't stay seventeen forever.'

Curt: 'I'm looking for this girl . . .'
Wolfman: 'Aren't we all?'

John: 'I don't like that surfer shit. Rock'n'roll's been going downhill ever since Buddy Holly died.'

Driver: 'Hey Toad! Is that you in that beautiful car? Jeez, what a waste of machine!'

Curt: 'She wants me! Someone roaming the streets actually wants *me*!'

Wolfman: The Wolfman is *everywhere.*'

Carol: 'You know what? Your car's uglier than I am.'

MUSICAL NOTES: Lucas originally wanted to use some Elvis Presley tracks but his management refused to negotiate with Lucasfilm. The Sonny Til & the Orioles version of 'Crying in the Chapel' was substituted instead, and other songs found to fill the void caused by the absence of the King of Rock'n'Roll. Lucas had more luck with the Beach Boys. Dennis Wilson had appeared in a film which Gary Kurtz produced and Kurtz's familiarity with him led to Dennis agreeing a bargain-basement usage fee of $2,000 per song. This set a precedent for other artistes. The two Beach Boys tracks used are 'Surfin Safari' (which Milner dismisses as 'shit') and 'All Summer Long', used extremely effectively over the closing credits.

Others among the 40 original, period recordings used prominently in *Graffiti* include 'Runaway' (Del Shannon), 'Green Onions' (Booker T and the MGs), 'Rock Around the Clock' (Bill Haley and the Comets), 'Sixteen Candles' (The Crests), 'Why Do Fools Fall in Love' (Frankie Lymon), 'The Great Pretender', 'Smoke Gets in Your Eyes' and 'Only You' (The Platters), 'Ain't That a Shame' (Fats Domino), 'Do You Wanna Dance' (Bobby Freeman), Buddy Holly's 'Maybe Baby' and 'That'll Be the Day' and Chuck Berry's 'Johnnie B Goode'. The most difficult track to acquire the rights to was the Big Bopper's 'Chantilly Lace': Bopper was dead, killed in the same air tragedy that robbed the world of Buddy Holly, and no one was sure who owned the copyright in his recordings. Lucas eventually tracked down Bopper's mother in retirement in Tennessee and asked her for permission, which she granted.

In order to try and create sufficient atmosphere – and to avoid the source records used sounding too 'clean' – Lucas and Walter Murch devoted a great deal of time and effort to playing their selected records 'live' in concrete buildings and airy surroundings, and then recording the results on reel-to-reel tapes. It is these 'tainted' copies that were then mixed into the finished film's sound. One of the most interesting uses of this technique comes when Steve and Laurie dance to The Platters' recording of 'Smoke Gets in Your Eyes'. Initially the sound of the track has been re-recorded to cover it in the echoey noises you'd expect to hear when a record is playing in a large room, but as Steve and Laurie dance and the scene become more intimate the sound gets smaller and smaller, losing its distortions until it's indistinguishable from the record as released.

The music track in *Graffiti* is virtually omnipresent, a result not simply of the writing process (see **SCREENPLAY**) but of Lucas's keenness to suggest the colossal importance that old time rock'n'roll had to his generation of teenagers. Murch realized when mixing the sound that whereas on a normal picture one would use sound to create the atmosphere and music to emphasise particular moments of the drama, on *Graffiti* the reverse was true. The music was there to create the ambience, and in the few music-free sequences (such as where Terry and Debbie are drunkenly, irrationally convinced that they are being stalked by a serial killer, or as Curt attaches a cable to the back of a police car at the insistence of Joe's Pharaoh Gang) he was mixing levels of effects together in order to increase and underscore the dramatic. As innovative and technically fascinating as the picture's visual style, Murch's sound work is a key element in the picture's success.

RECURRING CONCERNS: *Graffiti* is the Lucas theatrical feature which most clearly showcases his interests in cars and speed. 'The car is the most important symbol in the film', noted *Film Reader* a year or so after its release. Here, as in *THX*, cars are a means of establishing an individual's identity; the way someone expresses themselves. Thus Milner's car is unusual, impressive and fast-moving but appears to be (despite its exotic look and modifications) within the law; Steve's is solid, dependable and straightforward (though desirable to some) and Falfa's promises more than it delivers, being in the end all show. Terry is reduced to riding a Vespa scooter and it is only when Steve lends him his car that Terry acquires the ability to pick up girls – almost as if Steve has somehow passed on some arcane knowledge along with the keys to the ignition (you could make the keys some sort of lazy sub-Freudian symbol of Terry's new potency as well, although the film very wisely doesn't bother).

Interestingly though, whereas in *THX* the car is a symbol of escape – it is only after acquiring one that THX has even the slightest chance of getting out of the undercity – in *Graffiti* the very opposite applies; cars are what keep them in California. Steve abandons his plan to leave and reclaims his car from Terry, and it is confirmed in the epilogue that Steve never leaves Modesto, whereas Terry, left car-less, escapes the town within three years (see **More American Graffiti**). Curt, the only one of the boys without his own car, is the only one to escape Modesto within the film itself and Milner – the one most obsessed with cars – is not only still stuck in their home town even though he's older than the others, but there is the implicit suggestion that it is his obsession with cars eventually costs him his life.

It is also worth noting that in Lucas's next two directorial features both Luke and later Anakin Skywalker can only escape their mundane home lives when they've respectively sold and abandoned their car-type vehicles respectively. This altered symbolism seems to mark a shift in Lucas's thinking, from the adolescent mind-frame visible in *THX* and his student films to the more contemplative, thoughtful persona glimpsed in his later features. Simply, desperately believing a car to be the most important thing in the world is something only teenagers and the permanently adolescent do.

VISUAL INTERESTS: Lucas had always planned to shoot the picture with very low light levels, utilising mostly street lamps and real in-camera sources of lighting to expose the film. He hoped it would give the finished movie a look which combined a realistic night-time environment with isolated, gaudy, glowing lights which would make it look, in his oft-repeated phrase, 'like a jukebox'.

This was always going to be technically difficult, and a short way into production he realised that in many shots the depth of field was simply too shallow, resulting in footage which would – when blown up – appear too murky on cinema screens. Lucas called Haskell Wexler, who was directing commercials in Hollywood, and begged him to come and help. Between them Lucas, Coppola and Wexler worked out a system whereby they could retain the film's look whilst increasing the light available to the camera. Wexler placed car lights on the back seats of the vehicles, which meant that the interior of each car was much brighter than it might otherwise have been. The trick was that because the light was sourced in the vehicle itself it seemed a natural part of the environment, and provided a strong contrast between the exterior darkness and the vehicle's interior. Local store owners were persuaded to let crew members into their shops, or to turn on all their lights before closing for the evening, giving in-camera and naturalistic sources of light for many shots.

1,000 and 2,000-watt bulbs were placed on top of Petaluma's actual streetlamps, achieving again the required light for exposure without sacrificing the picture's 'glowing' aesthetic.

One scene shot beside a lake was especially tricky and had to be accomplished near dusk across several days – shot at a time when there was enough ambient light reflecting off the lake to expose the film whilst retaining a night-time look to the finished footage.

Aside from the actors it thrust into the limelight, *American Graffiti*'s most enduring legacy may be what has (unsurprisingly) become referred to as 'The *American Graffiti* Ending', the flashing up at the end of caption cards which inform the audience what has happened to the characters since the events of the film; by treating fictional people as if they are historical figures this technique adds a strange resonance and verisimilitude to fictional events. Contrary to speculation the captions are in the original screenplay for the film, and Lucas pushed hard for their inclusion against the advice of people who didn't want the film to end on a down note, failing to understand that what the captions actually do is reinforce the film's own prevailing sense of melancholy, and as such are an entirely appropriate ending to the picture. The technique has been used on far too many films to note here, and has become a standard filmmaking technique.

EXTERNAL REFERENCES: Milner's yellow car has the registration plate THX 138, a compromise between the title of Lucas's first feature and the simple fact that California licence plates then consisted of only three letters and three numbers. The bright yellow colour is reminiscent of the colour of the car in Lucas's own *1:42.08 to Qualify* (1966) (and see also **Attack of the Clones**).

Visible in the background in several shots is a cinema showing *Dementia 13*, producer Francis Ford Coppola's first film as a director. Although a neat conceptual nod to his friend and mentor, it's unfortunate that *Dementia 13*'s release was in early 1963, several months after *Graffiti*'s setting of September 1962.

Rather wonderfully Curt leaves on a plane belonging to 'Magic Carpet Airlines'.

RELEASE: *American Graffiti* previewed for the first time at the Northpoint Theater, San Francisco on 28 January 1973. Universal's Ned Tanen was in attendance. The audience – demographically selected to the studio's specifications – loved the movie. Tanen hated it. Furious, he rounded on Kurtz, Coppola and Lucas after the screening. He claimed to have gone into bat for them, to have believed in them, and he insisted that by producing a film which he claimed was 'unreleasable' they'd betrayed him. Lucas was cowed but Coppola was furious – he demanded to know what Tanen was thinking, what he thought he was doing. Had he not seen the reaction in the screening room? Coppola told Tanen that rather than chewing Lucas out he should 'Get down on your knees and thank this young man for what he's done for you'. He then whipped out his chequebook and offered to buy Universal's share of it on the spot, suggesting Tanen should either sell the film to him or stop complaining. Coppola and Tanen didn't speak again for another twenty years.

Whilst Universal demurred over what to do with their 'unreleasable' film, further preview screenings took place on the lot. Lucas and Coppola ensured that every time someone – for example an executive from marketing – needed to see the picture it was booked into one of the larger preview theatres, and that that theatre was filled (he extended open invites to the lower-level Universal staff, secretaries and functionaries, to attend any screening). Audiences always responded so positively to the film that this ensured that its reputation on and off the lot began to grow. The management still wanted to sell the feature directly to television, but it was at least partially because of the buzz created by the pure enthusiasm of low-level Universal employees that *American Graffiti* reached movie theatres at all.

A preview was held at the Writer's Guild Theater in Beverly Hills, and the response was ecstatic. Half a dozen more followed, but still Tanen was unconvinced. Primary among his objections was the film's use of the (now commonplace) technique of running several stories simultaneously and then intercutting between them. Although it seems incredible today that this is the case, one of the reasons Lucas had difficulty getting backing for the *Graffiti* screenplay was its adoption of this mode of storytelling. It was regarded as needlessly 'arty' by many who read the screenplay, and as something that wouldn't be understood by the audience of a mainstream picture. This was a complaint levelled at the finished film by studio management and the principal reason behind it being labelled 'unreleasable'; there was no conceivable way to recut the film to make the stories run sequentially rather than contemporaneously.

When Fox's Alan Ladd Jr – then in negotiation with Lucas over the director's next project – called Tanen to say that he'd seen the movie and that if Universal weren't going to release it Fox would, Tanen was confused. When Paramount made a similar approach days later he was astounded. Conceding that maybe he and his teams really were the only people who didn't love the film, he arranged for it to be released, initially at the Avco in Hollywood and the Sutton in New York, and it proved to be a success across the country two weeks later.

The general release date was 1 August 1973, and *Graffiti* took a breathtaking $55 million in net rentals. In its first week it made $35,000, which was then a record. When compared with the movie's direct cost ($775,000 plus $500,000 for prints and other sundries) it was even more impressive. Lucas's cut netted him $7 million ($4 million after taxes). The film earned back its budget quicker than any other film in history. In fact, until *The Blair Witch Project* (Daniel Myrick, Eduardo Sanchez, 1999), *American Graffiti* would hold the record for the largest budget-to-profit ratio in motion-picture history. The picture continues to make money; to date it has made $115,000,000 profit in cinema takings in the US alone, and its lavish DVD edition of 1998 was (in the US at least) an enormous seller.

Coppola and Lucas chose to share the success of their film; Coppola gave co-producer Gary Kurtz 5% (as agreed before production) and Visual Consultant Haskell Wexler received 3% from Lucas and 2% from Coppola. Lucas gave the Huycks 1% and split another between the ten principal cast members, all of whom had worked for the industry standard of $480 a week during production. He bought Verna Fields, Walter Murch and Fred Roos new cars and other crew members received smaller gifts or bonuses of $10,000.

CRITICISM: At the time of the picture's release Lucas was upset and angry at the reviews in his native San Francisco; this was not because the papers were having any influence on the picture's box office or wider critical success, but because the only US papers to review the film negatively were those journals his parents read. *American Graffiti* was an almost total success critically and financially, but it didn't appear a success to Lucas's own family. The *San Francisco Chronicle* famously called it the worst movie ever made, whilst the *Modesto Bee* was little kinder, calling the film 'monotonous' and repeatedly criticising it for being 'made up'. The reviewer noted that it was part of a current crop of 'nostalgia pics' and opined 'I hope it will be the last for a while'. In a piece of outlandishly inaccurate prediction he also commented that '. . . the stars are nice clean-cut kids whose names will probably not be remembered' when describing a cast that included a future Oscar-winning actor, a future Oscar-winning director, the stars of three of network television's most successful ever sitcoms and (in Harrison Ford) an actor who would achieve the unprecedented, and not since replicated, feat of starring in no less than seven of the ten highest-grossing box office films of all time (only one of which, *The Fugitive* [Andrew Davis, 1993], wasn't co-written and produced by Lucas).

Elsewhere reviews were better; a great deal better, in fact. *Variety* enthused that the film was 'a most vivid recall' of the adolescent experience with 'humour and heart', and what's more one told with 'outstanding empathy and compassion' thanks to 'brilliant interplaying and underplaying' from an 'exceptionally talented' cast. 'Lucas has done a truly masterful job', the review concluded. The *New York Times* was equally impressed, claiming that the film was 'full of the material of fashionable nostalgia' but never stooped to exploit it. Comparing it to early Fellini, the reviewer rated it 'a very good movie . . . funny, tough, unsentimental' and full of 'marvellous performances'. Its ultimate conclusion was that 'The nostalgia boom has finally produced a lasting work of art'. The same paper took two more opportunities to praise the film, one a month later and another in early 1974, when it elected it one of the ten best films of the previous year. The summary of 16 September praised the Terry and Debbie sequences as amongst 'the funniest I've seen in any film in months' and compared the film with the 1948 movie version of William Saroyan's *The Time of Your Life*. The January review revered the film's lack of sentimentality and praised the prevalent mix of 'toughness and high humour'; it was in total 'a remarkably successful example of American moviemaking'.

Akira Kurosawa

Born in Tokyo in 1910 to an old samurai family, Akira Kurosawa remains the Japanese film director best known to western audiences. A former painter, screenwriter and assistant director, he broke into directing with *Sanshiro Sugata* in 1943. Although he was a remarkable technical filmmaker and a screenwriter with an instinctive understanding of pace and structure, the obvious influence of European and American film on his work (he claimed more than once that he saw John Ford as his creative father) has often caused him to be underrated in his own country.

In 1951 his *Rashomon*, a film which retells the same event from four different perspectives and has a good claim to being the finest movie ever made, was shown at the Cannes Film Festival and seized upon by the western media as the first great Japanese movie. Only later was it acknowledged in the west that Kurosawa was part of a tradition of Japanese filmmaking that included such indisputable, if little-known, masters as Yasujiro Ozu and Kenji Mizoguchi.

Kurosawa's other films include *Stray Dog* (1949), *The Seven Samurai* (1954), *The Hidden Fortress* (1958), and *Yojimbo* (1961). A humanist intellectual with a compassionate outlook and a keen knowledge of cultures outside his own, he also made two outstanding Shakespeare adaptations: *Throne of Blood* (Macbeth – 1957) and *Ran* (King Lear – 1985) and made movies based on Dostoyevsky (*The Idiot*, 1951) and Gorky (*The Lower Depths*, 1957).

Revered by the movie brats generation of filmmakers (not just Lucas but also Coppola, Spielberg *et al.*) for his fierce editing, beautiful framing, use of film wipes and attention to lighting, Kurosawa's mainstream popularity and recognition increased by association with some of New Hollywood's brightest stars. He won an Oscar in 1975 for *Dersu Azala*, a technically exquisite, if difficult to like, Russian co-production about a man mapping Siberia. It was his comeback film after attempting suicide following the failure of *Dodeska-den* (1970), his hugely ambitious study of shanty towns. Kurosawa's 1980 epic *Kagemusha* (aka *Shadow Warrior* aka *The Double*) was produced by Lucas and Coppola, who were keen to support a man who had influenced them so much.

Kurosawa continued to make films until 1993; his last was *Madadayo*, a story of old age and responsibility framed around the life of Japanese intellectual Uehida Hyakken-sama. Undeniably a lesser Kurosawa work, its restrained emotional complexity makes it a fine farewell to his art by a master director. Akira Kurosawa died in 1998.

In the UK the critical consensus was generally very positive indeed, but unlike in the US it didn't translate into mainstream commercial success. One reviewer failed to see why he should be interested in the experiences of people of a different generation on a different continent, and attacked the film's tagline with misplaced sarcasm – 'Where were you in '62?' he pondered. 'I was *here*, reviewing Fellini'. The *Daily Telegraph* called it 'endearing and entertaining', and 'very clever' to boot, whereas the *Spectator* found it 'convincing and delightful', especially the way the characters' innocence was captured 'with a sympathetic appreciation of its fragility'. The much-discussed ending was one of the reviewer's favourite aspects of the film: 'The rainbow fades, the fairground closes, we are back in the present'.

American Graffiti is charming, bittersweet, compelling and emotionally literate; most importantly, for such a personal project its utter lack of sentimentality and the restraint and distance with which it views its writer/director's own experiences are remarkable. The cast are consistently excellent, but Richard Dreyfuss in particular is extraordinary, giving a performance of repressed energy and reluctant sarcasm, of depth and intelligence, a seemingly effortless portrayal of a young man with enormous potential for greatness. Lucas and Wexler's photography remains unique; and this still looks unlike any other film ever made despite having spawned not merely a sequel but a *genre*.

While it never loses its sense of time and place for a moment *American Graffiti* also transcends the confines and specifics of its setting to become one of the definitive movies of adolescence: awkward, beautiful and witty. The American Film Institute's 1999 declaration that *American Graffiti* is one of the 100 best American motion pictures ever made is entirely appropriate.

AWARDS: The March 1974 Academy Awards saw *Graffiti* nominated for five Oscars; these included the so-called 'Big Two' of Best Picture and Best Director, as well as Best Film Editing for Marcia Lucas and Verna Fields, Best Original Screenplay and Best Performance by an Actress in a Supporting Role for Candy Clark. None of these nominations translated into actual awards, largely thanks to *The Sting* (George Roy Hill, 1973) making a clean sweep of the major awards that night.

The movie did, however, pick up the Golden Globe for Best Motion Picture (Comedy) and Paul Le Mat won the Most Promising Newcomer award at the same ceremony. The script won both the New York Film Critics and the National Society of Film Critics Awards for Best Screenplay and was nominated by the Writer's Guild of America as Best Comedy Written Directly for the Screen.

TRIVIA: On the trailer Lucasfilm is still spelled 'Lucas Film' as it is on *THX-1138*, but by the time the picture was released the company's name had been conflated to one word. The released version of *Graffiti* uses a version of the simple green typeface Lucasfilm logo used up to and including *Radioland Murders*.

Lucas's casting of Wolfman as much-admired sage and counsel to a generation of teenagers was aped by Kevin Smith in his film *Mallrats* (1995), where he used famed comics creator Stan Lee (the inventor of the X-Men, Spider-Man, the Incredible Hulk, the Fantastic Four, Daredevil and dozens of others) in exactly the same way, giving him scenes in which – playing himself – he imparts advice to Brodie (Jason Lee) which causes him to realise what's important in his life.

EXPERT WITNESS: 'George let us ad lib practically whenever we wanted; changed dialogue at will; let the scenes run on and on. We did many, many takes on every scene and printed lots of them.' Actor Charlie Martin Smith.

LUCAS ON AMERICAN GRAFFITI: 'It all happened to me . . . I went through all that stuff, drove the cars, bought liquor, chased girls . . . but I sort of glamorised it.'

'The film is about teenagers; about moving forward and making decisions . . . but it's also about the fact that you can't live in the past . . . things can't stay the same . . . essentially that's the point.'

Star Wars (1977)

(160 minutes original edition/120 minutes special edition)

20th Century Fox
A Lucasfilm Limited Production
Director of Photography: Gilbert Taylor, BSC
Produced by Gary Kurtz
Special Edition Produced by Rick McCallum
Production Designer: John Barry
Music by John Williams
Executive Producer: George Lucas
Edited by TM Christopher (Special Edition only), Marcia Lucas, Paul Hirsch, Richard Chew
Written and Directed by George Lucas

PRINCIPAL CAST: Mark Hamill (*Luke Skywalker*), Harrison Ford (*Han Solo*), Carrie Fisher (*Princess Leia*), Peter Cushing (*Grand Moff Tarkin*), Alec Guinness (*Ben [Obi-Wan] Kenobi*), Anthony Daniels (*See-Threepio [C-3PO]*), Kenny Baker (*Artoo-Detoo [R2-D2]*), Peter Mayhew (*Chewbacca*), David Prowse (*Darth Vader*), James Earl Jones (*Voice of Darth Vader*), Phil Brown (*Uncle Owen*), Shelagh Fraser (*Aunt Beru*), Jack Purvis (*Chief Jawa*), Alex McCrindle (*General Dodonna*), Eddie Byrne (*General Willard*), Drewe Henley (*Red Leader*), Denis Lawson (*Red Two [Wedge]*) Garrick Hagon (*Red Three [Biggs]*), Jack Klaff (*Red Four [John 'D']*), William Hootkins (*Red Six [Porkins]*), Angus MacInnes (*Gold Leader*), Jeremy Sinden (*Gold Two*), Graham Ashley (*Gold Five*), Don Henderson (*General Tagge*), Richard LeParmentier (*General Motti*), Leslie Schofield (*Commander #1 [Chief Bast]*)

TAGLINE: A long time ago, in a galaxy far, far away (1977).

Return to a galaxy far, far away. (1997 reissue).

SUMMARY: A long time ago in a galaxy far, far away a civil war is raging. The Empire, a multi-planetary military dictatorship controlled by a distant, unseen Emperor and enforced by the armoured Lord Darth Vader and his shock troops or 'stormtroopers', is fighting a growing rebel movement. Princess Leia of the planet Alderaan, a member of the Imperial Senate subservient to the Emperor, has discovered the existence of the Death Star, an armoured space station with enough firepower to destroy an entire planet. Having appropriated the plans to this still secret project (she plans to turn them over to insurrectionist forces – the Rebel Alliance, with whom Alderaan has some political sympathies) she is on her way back to Alderaan, and is planning to stop off on the desert planet Tatooine to make contact with Obi-Wan Kenobi, an old man who – some unspecified number of years in the past – was both a friend of her father's and a Jedi Knight, one of a now extinct sect of warrior-mystics who administered order and justice in the time before the Empire. Intercepted by Vader and his men in orbit and taken prisoner, Leia sends the droid R2-D2 (Artoo-Deetoo) along with the humanoid interpreter robot C-3PO (See-Threepio) down to Tatooine to ask Kenobi for his assistance, and request that he deliver the stolen plans to her father on Alderaan.

Once on the planet Threepio and Artoo are captured by Jawas –
scavengers who haunt the planet's deserts looking for scrap – and
are subsequently sold to a moisture farmer named Owen Lars,
who lives with his wife Beru and his nephew Luke Skywalker.
Obsessed with his mission – about which Threepio knows little –
Artoo runs away from his new owner, and so Luke is forced to
follow him out into the desert with Threepio at his side. All three
meet 'Ben' Kenobi, a hermit-like old man who, when questioned,
admits that he is indeed Obi-Wan. Having received the message
from Artoo, Kenobi accepts the mission, and tries to persuade
Luke to come with him. He tells Luke that his late father – whom
Luke always believed to have been 'a navigator on a spice
freighter' – was a Jedi himself, and that Owen has been lying to
him all his life. As proof he gives Luke his father's lightsaber – a
Jedi weapon which is like a sword but with a beam made of
energy instead of a blade of steel. He also tells Luke that Luke's
father was betrayed and murdered by Darth Vader, a young Jedi
who – he reveals – was a pupil of Kenobi's before turning to evil.
Luke refuses to leave with Ben, but on returning home he
discovers his aunt and uncle dead – murdered by stormtroopers
sent down to the planet to retrieve the stolen plans.

Luke changes his mind, and together he, Kenobi and the droids
charter a space freighter to take them to Alderaan. This ship, the
Millennium Falcon, is owned and operated by Han Solo, a
cocksure smuggler, and his very tall, monkey-like Wookie
companion Chewbacca. Solo accepts the charter because he owes
a substantial amount of money to Jabba the Hutt, a crime lord
who controls much of the planet (Solo smuggles for Jabba, but
dumped a consignment of merchandise into space because he
feared he was about to be boarded by stormtroopers).

Imperial forces nearly prevent the *Falcon* from blasting off from
Tatooine, but the ship escapes and makes its way to Alderaan.
Upon reaching Alderaan's co-ordinates they discover that the
planet is no longer there. It has been destroyed by the Death Star,
which, under the command of the officious Grand Moff Tarkin, is
floating in space near where the planet used to be. The *Falcon* is
dragged on board the station via a tractor beam, and the crew first
hide, and then make their way onto the Death Star under cover.

Luke discovers that the Princess is being held prisoner on the
station and decides to rescue her, which he and Solo do. Kenobi
volunteers to deactivate the Death Star's tractor beam, so that the

ship can leave. He does so, but on his way back to the *Falcon* is intercepted by Vader. Kenobi fights Vader in a lightsaber duel, which gives Luke, Han, Leia, Chewie and the droids enough time to get to the *Falcon* and escape. Kenobi allows himself to be killed by Vader after uttering a final cryptic warning (see **QUOTES**) but the old man's corpse disappears, a fact that visibly puzzles his former pupil. Tarkin has, however, ensured that a homing device is placed on the *Falcon*, and so the Death Star follows the ship to the moon of Yavin, the base of the rebel forces. The station is going to destroy the moon. Han, having been paid – and much to Luke and Leia's disgust – decides to leave immediately.

The plans which Artoo has been carrying have been studied and suggest a way in which it may be possible to destroy the station, by flying a small one-man ship through its defences and manually aiming and firing a torpedo into a very small thermal exhaust port. Luke joins the rebellion and – thanks to his skill as a pilot – is given one of the few available ships (an X-wing) to participate in the desperate attack on the advancing Death Star. Most of his comrades die in the attempt – partially due to Vader attacking them from a small ship of his own – but thanks to a last-minute intervention by the returned Solo and Chewbacca, and guided by Obi-Wan's spectral voice, Luke succeeds in destroying the space station. Tarkin is killed, but Vader escapes. Han and Luke are presented with medals in a large ceremony celebrating the rebels' first victory against their oppressors.

SCREENPLAY: Just when Lucas initially came up with the idea for *Star Wars* is hard to pin down. During the production of his first feature *THX-1138* in 1970, Lucas told composer Lalo Schifrin that he wanted to make a Flash Gordon picture, a technical updating of the 40s SF movie serials that he'd so enjoyed as a child. It would be those serials rendered not as they were (he and fellow student Don Glut had viewed many at USC and found them lacking *in extremis*), but how he remembered them as having been. He began to seek the rights, but when these proved unavailable (having been bought up by producer Dino Di Laurentiis) he began to work on similarly themed SF movie ideas of his own, hoping to create something that was similar to *Flash Gordon* or *Buck Rogers* but which he would own himself.

In January 1973, during the pre-release problems encountered by his second movie *American Graffiti*, Lucas began work on a story outline and first-draft screenplay for his space adventure. Famously, the first sentence of this near-incomprehensible document (which contained most of the characters, names, concepts and events of what would become *Star Wars*, albeit not in a form that anyone who had seen the film would recognise) was: 'The Story of Mace Windu. Mace Windu, a revered Jedi-Bendu of Opuchi who was related to Usby CJ Thape, Padewaan learner to the [a] famed Jedi'. Jedi was a word Lucas had coined to describe a clan of warrior mystics, samurai monks, who were always essential to his conception of *Star Wars*. Ever respectful of (some might say obsessed with) Japanese culture, he had named them after the branch of Japanese drama that drew moral and instructive lessons from stories set in the past – *Jidai geki*.

This draft version is set in the thirty-third century and features a teenage princess, droids, an evil Empire and a grizzled Jedi warrior, General Skywalker, whose plot role resembles Luke's from the finished film even though his character is essentially that of Obi-Wan Kenobi. The plotline climaxes with a space-borne dogfight and ends with a medal-awarding ceremony. Among the planets named are Alderaan (here the Imperial capital) and Yavin, at this point the Wookie's homeworld. Some character names from this draft (Valorum, Mace Windu) would eventually find a home in *The Phantom Menace* twenty years later.

By May of 1973 Lucas had a revised 132-page draft script, one written in his office at home under the benevolent gaze of the portrait of revered filmmaker Sergei Eisenstein that hung above his desk. By now General Skywalker had acquired the first name Luke but was no longer the film's protagonist. This was now Anikin (*sic*) Starkiller, one of many sons of General Skywalker's old comrade, the partially mechanical Kane Starkiller. Here Anikin has to protect a princess figure – called Zara – and is aided by two robots, R2-D2 and C-3PO. This is the version entitled *The Adventure of Anikin Starkiller*.

Shortly after the film's US release Lucas claimed to have written 'four entirely different screenplays' for *Star Wars*, and more than one draft of each of those. He also called *Star Wars* 'a good idea in search of a story'. But what was that 'good idea'?

An unabashed fan of research, Lucas had begun his preparations for the film not yet called *Star Wars* by working backwards from Flash Gordon. He was looking to uncover the character's cultural origins and the source of his appeal –

something he was hoping to transfer to his own story. Once he'd worked his way through Gordon's creator Alex Raymond's original comic strips he tackled Edgar Rice Burroughs's novels, not merely *Tarzan* but also the then unfashionable *John Carter of Mars* series, plus Jules Verne's canon and Edwin Arnold's obscure 1905 novella *Gulliver on Mars*. Conversations with his New Hollywood peers about the nature of the archetypes thrown up by his reading – and which he increasingly saw everywhere he looked – brought him into contact with the work of Dr Joseph Campbell. Lucas's initial focus was Campbell's then newly published collection *Myths to Live By* (1972), an anthology of lectures and essays from his academic career, which had been devoted to hunting down and identifying the basic archetypal characters and situations which he felt underpinned all of the human race's mythologies; he would later describe them as evolving in parallel with human language. 'The book began to focus what I had already been doing intuitively', Lucas later said, an idea which seemed to him itself to reinforce Campbell's own contention that such archetypes and situations dwelled in the collective unconsciousness of the human race. He expanded his reading to include epics of all kinds, and began planning a visual style that would combine the vistas of Kurosawa with the kind of static-camera realism which he'd used on *American Graffiti*, despite his natural instincts as a cameraman pushing him towards the more roving-camera style he'd utilised in his student work.

He wanted over-exposed colours and lots of shadows, but shot in a way that made them seem unremarkable, a 'cohesive reality'. Seeing the Apollo missions return from the moon 'littered with weightless candy-bar wrappers and old Tang jars, no more exotic than the family station wagon' had illustrated to him the problem with every fantasy movie ever made. The worlds therein never looked like people actually *lived* in them; his film would depict a 'used future'. Describing the aesthetic he'd sought to the technical specialist magazine *American Cinematographer*, he explained that he 'wanted the seeming contradiction of . . . fantasy combined with the feel of a documentary'. To Lucas *Star Wars* wasn't science fiction at all; it was, as *THX* had been, a 'documentary fantasy'. This is something that senior crew members were all aware of by the time it began filming; John Barry (production designer) told reporters that Lucas had insisted the film look 'like it's shot on location on your average everyday Death Star or spaceport'.

Whilst Lucas drafted and redrafted his story to take in his ideas and research, he also began simultaneously hunting for funding for the film he hoped to make from it. United Artists had first refusal on the idea as part of the initial deal made for the first-draft screenplay of *American Graffiti*. As a studio UA had little interest in epics and – aside from their stake in the James Bond series – even less in the youth market. David Picker politely and swiftly rejected the idea, as Lucas had probably hoped he would. Univeral's Ned Tanen was also contractually allowed to see the outline before Lucas could show it to any other party, but there was never any danger of Universal backing an ambitious project from a director they honestly believed had recently delivered to them, in *American Graffiti*, an unreleasable movie.

This freed Lucas to approach the one executive he felt had any hope of understanding what he was trying to achieve: Alan Ladd Jr, the son of the movie legend. Lucas's agent smuggled a print of *American Graffiti* to Ladd, who viewed the film, enjoyed it enormously and agreed to meet with the writer/director.

Lucas warmed to Ladd immediately: like Lucas and his contemporaries in New Hollywood, Ladd was a man driven by a love of motion pictures. Lucas could communicate with Ladd through a shared vocabulary, one steeped in film history and movie lore; he could explain the idea with reference to movies they both loved: Michael Curtiz actioners like *The Sea Hawk* (1940) or *Captain Blood* (1935); or by describing a scene as being like something from *The Searchers* (John Ford, 1956) or *Fahrenheit 451* (Francois Truffaut, 1966). Ten days after his initial presentation to Ladd Lucas signed a development deal with Fox, Ladd had reportedly told him, 'I'm interested, I don't understand this, but I loved *American Graffiti* and whatever you do is OK with me . . .'

Fox agreed to pay Lucas $15,000 to develop a script, $50,000 to write the movie and another $100,000 to direct it. Gary Kurtz – named as producer – received $50,000. The ecstatic reaction of preview audiences to the as-yet unreleased *American Graffiti* appears to have changed the direction and tone of *Star Wars* slightly. The reception of the film suggested to Lucas that there was nobility as well as commercial advantage in making uplifting films. Until then almost everything he'd been involved in had been angry and/or abstract, like *THX-1138* and *Apocalypse Now* or his student films. Early drafts of *Star Wars* feature suggestions of mutilation and torture and far more unpleasant violence than the almost slapstick gunplay of the film he eventually shot. *Star Wars* consciously became that which perhaps it had always been in essence: fun. In his notes in the *Star Wars* novelisation Lucas calls it 'a movie for the kid in all of us', and a film which he hoped would drive away 'the grimness of everyday life' and prevent it from 'following us into the movie theater'.

This desire to produce something positive, something he would spend the rest of his life describing as 'a fairy tale' but which tied into Campbell's ideas of inescapable archetypes, took over the *Star Wars* project – or as Lucas increasingly seems to have come to see it, Campbell's theories exerted a conscious rather than unconscious influence.

The script development money from Fox gave Lucas enough to live on whilst he continued to work on the screenplay. As he did so it changed radically again; a 'Kiber Crystal' (a physical embodiment of the force) was written in and then written out. Luke Skywalker became Deak Starkiller's overweight younger brother before finally becoming the idealistic farm boy familiar from the finished film. Characters swapped names and roles again, Deak taking, for example, the plot function the shooting draft gives to Leia. A new character named Darth Vader – sometimes a rogue Jedi, sometimes a member of a rival clan called 'the Knights of Sith' – had his role expanded. Some drafts killed him off during the explosion of the Death Star, while others allowed him to survive; across subsequent drafts his role continued to grow. Some previously major characters disappeared altogether, pushed into a 'backstory' which in Lucas's own mind explained the build-up to the events of the film. It is somewhere around this point that he claims to have written an outline which comprised in essence the events of *Star Wars* and its two sequels.

This claim, often dismissed, does have *some* internal logic and helps to explain the appearance of a second Death Star in *Return of the Jedi*. It is possible that the Battle of Yavin and the fall of Hoth were originally one event, and that the Death Star was merely damaged during it, rather than destroyed. Luke and Ben (who does not die even in the shooting draft of the film) would then flee to another world so that the elderly Jedi could instruct the younger man in the ways of the force. Leia and Han would be betrayed and then captured by Vader in the outline's middle third, with the final destruction of the Death Star and Luke's defeat of Vader in a lightsaber duel coming at the very end. If this version of the story ever existed it never got nearly as far as full script form, and was quickly put aside by Lucas who chose instead to develop the more easily realisable and saleable aspects of the plot, abandoning the middle section and much of Luke's training and bringing forward the destruction of the Death Star so that it could serve as the climax to a shorter story. During the writing of *Star Wars* Lucas consulted numerous friends and colleagues, asking them to read drafts and suggest amendments. Among them were fellow writer/director Brian De Palma[1] (whose sarcasm regarding 'the farts of others' saw Lucas's mystical energy field 'the force of others' lose the second half of its name), Willard Huyck and Gloria Katz (see **American Graffiti**) and film critic Jay Cocks.

In August 1973 *Graffiti* was released and became a box office phenomenon. Not only did the profits make Lucas rich, but its success also meant that he was able to renegotiate the terms of his Fox development deal. Rather than making demands in the more traditional arenas of salary and percentages, Lucas wanted control of the merchandising, music and sequel rights to his creations. Fox conceded him 60% of the merchandising rights, aware of its potential value to them, but eventually agreed that Lucas's share would rise by 20% a year for two years after the film's release. Few films made money from spin-off products for a whole 24 months after release and Fox assumed that *Star Wars* would be no different. Lucas got the sequel rights as well, albeit with the proviso that any sequel had to be in production within two years of the film's release.

Most important amongst Lucas's demands was that, if it went ahead, he wanted the film to be officially made by his own company, not by Fox. That way he could stay in total control over the budget and ensure that all charges and costs made for the production were legitimately spent on the production. The experience of watching *Mackenna's Gold* being made a decade earlier had taught him just how much money a studio could unconsciously waste on any production, and on a film like *Star Wars* – which was enormously ambitious and would inevitably be

[1] Brian De Palma, director *Murder a la Mode* (1968), *Carrie* (1976), *Blow Out* (1981), *Scarface* (1983), *The Untouchables* (1987), *Carlito's Way* (1993), *Mission: Impossible* (1996), *Snake Eyes* (1998).

chronically under-budgeted – it was crucial that this did not happen. Theoretically this was Lucas's smartest, most significant demand. He set up a company, the imaginatively named 'Star Wars Corporation', which contractually would own 40% of the net profits on the film once it was released.

Control of the music rights also had a logical precedent; Universal were currently making a fortune out of an *American Graffiti* soundtrack that was nothing more than a repackaging of old hits featured in the movie. Of the profits of this Lucas saw nothing, despite having selected the tracks used and fought long and hard for their inclusion in his film.

By this time the story of *Star Wars* had changed so many times that it becomes possible to claim that almost anything was 'always' part of it. Characters bounced in and out right up to the preparation of the shooting draft, dated 15 January 1976. This was tailored to be as close to the film's proposed budget of around $10 million as possible, and contains as many of the ideas, characters and situations Lucas had spent the past few years developing as he considered feasible. It's easily recognisable as the film that was released, minus a few subtractions here and there (see **CUT SCENES**), most of which found their way into the novelisation and comic-book adaptation. This draft is the first version of the script in which Obi-Wan Kenobi dies after fighting Vader on the Death Star. Previously he had been injured in the fight, but escaped to Yavin with Luke's party. Alec Guinness, who had already been cast, was initially unhappy with this change, but was eventually persuaded by Lucas that an heroic death followed by several appearances as a spectral, comforting voice would prove more memorable to audiences than his spending the last third of the film sitting on Yavin whilst the X-wings went into battle.

Alan Ladd Jr took this script to the Fox board during March 1975, just before the Oscars, and argued hard for it. The board passed the screenplay and budgeted the film at $8.5 million. *Star Wars* was going to be made.

It has recently become fashionable – bordering on *de rigueur* – to claim that *Star Wars*'s Oscar- and WGA-nominated, multiple award-winning screenplay is, in some sense, a bad script. Although Lucas himself has often publicly doubted his talents as a writer ('I'm not a good writer. It's very, very hard for me. I don't . . . have a natural talent for it'), the script for *Star Wars* – like that for *Graffiti* – is an excellent piece of work, perhaps thanks to the almost endless redrafting process it went through before being filmed.

For a start, it has a perfect three-act structure (Tatooine/the Death Star/the Assault on the Death Star) and is well paced. The characters are introduced at apt intervals and given early scenes which demonstrate their basic personalities admirably, and all have distinct voices expressed clearly through dialogue. Admittedly that dialogue occasionally veers from the blandly functional ('What are you doing hiding back there?') to the overwrought ('This will be a day long remembered, it has seen the end of Kenobi and it will soon see the end of the rebellion'), but it also effortlessly tells the audience everything they need to know about the fiction they are watching while simultaneously offering casual hints of a wider universe off screen ('The Imperial senate will no longer be of any concern . . .', 'Dantooine is too far out . . .', '. . . the outer rim territories . . .'). It not only shows rather than tells, but also simultaneously and subtly tells the audience a great deal more as well.

Furthermore, nobody ever 'info-dumps', simply telling another character something they already know just to inform the viewers (a far more common problem in movies than is often noted), and this, combined with the script's absolute refusal to discuss at length the technology which surrounds its characters, renders what is uneventful to the characters remarkable to the audience. The 'casual' dropping of the names of other worlds and technical terms ('I'm talking about the big Corellian ships', '. . . my T16 back home', 'ever since the XP38 came out . . .') is particularly useful in this respect. The subtleties of the screenplay are just as important to, and just as effective a part of, the world-building exercise going on as the pre-distressed models and dirty clothes on screen.

CASTING: As on *American Graffiti* Lucas hired Fred Roos and participated in open 'cattle-call' castings. Because they required several cast members of similar ages and builds, Lucas and fellow director Brian De Palma agreed to pool their resources, holding joint casting sessions for both *Star Wars* and De Palma's current project, an adaptation of Stephen King's *Carrie* (for example Sissy Spacek and Carrie Fisher each read for both the lead in *Carrie* and Princess Leia). The two directors sat together, occasionally joined by an interested but uninvolved third party such as mutual friend

Steven Spielberg, then riding high on the success of *Jaws*, which had recently been released by Universal. Mark Hamill had been a working actor for several years, including a long stint in TV soap *General Hospital*, but the television series he'd been starring in, *The Texas Wheelers*, had been unexpectedly canned by the network, and almost desperate for acting work he subjected himself to the cattle-call process. He read for both Luke and the character in *Carrie* eventually played by John Travolta. Hamill was 24 but looked younger, and something about his performance impressed Lucas, who put Hamill on his list of 50 actors to ask back for a video test. Among the others asked back was Will Seltzer, whom Lucas would eventually cast in *More American Graffiti* five years later. Carrie Fisher was a Roos suggestion; others on the shortlist to play Leia included Amy Irving and Jodie Foster. Foster was too young and, whilst she was as tough as the character was intended to be, her performance was somehow inappropriate. Irving wasn't keen, and later made remarks suggesting that she would have turned down the role if asked. She *was* never asked, but she did begin dating Steven Spielberg shortly after.

Fred Roos was also convinced that Harrison Ford would be ideal for Han Solo, although other options considered by Lucas included Nick Nolte, *Graffiti*'s Paul Le Mat, Christopher Walken, Glynn Turman and Bruce Boxleitner. Since *American Graffiti* Ford had had a small but impressively sinister role (which he described as 'young gay man') in Coppola's *The Conversation* (1974), but had mostly returned to carpentry. He was building a desk for Fred Roos during Lucas's conversations with the casting agent, something he regarded as a humiliating experience – he'd worked for Lucas as an actor and now he had to saw wood in front of him. It was all part of a subterfuge by Roos, who wanted to get the director and actor in the same room again. Lucas cottoned on to what was happening, and invited Ford to read with the actors who were coming in for video tests.

As they had been on *Graffiti*, Lucas and Roos were looking to cast a group rather than individuals. Short-listed candidates were brought in together and read as a company. Fisher and Hamill's initial screen tests are still extant; they both read their scenes with Ford. In the end it came down to a straight choice of two of the groups of three they'd compiled – Christopher Walken, Terri Nunn and Will Seltzer and Ford, Fisher and Hamill. Lucas chose the latter.

   For Obi-Wan Kenobi Lucas initially thought of Toshiro Mifune, the Japanese character actor who'd played so many of the figures Obi-Wan was patterned after. Mifune, though, was almost an unknown in America, at least outside the hippest movie-watching circles, and instead Lucas alighted on Sir Alec Guinness, a theatre-trained performer famous for his acting technique. Theatre legend has it that when playing the minor role of a messenger in *Hamlet* as a young man he'd run around the outside of the theatre before going on stage; it was the only way he could find to replicate the messenger's breathless hurry with conviction. Guinness had gained a Best Actor Academy Award for his startling performance in David Lean's prisoner-of-war epic *The Bridge on the River Kwai* (1957) and still occasionally worked in American films. Guinness met Lucas for lunch (the actor was in Hollywood playing the butler in Neil Simon's *Murder by Death*); although he was aware of the occasional inadequacies of the draft of the script he had been given, Guinness had found it a compulsive read. Attracted by the opportunity of a role which offered a physical challenge rarely given to actors in his age bracket (he was 62), he told Lucas he was interested, assuming they could rethink the money. The $1,000 a week they were offering the featured players (the rest of the cast were getting SAG/Equity minimum) was simply insufficient. Could there be a portion of the profits involved? Lucas wanted Guinness, and so offered him 2¼% of his company's 40% of the film's takings. Guinness agreed.

   Peter Cushing had begun his film career in the 1930s with small roles in *The Man in the Iron Mask* (James Whale, 1939) and the Laurel and Hardy comedy *A Chump at Oxford* (Alfred Goulding, 1940) before impressing as Osric in Laurence Olivier's *Hamlet* (1948). Forever associated with the roles of Van Helsing and Dr Frankenstein in Hammer's *Dracula* and *Frankenstein* series respectively, Cushing's other work had included an astonishing performance as Cassius in *The Spread of the Eagle* (a 1958 adaptation of Shakespeare's Roman plays) and the role of Winston Smith in Nigel Kneale's television play of *Nineteen Eighty-Four*, both for BBC television. Far more precise and versatile an actor than many would give him credit for, he was also the cinema's first *Doctor Who* in two gaudy, popular films of 1965 and 1966. Although Tarkin was in no sense a departure for the actor, he brought a sense of dignity and calculation to a role that in lesser hands could have become distinctly unmemorable.

Anthony Daniels, who was unknowingly embarking on a *career* rather than simply a *movie* as C-3PO, had only graduated from drama school two years before; after a spell as a member of the BBC radio repertory he was playing the English Ambassador in a well-received revival of Tom Stoppard's *Rosencrantz and Guildenstern are Dead* at the Young Vic, part of the National Theatre, when he met Lucas. For Threepio Lucas had met mimes as well as actors, but saw in the slight, well-spoken Daniels something which might translate well into the character. Although Lucas had originally conceived Threepio as speaking like a New York car dealer, Daniels was a physically skilled actor and appeared to understand the movements involved. Daniels was initially underwhelmed by both Lucas and the idea of a part in a film such as *Star Wars*, but warmed to the idea after his first call back, during which he saw Ralph McQuarrie's beautiful production sketches of Threepio, patterned after the Maria robot in Fritz Lang's *Metropolis* (1926). Initially Lucas considered redubbing Threepio with the voice of another actor after the shoot was done, but so totally did the actor claim the character as his own that no other voice seemed remotely right when dubbed over the footage. Daniels remains the only one of the speaking principals to appear as the same character across all five *Star Wars* pictures, and is to appear in the sixth also. He is an enthusiastic ambassador for the series, and has also reprised Threepio in all three *Star Wars* radio serials, the *Droids* cartoon series and on *The Muppet Show*.

Many of the more minor cast members were London-based actors signed up when it was decided the production would be shot near there (Daniels and Cushing were also cast after the decision to go to London was taken, but neither of their roles could feasibly be described as minor); this fact, combined with the casting of Guinness, Daniels and Cushing, meant that the bulk of the cast were British. In order to make this less obvious many minor roles (such as the officer in the cell block, played by uncredited British stage actor Malcolm Tierney) were overdubbed later by American voice-over artistes. This was also partially done to avoid the film falling too readily into the then already overworn Hollywood cliché of using English villains.

Peter Mayhew, playing Chewbacca, was a hospital porter, and at 7ft 2in Britain's second tallest man. One of the country's shortest was Kenny Baker, a seasoned performer hired to be inside

R2-D2. It was his task to activate the motors that moved the droid around, although on some scenes a remote-control version was used instead. What Lucas discovered to his surprise during the Tunisia shoot was that he actually preferred the sequences shot whilst Baker was inside Artoo to those featuring the more sophisticated remote-controlled robot. Baker's habit of fidgeting inside the droid even whilst it was stationary made Artoo judder; it gave him body language, realism, life. Baker would find himself called back to perform scenes (mostly close-ups) as R2 in *Star Wars*'s sequels and prequels. Baker's cabaret partner, Jack Purvis, also has a role in *Star Wars* as the Chief Jawa, as well as playing other minor creature roles in *Empire* and *Jedi*.

David Prowse, the man behind Darth Vader's mask, was a bodybuilder, gym owner and occasional actor who had appeared in Kubrick's *A Clockwork Orange*; to the British generation of the 1970s he was also the Green Cross Code Man, the stern-faced spandex-clad superhero who taught the rules of road safety on children's television. It is a point of some controversy that Prowse insists to this day that he believed he would provide Vader's voice as well. Given that Prowse had a strong Bristol accent – an accent considered inherently comic by many in Britain and virtually incomprehensible by many in the United States – it seems unlikely that this was ever a serious possibility. Tellingly, he was also over-dubbed as the Green Cross Code Man. Anyone interested in hearing how Prowse might have sounded as Vader can hear his voice in BBC television's *The Hitch-Hiker's Guide to the Galaxy*.

Prowse's lines in *Star Wars* were redubbed in America by actor James Earl Jones. Jones had received an Oscar nomination for his role in *The Great White Hope* (Martin Ritt, 1970), a biography of early twentieth-century boxer Jack Johnson, and although often on TV and in films, he was best known as a stage actor. He received payment but no credit for the work he had done on the film. He would later say that this was because he felt the amount of work he had done simply didn't justify billing ('I just went in with a single microphone and recorded my voice in a day' he said of the underwhelming experience), although it is possible that he refused credit because the film was widely expected pre-release to do badly. By *Jedi* he would be credited above David Prowse on the cast list.

PRODUCTION: The filming of *Star Wars* began on location in Tozeur, Tunisia on 22 March 1976 – almost exactly a year after the final green light had been given. The first sequences shot were the scenes of Luke buying Artoo and Threepio from the Jawas outside his foster parents' home. Producer Kurtz had allowed eleven days for the shoot; after that a borrowed army C130 Hercules was scheduled to pick up the cast and crew.

A few days into shooting creature make-up man Stuart Freeborn was taken ill and had to be flown back to Britain where he was diagnosed with pneumonia. Others in the crew contracted dysentery. On 26 March Tunisia experienced its first winter rainstorm for over half a century, damaging equipment and the exterior dressings to native buildings being used on location, and delaying filming of key scenes.

Locations used included the Hotel Sidi Driss in Matmata, near the Mediterranean coast, a deep, underground dwelling built by the native Burbur people and still in use. This would become Luke Skywalker's home and go down in *Star Wars* lore as 'the Lars homestead'.

Lucas wanted the stormtroopers who were sent down to Tatooine to find Artoo and Threepio to ride 'dewbacks', large dinosaur-like domesticated beasts that allowed the troops to move across the desert. One dewback was built out of foam rubber stretched over a wire frame. It could only be used in the background and no one was ever seen riding one, a failure which annoyed the writer/director greatly (see **ALTERNATIVE VERSIONS**). The other live animal Lucas wanted to portray was a bantha, a huge horned, shaggy beast reminiscent of a prehistoric mammoth. It was to be the primary mode of transport for the Tusken Raiders of Tatooine, the faintly Bedouin, vaguely mechanically-enhanced creatures who attacked Luke when he was out looking for Ben Kenobi in the Jundland wastes. In the end creating the beasts proved impossible, and whilst they were referred to in dialogue in scenes that were shot ('bantha tracks . . .') none of the sequences was lensed.

As hard as the shoot was on Lucas, at least he knew what he was aiming for; he had a vision – or at least an idea – of how it would all fit together. The actors, suffering stomach troubles and sunburn and long days, were less clear. Anthony Daniels, trapped inside an almost immovable fibreglass body-suit, suffered perhaps the worst. Twenty-five years later he would give much of the credit for helping him to get through the Tunisia sequences to the vastly more experienced Alec Guinness: 'He was incredibly kind to me . . . I firmly believe that I wouldn't have completed that arduous task of shooting without him.'

Once the Tunisia shoot was over the cast moved to EMI Elstree Studios in Borehamwood, outside London. *Star Wars* was being made in the UK because it simply wasn't possible to shoot the film in Hollywood at that time, not that Lucas – with his lifelong hatred of LA – would have wanted to anyway. *Star Wars* required nine stages simultaneously, something that no Hollywood studio complex could guarantee at anything like sufficient notice. In March 1975 producer Kurtz had flown to Italy to look at studio space, but found nothing remotely suitable. He then caught a plane to London, where Lucas joined him.

Together Kurtz and Lucas scouted all the major UK film studios. Pinewood was a possibility for a while, but the management insisted that Lucasfilm hire their technicians to make the film, a condition at which both men baulked and which became a deal-breaker. Neither Shepperton nor Twickenham had enough soundstages (although the giant Stage H at the former – bigger than any individual stage at Elstree – would ultimately house one scene of the film), which left only EMI Elstree. Then losing £1 million a year, Elstree was being kept open more or less on the insistence of Harold Wilson's government, whose allies in the Trade Union movement considered the closing of the facility unconscionable. Elstree had no staff, and any film producer who wished to rent it had to supply their own technicians and some of their own equipment. This was off-putting to many, but it sealed the deal for Lucas and Kurtz, who wanted to move their own people in. They hired the facility for seventeen weeks, starting at the beginning of March 1976.

To design and build the sets needed to turn to Elstree into a realisation of Lucas's screenplay they hired John Barry, a British designer who had worked under Ken Adam on *Barry Lyndon* (Stanley Kubrick, 1975), a film Lucas admired enough to hire its costumier John Mollo as well. Barry came into contact with the writer/director whilst working on the Willard Huyck/Gloria Katz-scripted *Lucky Lady* (Stanley Donen, 1975). An eclectic with interests in many cultures and many kinds of film, Barry brought with him his assistant Norman Reynolds; one of the pair's first jobs for Lucas was to scout Tunisia with him.

Elstree's two largest studios were given over to the Mos Eisley spaceport and the interior of the Death Star. Both the Mos Eisley hangar bay and the one inside the Death Star which replaced it on the same stage were constructed around Norman Reynolds' full-size *Millennium Falcon* set. Built by naval engineers at Pembroke Docks, Wales, it was 65 feet in diameter, 16 feet high and 80 feet long, and weighed 23 tonnes. The shoot wasn't easy on Lucas, whose English crew – led by director of photography Gilbert Taylor – refused to work paid overtime and stuck rigorously to work-to-rule dictates. They worked exactly eight hours a day, minus lunch and two mandatory tea breaks, despite frequent appeals from Lucas and Kurtz who knew that their film was on a knife-edge schedule and that any further lost time would be disastrous. Kurtz felt the crew made no real secret of their contempt for the production they were involved in (Taylor had had similar clashes with Stanley Kubrick on 1963's *Dr Strangelove*, for which he'd been hired because of his expertise with black and white shooting). He'd worked with Hitchcock and on Polanski's drearily literal 1971 *Macbeth* adaptation, and seemed to producer Kurtz to consider the assignment beneath him.

Taylor was a last-minute replacement for Lucas's chosen DOP Geoffery Unsworth, who'd done extraordinary work on *2001: A Space Odyssey* (Stanley Kubrick, 1968) and won an Oscar for *Cabaret* (Bob Fosse, 1972), but whose prior agreement to shoot *A Matter of Time* for Vincente Minelli in Rome unexpectedly conflicted with Lucas's offer of work.

Shooting was hard work and marked by a cold-war animosity between the cast and US crew, who mostly sided with Lucas, and the UK-based crew, who mostly sided with Taylor. Matters got worse when Lucas, never the most actor-communicative of directors, lost his voice after developing a cold which gave him a vicious cough.

The absence of Stuart Freeborn, still recovering from Tunisia, meant that most of the aliens seen in the Mos Eisley cantina sequence were completed by assistants and lacked any articulation at all. Deeply unhappy with the scenes as shot, Lucas resolved to do to reshoots back in the US later.

The last scenes to be shot were for the opening battle as Vader and his stormtroopers board the Blockade Runner. The sets had been built once Fox had released a few thousand extra dollars to allow for them. With little time Lucas used six cameras to capture the battle, manning one himself (Gary Kurtz manned another), and shot the entire sequence in two takes. Judicious editing would later make the finished sequence look as if sufficient coverage had been shot. The six cameras produced so many different perspectives on the action that even the duplicated images that are in the film are unnoticeable. The finished sequence, chaotic though the creation of it was, is amongst the best put-together moments in the movie, a superb evocation of Lucas's 'documentary fantasy' approach as his cameras dart in and out of the action like reporters shooting newsreel footage. Virtually the first live action seen in the picture, its style later went a long way towards convincing audiences that what they were seeing was somehow real.

Principal photography was completed on 16 July 1976, although some reshoots and pick-up shots for the Tatooine sequences were undertaken in Yuma, Arizona in early 1977. Amongst the later scenes shot were those featuring the Banthas; Lucas borrowed a trained elephant from Marine World, and had it dressed to resemble a more hirsute, fearsome kind of pachyderm. Mark Hamill was unavailable to participate in the reshooting, as he'd crashed his car on the Antelope Freeway in LA shortly before and was undergoing painful facial reconstructive surgery. Although Hamill would have been involved in the reshooting of scenes of the landspeeder moving across the desert Lucas had no choice but to film them without him; he took a double to the shoot, dressed him in Luke's costume and favoured Threepio in the shots.

Also reshot were portions of the cantina sequence, shot over two days in La Brea, California. New cutaways and background shots were filmed, to be inserted into the footage shot in London and eliminate as many as possible of the unsatisfactory masks; it is this reshooting that has produced the peculiar phenomenon of two separate actors, Paul Blake and Maria de Aragon, both touring signing autographs for having played one minor role (Greedo) when a third person, Berkeley linguist Larry Ward, was actually responsible for supplying the voice (Greedo speaks in Quechua, the language of the ancient Inca people of South America).

The last scene shot for the film was undertaken by Industrial Light & Magic (ILM)'s Richard Edlund, Lorne Peterson and Dick Alexander, who travelled to Guatemala to capture second-unit jungle footage and shots of ancient buildings to be used to represent Yavin at the very end of the film. Peterson himself is the rebel sentry standing guard 300 feet in the air atop an Inca temple, seen in the films as the X-wings depart for their attack on the Death Star.

Whilst supervising editing of the film Lucas experienced chest pains, and was rushed to hospital where he was treated for a suspected heart attack. Later diagnosed with hypertension and exhaustion, both exacerbated by his diabetes, the scare pushed Lucas into declaring that *Star Wars* – whether it was a success or failure – would be his final film as a director.

Fox, whose faith in the (un)finished film had now collapsed to the point where they'd considered selling off their share of the profits to German investors as a tax loss, were trying to book screens to show it from May. It was part of an uninspiring selection of Fox films offered to exhibitors that year, a selection which contained such critical and financial turkeys as *The Duchess and the Dirt Water Fox* (Melvin Frank) and *Mother, Jugs and Speed* (Peter Yates). Fox wanted $10 million in advance bookings for *Star Wars*, but they secured less than $2 million and that only by implying to theatre chains that they wouldn't be offered the anticipated *The Other Side of Midnight* (Charles Jarrott, 1977), which Fox would be offering for exhibition later in 1977, if they didn't sign up for *Star Wars*. Several exhibitors complained at this technically illegal 'block booking' and the company was fined $25,000 for it; punished for virtually forcing cinemas to show something which turned out to be one of the most successful movies of all time.

In early 1977 Lucas screened *Star Wars* for a group of friends. It was very nearly finished, although the opening crawl was substantially longer and many of the special effects shot were absent, represented instead by sequences from World War II films and real combat footage shot by the USAF during that conflict. Among those present were the Huycks, Brian De Palma, Marcia Lucas, Alan Ladd Jr, Steven Spielberg and Jay Cocks. Martin Scorsese had been invited but his fear of flying coupled with the troubles editing his own, equally fraught *New York, New York* meant he didn't turn up.

After the screening Ladd was confused, Marcia upset and De Palma reportedly near-hysterical. At a restaurant afterwards he tore into Lucas's film, attacking everything from Carrie Fisher's hair to the first appearance of Darth Vader – he hated everything about it. Lucas was upset but the Huycks and Spielberg were probably unsurprised: De Palma had behaved in exactly the same way after the first screening of Scorsese's *Taxi Driver*, laughing loudly through most of Cybill Shepherd's scenes with Robert De Niro and pouring scorn on the entire enterprise during the post-screening discussions. Only Spielberg was impressed, famously telling Lucas that he thought it'd make him $100 million. Lucas baulked at such high expectations, pointing out that nothing made $100 million and arguing that Spielberg's own *Close Encounters of the Third Kind* would undoubtedly do better at the box office. The two directors wrote what they considered genuinely realistic estimations of what each other's film would make in their first six months of release on the inside of matchbooks which they then traded. By the time Lucas got round to opening Spielberg's matchbook and saw the figure $33 million in his friend's scrawling hand *Star Wars* had already made ten times that.

On 30 April the now completed movie received its first public showing: a preview for a demographically selected audience held at the Northpoint Theater, LA, the same preview venue where *Graffiti* had tested so well. Before the screening Marcia Lucas (who had taken time off from working on *New York, New York* to help cut the film) told her husband that if the audience didn't cheer when the *Millennium Falcon* rescued Luke from Vader at the end then they'd know that there really was a lot of work to do. Lucas was morose, and insisted that previews always meant at least some re-cutting. In the end the film's first public audience didn't cheer when the *Falcon* rescued Luke – they stood and raised their arms, clapping in a manner editor Paul Hirsch could only describe by comparing it to an audience reacting to someone striking a home run in the ninth innings of the seventh game of the World Series.

After the film finished showing, an upbeat Paul Hirsch deadpanned, 'I guess we won't be recutting then' at the rest of the editing team. Alan Ladd Jr was at the screening and though he'd maintained his faith in the project when all else at Fox had long given up on it, even he was surprised. 'I didn't expect that,' he told the filmmakers above the din. 'I didn't expect that.'

ALTERNATIVE VERSIONS: The most notable alternative version of *Star Wars* is the Special Edition reissue released to cinemas in the US on 31 January 1997, although there are considerably more than two editions of the film in existence, even ignoring changes in picture and sound quality caused by the subtly different speeds of NTSC (American) and PAL (British) VHS tapes. The version of the film rereleased on 21 July 1978 had had several alterations made to it. One brief scene had been added (the sequence in which a 'captive' Chewbacca roars at the Death Star's tiny wheeled 'mouse robot' and it speeds away in terror – the scene occurs 109 minutes into the Special Edition) and the voice of actress Shelagh Fraser (Aunt Beru) had been re-dubbed. Other small alterations were made to later copies of the film made available on videocassette and to television stations.

The version shown on British and American television during the 1980s is identical in most respects to the 21 July 1978 version (although see also **TITLE TATTLE**); what differences there are are minor but of circumstantial interest. In the TV cut the stormtrooper searching for the droids in Mos Eisley (49 minutes in) says, 'This one's secure, move onto the next one', whereas in the 31 July 1978 cut (then available on VHS) he says 'locked' instead of 'secure'. The VHS version (in line with later VHS reissues and the Special Edition) adds an acoustic to the voices of the X-wing and Y-wing pilots during the Battle of Yavin so they sound to the audience as if they are talking through microphones. On the TV edition the voices are untreated. Also on television Luke has the line 'Blast it, Wedge, where are you?' (1 hour 44 minutes in), whereas the VHS (and indeed Special Edition) has him saying 'Blast it, *Biggs*, where are you?' (the latter makes far more sense, given that Luke knows Biggs well, but has never spoken to Wedge – although it is Wedge, not Biggs, who ultimately helps Luke). The British 1991 widescreen VHS release cuts one line (stormtrooper: 'Close the blast doors, close the blast doors' at 1 hour 26 minutes), which had been extant in all previous versions of the film. By the Special Edition the line had returned.

The Special Edition grew out of Lucasfilm's simple plan to rerelease *Star Wars* to theatres on or around the twentieth anniversary of its opening. New prints were required for such a rerelease, and it was decided that the picture would be given a THX sound mix and undergo a degree of picture clean-up as part of the process of striking these new prints. Investigation of the master tape quickly demonstrated to Lucasfilm that the master negative of the film had degraded badly in the decade or so since it had been looked at. This was partially an ironic result of the film's initial success: Fox had struck so many prints from the master once the film had become a success that they had literally worn it out. Worse still, the original negative was of a low quality anyway – *Star Wars* was not an expensive film and the rapidly disappearing budget and pressure of time forced Lucas and his team to use no less than five different types of film stock on the master. One of these was an extremely low quality 'reversal stock' on which many of the special-effects shots were printed. This discovery prompted a more extensive remastering and cleaning-up process (including recombining all the special-effects shots digitally from their original elements), but this process very quickly mutated into something else.

Lucas began to tinker with *Star Wars*, adding scenes not present in the initial cinema release and supervising the addition of new special-effects sequences. He later explained to journalists that there were always things in *Star Wars* that he '. . . wasn't satisfied with, special-effects shots that were never really finished, scenes that I wanted to include [that weren't] included for reasons of money and time.'

Principal among these was a scene of Han Solo being confronted by Jabba the Hutt in the hangar bay in Mos Eisley. Lucas intended Jabba to be a non-human, probably 'a furry creature, like Chewbacca', but rather than having an elaborate costume made for an actor to wear on set he instead intended to shoot the scene with an actor playing Jabba and then matte a stop-motion creature over the top of the actor during post-production. This decision was partially influenced by the failure of the initial attempt to shoot the Mos Eisley cantina sequence (see **PRODUCTION**), itself caused, in part, by creature-design maestro Stuart Freeborn's illness over this period. The Mos Eisley cantina scenes were reshot in America later, but the scene with Jabba took place in the hangar in front of the immovable 23 tonne *Millennium Falcon* mock-up: it had to be shot in London or not at all. The scene was shot with actor Declan Mulholland playing Jabba whilst wearing a large padded fur costume to increase his size. Back in America time and money would prohibit the addition of the stop-motion beast over Mulholland (although Freeborn produced several designs). The loss of the scene annoyed Lucas, and whilst it appeared in the radio, comic-book and novel adaptations of the movie its absence from the picture itself remained a sore point with him, especially after Jabba did make an appearance in *Return of the Jedi* in scenes which capped off the plot thread concerning the price on Han Solo's head, which the hangar scene had been intended to help initiate (much of Jabba's expositional dialogue was added to that of the subtitled character Greedo in an earlier scene in an attempt to make matters as clear as possible). Explaining his reluctant excision of the scene Lucas commented, 'At that point . . . ILM was coping with so much work . . . we were way behind schedule . . . to add that sequence would have broken the back of the operation.'

The raw footage of Mulholland and Ford was included in the 1987 documentary 'The Making of Star Wars', which aired on NBC in the US and ITV in the UK; the feature also included Lucas expressing further his frustration at the scene never being included in the film. The rerelease of 1997 afforded the opportunity to put the scene in, advances in computer graphics allowing Lucas's team at ILM to drop a CGI Jabba modelled after the one used in *Jedi* into the footage. The CG took ILM nearly a year to do, and while it would be disingenuous to suggest that the opportunity to test out the technology for creating CGI characters which could then interact with previously filmed actors didn't play a part in the decision to add Jabba into *Episode IV*, it was clearly also the fulfilment of a long ambition on Lucas's behalf. Conversely the addition to the same scene of the bounty hunter Boba Fett (who had not been designed when *Star Wars* was shot – see **The Empire Strikes Back**) had nothing to do with settling old scores and was done seemingly for a combination of the following reasons: it pleased the character's fans, it was a further test of the technology that allowed the addition of new elements to pre-filmed footage, and Lucas was aware that the character would feature in at least one of his planned *Star Wars* prequels, his addition neatly adding to the illusion of unity that they would in part seek to imply. The other scene added to the Special Edition is a small scene of Luke greeting Biggs (see **CUT SCENES**) in the hangar on Yavin immediately before the X-wings leave to attack the Death Star.

The other alterations are mainly to the special effects; some new shots were added to the attack on the Death Star, and the explosions of both Alderaan and the Death Star itself were redone to make them more impressive. The 'dewbacks' whose minimal presence in the theatrical edit of *Star Wars* had so irritated Lucas were added (again as computer-generated items, their first appearance 14 minutes in) and numerous background characters were added into the scenes taking place in Mos Eisley in order to increase the scale and substance of the township. One of the more subtle additions is (at around 53 minutes) when the *Falcon* leaves Mos Eisley – in the originally released version there was no shot of the ship actually taking off (it was technically impossible to achieve), so for the reissue ILM added a CGI shot of this moment to the film.

As Lucas saw it there were two types of changes made to the Special Edition: 'One is restoration . . . to make it a cleaner, clearer picture of high quality that will be preserved longer . . . the best possible picture, the clearest quality sound; that's just for posterity and my own emotional well-being. A lot of the ILM changes we made were . . . for aesthetic reasons.' At the suggestion that he'd make further changes Lucas was dismissive: 'There's no real emotional things on the creative side [left to] come along.'

The most controversial change made to the Special Edition was to the Mos Eisley cantina, where the bounty hunter Greedo threatens Han Solo at his table. In the film as released Han shoots Greedo dead during the course of their conversation; in the Special Edition Greedo fires first and Han returns fire, killing him. 'In terms of Han's character I didn't like the fact that the first thing he does is gun someone down in cold blood,' claimed an unrepentant Lucas. The alteration remains one of the most discussed aspects of the reissue and is even the source of a joke in box office hit comedy *Jay & Silent Bob Strike Back* (Kevin Smith, 2001). In this Holden McNeil (Ben Affleck) responds to a friend's suggestion with the observation that it is 'the worst idea since Greedo shooting first'.

The cost of preparing the Special Edition of *Star Wars* was ultimately a little higher than the film's original $10 million budget. In a similar piece of up-scaling the new cut was released to 2,100 screens, many more than the paltry number that exhibited the original cut (see **RELEASE**). The rereleased *Star Wars* took over $32 million in its opening weekend, breaking box office records for January. The film subsequently returned to the top of the all-time box office receipts chart.

CUT SCENES: Although the Special Edition of 1997 (see **ALTERNATIVE VERSIONS**) restored some missing material, several scenes remain extant which have not been incorporated into any version of the film.

Most important amongst these is the original introduction to Luke Skywalker. Luke is seen out in the desert by his uncle's farm attempting to fix a tall thin piece of machinery, and is being hindered by mechanical failures with a droid which is meant to be helping him. Activity in orbit (the space battle which opens the film) causes him to abandon his chores and rush away.

In another cut scene he arrives outside a building in the nearby town of Anchorhead. He goes inside and meets up with various friends of his, including Cammie (Koo Stark) and Biggs (Garrick Hagon), a character occasionally referred to in dialogue in the completed film ('Biggs is right, I'm never going to get out of here') and who later appears as one of the X-wing pilots who dies during the attack on the Death Star. They then go outside and use Luke's binoculars to try and see the space battle, but the firing has finished. Luke's friends tell him that he must have been mistaken and then mock him for insisting that he's right. This scene is particularly interesting for its subtleties. Biggs speaks of the Empire positively, and discusses a potential rebel attack on Tatooine and the idea that the Empire would have to 'fight to save the system'; his use of the word 'save' carries with it an implicit endorsement of the Emperor's rule. This sequence with Luke's friends would, if included, have been the only scene in the trilogy where the audience observed ordinary people, as opposed to rebels and servicemen, discussing the nature of the Empire.

A later scene shows Biggs telling Luke that although he has recently qualified from 'the academy' (the same academy Luke wants to attend, as referred to in later dialogue) he's going to jump ship and join the rebellion against the Empire instead. This revelation indicates that his earlier, positive comments about the Empire were made because they were in public, and nicely creates the idea of an undercurrent of paranoia relating to public opposition of Imperial rule. Interestingly, Biggs's explicit criticisms of the Empire in this scene make it sound more Communist than Fascist. Biggs talks of the Emperor 'nationalising commerce', and scathingly informs Luke that unless somebody does something soon his Uncle Owen will become 'a tenant, slaving for the greater glory of the Empire'.

In this scene Biggs explains to Luke that he's telling him that he plans to join the rebels because he wants someone to know what really happened to him. The scene was cut for a number of reasons. Not only is it rather long (and therefore slows down the pace of the early part of the movie), but it's also almost one continuous single take. This meant either losing all of it or keeping all of it, as editing it down would prove complex. Additionally it bears a strong resemblance to several scenes in *American Graffiti*, particularly those involving Steve and Curt or Curt and Wolfman Jack, and Lucas didn't want to be seen to repeat himself so obviously one film on. Perhaps most importantly, given where it was originally positioned in the screenplay and the first cut, it disrupts the progress of the film's first act. In this, structurally speaking, the audience encounters one character who then introduces them to the next (Artoo and Threepio introduce us to Luke who introduces us to Ben who introduces us to Han and so on). This scene removes that aspect, something Lucas was keen to keep in, by cutting back and forth from Luke to Artoo and Threepio's story.

Cut from the shooting draft at a relatively late stage and subsequently never shot was the lightsaber fight between Luke and Vader. The script progressed almost identically to the finished film, except that in the script, when Luke is called upon to fire a photon torpedo into the Death Star's exhaust port, the weapon fails to fire. He lands his X-wing on the exterior of the Death Star and with Artoo's help drops the payload from the torpedo in by hand. Vader also lands his ship and attacks Luke, who is forced to defend himself with his lightsaber before escaping.

QUOTES:
Obi-Wan: 'The force is what gives a Jedi his power. It surrounds us and penetrates us and binds the galaxy together.'

Princess Leia: 'Governor Tarkin, I should have expected to find you holding Vader's leash. I thought I recognised your foul stench when I was brought on board.'
Tarkin: 'Charming to the last.'

Vader: 'I've been waiting for you, Obi-Wan. We meet again at last. When I left you I was but the learner, now I am the master.'
Ben: 'Only a master of evil, Darth.'

Han: 'I ain't in this for your revolution . . . I expect to be well paid.'

Princess Leia: 'If money is all that you love, then that's all you'll receive.'

Luke: 'I want to come with you to Alderaan, I want to learn the ways of the force and become a Jedi like my father.'

Obi-Wan: 'You can't win, Darth – if you strike me down I shall become more powerful than you could possibly imagine.'

MUSICAL NOTES: The rough edit of *Star Wars* had a temporary track which used pieces of Gustav Holst's *The Planets* suite, snatches of Alex North's score for *Cleopatra* (Joseph L Mankiewicz, 1963) and selections from Bernard Hermann's music for Alfred Hitchcock. Whilst these stock tracks helped create the right mood, there was never – as has been suggested since – the possibility of actually releasing the film with such a track. Lucas wanted a rich, orchestral score, something old-fashioned and outdated at the time. He knew it should be reminiscent of Erich Wolfgang Korngold, the multi-award-winning film composer who had scored *The Adventures of Robin Hood* (Michael Curtiz, 1938) and *The Sea Hawk* (Michael Curtiz, 1940), two of his models for *Star Wars*.

Steven Spielberg introduced him to John Williams, who had provided a folksy score for his own *The Sugarland Express* (1974) and an iconic motif for *Jaws* (1975). Excited by the project, and intuitively understanding Lucas's belief that a film this odd needed an instantly understandable score, Williams watched the rough cut alone in a preview cinema and then spent three intensive days with Lucas discussing themes. Williams's music was recorded by the 97-piece London Symphony Orchestra throughout March 1977. Williams had written over ninety minutes of music for a two-hour film. Lucas was awed by the experience of watching the orchestra work, and later played tapes of the soundtrack down the phone to Steven Spielberg in LA.

The final sound mix for the film was made at the Samuel Goldwyn Studios in Hollywood mere days before the release. At the suggestion of Walter Murch (see *THX-1138*) Lucas had recorded in Dolby, a system that promised that the sound in commercial cinemas would sound exactly as it had done in the dubbing theatre. It was as yet untried, and difficulties with it delayed the film's exhausted crew – especially sound-effect editor Ben Burtt, another USC graduate who'd left a teaching position at his alma mater to join Lucas on *Star Wars* – still further.

RECURRING CONCERNS: As with *THX* and *Graffiti* this is, at heart, about a young man who abandons the environment in which he was raised and embarks on an adventure of his own; as such it could be considered autobiographical on Lucas's part.

Lucas's obsession with metaphorical circles is frequently referenced in dialogue (most famously in Vader's 'The circle is now complete') and, by beginning the *Star Wars* saga in the middle, Lucas ensures that form imitates content, as anyone watching the films in production order is forced to approach the story in one epic circle, ending (in 2005) shortly before they began (in 1977). Visual circles include the Death Star (a series of concentric circles), Tatooine's twin suns and the endless curving architecture on Tatooine. More importantly, when the camera does move it is always in arcs (the Death Star briefing scene which begins with Tagge saying 'Until this battle station . . .' or Luke's arrival at the burned-out homestead.)

In a story and thematic sense *Star Wars* is the least dense of the series it spawned; this is simply because it is the foundation on which the rest of them are built.

Lucas's interest in speed has been previously noted, but *Star Wars* finds a new outlet for it. Before this film the use of speed in Lucas's own work had been restricted to discussion and representation of it; neither *THX* nor *Graffiti* are fast-moving films and it is in, perversely, their slowest, talkiest scenes that characters talk about moving fast. The striking thing about *Star Wars* in 1977 was – and indeed still is – just how fast it moves, both in terms of narrative and within specific individual sequences. Put simply, its use *of* speed: the action movie just didn't exist in 1977, at least not in the way audiences now understand it. Not since the days of Lucas's beloved Michael Curtiz had adventure movies really involved any more than people trying to escape from burning buildings or one-on-one fights. Try watching the De Laurentiis *King Kong* (1977) with twenty-first century eyes; for something that's ostensibly an action-adventure movie it's crushingly, unbearably slow. The Death Star trench sequence was unthinkable in its day not simply because of the effects technology but because of the very way it moved; while this was remarkable in cinema as a whole, it was doubly so in terms of science fiction, where – as on *Star Trek* – a space battle would previously involve two near-static spaceships firing occasional beams of thick yellow light at each other. Lucas's instructions to the ILM effects people were to try to make the trench run as exciting as the car chase from *The French Connection* (William Friedkin, 1974). That this was the only recent model he could think of is telling in itself; that *Star Wars* so outstripped that rightly famous sequence in terms of outright visceral thrills is all the conclusion you need. The Death Star run remains, in spite of all its imitators, a hugely tense, fraught, frantic, exciting sequence, staggeringly well edited and utterly compulsive. *Star Wars*, unlike *THX*, isn't about vehicles that carry you at great speed to a far-off place, providing an escape from the mundane and the oppressive in the process – it *is* one.

EXTERNAL REFERENCES: Before production began in earnest Lucas sat his crew down and made them watch four feature films which he felt between them defined the look and atmosphere he was after in *Star Wars*. They were Stanley Kubrick's *2001: A Space Odyssey* (1968) and Douglas Trumbull's 1975 *Silent Running* (the only two medium-to-large-budget special-effects movies ever made, as well as being the only 'space pictures' Lucas admired the craftsmanship of), Sergio Leone's *Once Upon a Time in the West* and Frederico Fellini's *Satyricon* (both from 1969). The Leone picture was full of the sunburned, sandblasted vistas Lucas wanted to evoke during the Tatooine sequences, and the Fellini film, with its aspects of travelogue and attempts to portray an entire society (Nero's Rome) both corrupt and alien to twentieth-century Americans in an almost fly-on-the-wall manner, gave an idea of the 'documentary fantasy' approach the director was carrying over from *THX-1138*. All four films shared one vital element: they're all windows into lived-in worlds remarkable to audiences but regarded as desperately ordinary by the film's protagonists – a key part of Lucas's approach to *Star Wars* and an important factor in its ultimate success.

Leia is imprisoned in cell number 2187, a reference to the Canadian documentary *21-87* (Arthur Lipsett, 1964) which suggested to Lucas much of his pseudo-documentary approach to filmmaking.

The assault on the Death Star resembles the battle sequence in *633 Squadron* (Walter Grauman, 1964); and the finale where Han and Luke are presented with their medals is (famously) a more or less shot-for-shot lift from Leni Riefenstahl's 1936 Nazi propaganda piece *Triumph Des Willens*, a film as technically magnificent as it is morally reprehensible: the scene copies Hitler, Himmler and Metze approaching the Nuremberg monument almost exactly.

The sequence where Luke returns to the ruined Lars homestead has often been said to be based on the scene in *The Searchers* (John Ford, 1956) where John Wayne returns to his brother's home to find it has been burned out by Comanche Apaches; but it has an equal amount of resonance with a similar moment in *Nevada Smith* (Henry Hathaway, 1966).

Lucas has suggested that Artoo and Threepio should be considered one personality, and that in Freudian terms Artoo is the Id, while Threepio is the Superego. He has also often noted that Artoo's way of communicating through bleeps and whistles is a conscious nod to Harpo Marx.

The Jawas are obviously a nod to the 1939 Victor Fleming version of *The Wizard of Oz*, whilst Threepio combines the characteristics of the tin man from both that version and the earlier, black and white silent version (Larry Semon, 1925), while looking more than a little like the Maria robot from *Metropolis* (Fritz Lang, 1926).

The Mos Eisley cantina is a deliberate evocation of the Korova Milk Bar from Kubrick's *A Clockwork Orange* (1971); production designer John Barry worked on both films.

Elements of the characters of Artoo-Detoo, See-Threepio, Princess Leia and Ben Kenobi are consciously modelled on (respectively) the runaway princess, peasants and samurai portrayed in Akira Kurosawa's 1958 *Kakushi toride no san akunin* (Trans: *Three Bad Men in a Hidden Fortress*), a film acknowledged by Lucas as a personal favourite, and a major influence on *Star Wars*. This resemblance is often strongly exaggerated in criticism however, particularly by people who haven't seen Kurosawa's film (there is often an assumption that the Death Star in some way resembles the fortress, a comment so ignorant of the content of Kurosawa's film it is simply laughable). It is worth noting that the final scene of *Star Wars* is – in story terms – also the final scene of *Hidden Fortress* despite the lifting of the mechanics of the *Triumph Des Willens* shot. That in itself is both a very clear expression of Lucas's casual eclecticism in influences and testimony to his film literacy. These nods to *Star Wars*' cinematic forebears, just a few of many, are the physical equivalent of Lucas's self-conscious acquisition of the character types and archetypal situations common to many epics and myths (see **SCREENPLAY**). The commonly used abbreviated title for Kurosawa's film is cheekily mentioned once in *Star Wars*, when General Motti speaks of the rebels' 'hidden fortress'.

The comic rivalry over Princess Leia that Han and Luke indulge in is a conscious evocation of the Bing Crosby/Bob Hope squabbling over Dorothy Lamour that featured in the *Road to . . .* film series.

RELEASE: Odd as it seems now, when every blockbuster and pseudo-blockbuster imaginable is prefaced by three months of breathless, unrelenting media 'enthusiasm', *Star Wars* wasn't released on a wave of hype or accompanied by an extensive marketing campaign. Quite the opposite, in fact: it was released (on 25 May 1977) to a paltry 32 screens, after a barely publicised premiere at Mann's Chinese Theater in Hollywood. It made $2.8 million in its opening week (then a record) but still didn't receive a wider nationwide release for another two months and then only after public demand. Despite its almost unprecedented success in preview screenings Fox were still unsure of what to do with Lucas's bizarre children's film. It only got a Hollywood opening at all because William Friedkin's *Sorcerer* – which had been intended for this slot at Mann's – was not yet ready. It is a measure of the studio's lack of faith in, and general bewilderment with, the project that no posters were produced to advertise the film's initial period of release (the iconic painting of Luke lifting his lightsaber above his head was the product of around a month later when the movie was already a success). There was a trailer. Featuring almost no clips from the movie it ran for less than a minute: against a moving field of stars a voice-over announces mournfully, 'This film is light years ahead of its time. The story of a boy, a girl and a galaxy. With thousands of creatures spanning the universe'. It is doubtful that a single person was tempted into the cinema to see *Star Wars* by the trailer alone.

So negative had the studio's advance feeling about *Star Wars* been that Lucas virtually fled the country; he was still in LA on the opening day, finishing the sound edit for *Star Wars* (he was unhappy with the copy playing downtown) and waiting for

Marcia to finish up on *New York, New York*, but the next day they both flew to the Manua Kea hotel, Hawaii, where they spent time with the Huycks and Steven Spielberg and Amy Irving. It was an attempt to escape what he felt would be the inevitable terrible reviews and consequent wrath of the studio. Even when Alan Ladd Jr called him to share his excitement over the movie's colossal opening weekend, Lucas was unmoved; all movies labelled science fiction did well in their first few days due to the business attracted by the neglected fanbase for such things. It was only when the film continued to do outstanding business and was expanded to more and more theatres that Lucas considered returning early from his holiday and began to realise that the film he'd just made had changed his life forever (see **Raiders of the Lost Ark**).

Between the release of *Star Wars* and the 23 May shares in Fox climbed to $11.50 each; over the next three months the value rose to $24.62, such was the film's unexpected value to the studio.

CRITICISM: '*Star Wars*,' wrote the *New York Times*' Vincent Canby on 26 May 1977, 'is the most beautiful movie serial ever . . . an apotheosis of *Flash Gordon* serials'. It was not merely that, though, but also 'a witty critique' with references to films and literature as diverse as *Quo Vadis* (Mervyn LeRoy, 1951), Arthurian myth, *The Wizard of Oz* (Victor Fleming, 1939) and the Gospel According to St Matthew. It was a view Canby would return to and refine in later years (see below); the following month he used an article in the same paper to respond with some ferocity to negative comments about *Star Wars* (which began once the picture was becoming such a success) that the picture was not 'a film of the Non-think age' as some other critics had implied, and reiterated his points about the film's extra-textual richness and the 'remarkable technique' its writer/director had demonstrated by putting it on the screen at all. *Variety* was more simplistic, but equally demonstrative in its positive reaction: '*Star Wars* is a magnificent film', it said, 'the biggest possible adventure'. There is a tension in some contemporary reviews, between those who see the film as something clever and perhaps important, and those who consider it to be simply a grandiose adventure. This tension is one the film itself is aware of, as there is conflict between the characters over the importance and significance of what they are doing. Solo dismisses the force as 'a load of simple tricks and nonsense', but comes in time to appreciate Luke's aptitude ('great shot, kid, that was one in a million'), while Kenobi, like Lucas, pines for what he feels has been lost from the world, and through Luke looks to revive it somehow.

Most contemporary reviews of *Star Wars* were overwhelmingly positive, reflecting both the critical respect Lucas's previous two films had created for him and, perhaps, critics' dislike of the general disdain displayed by the studio towards what was, after all, the work of one of the prime movers of New Hollywood. It was this critical reaction, combined with good word-of-mouth responses from audiences, that led *Star Wars* to charge up the box office rankings. Whatever might have been suggested since, the fact is that the success of *Star Wars* was a popular phenomenon, not (as the releases of many summer films have been since) a managed media event.

Box Office magazine's review called *Star Wars* 'a wow of a film' and 'one of the most entertaining films of its type yet done', praising the pace ('non-stop') and tone ('Few fantasies have been made with such a sense of humour'). While it conceded that the special effects would be the biggest draw for some viewers it was adamant that smarter viewers shouldn't 'overlook other elements'. The *Washington Post* was particularly keen on Lucas's direction and the way new 'perspectives and monsters' turned up 'with astonishing and amusing rapidity', citing as a particular favourite moment the cutaway in the Mos Eisley cantina where one alien is seen laughing at a joke that another has just told him, but which the audience has not heard. Also lauded was Guinness for supplying 'emotional equilibrium and authority', and critic Gary Arnold concluded that *Star Wars* was 'delightful . . . the kind of . . . movie you dream about finding, for your own pleasure as well as your kids' pleasure'.

Negative reviews really only began later, and then were limited to off-the-cuff comments linked to some nebulous idea that *Star Wars*' success somehow infantilised mainstream American film, or that every bad film with special effects could be blamed on George Lucas. It's an argument that's been made often and badly.

It is arguable that, for example, *Moonraker* (Lewis Gilbert, 1979), *Top Gun* (Tony Scott, 1986), and *Godzilla* (Roland Emmerich, 1998) are among the worst films ever made, and it is almost certainly true that none of them would exist in the form they do without *Star Wars*. It is equally true that many deeply unsatisfactory, but ultimately enjoyable, popcorn films have followed in *Star Wars'* wake: from the overrated and nonsensical *Superman – The Movie*, (Richard Donner, 1978) through to *Independence Day* (Roland Emmerich, 1996) and *Lost in Space* (Stephen Hopkins, 1998).

It is also true that the whole Don Simpson/Jerry Bruckheimer 'high concept' approach to filmmaking was in part a reaction to *Star Wars*, and an attempt to artificially recreate its success. This is something most people with a serious interest in film would consider deeply unfortunate. Indeed Lucas, as big a movie fan as there has ever been, has himself repeatedly gone on record as saying that America needs to stop dwelling on 'the monetary side' of movie-making, saying: 'How much does a film cost? How much does a film make? It's very depressing to dwell on that. No film is *about* what it *cost*.'

The response to this is simple: these things are no more George Lucas's or *Star Wars'* fault than every tenth-rate Western is John Ford's responsibility or every tedious vampire movie is somehow down to Friedrich Murnau. Lucas is no more to blame for *The Avengers* (Jeremy Chechick, 1998) than Paul Schrader is for *Rambo III* (Peter MacDonald, 1988) because he also wrote a film about a traumatised Vietnam veteran. It's simplistic nonsense to suggest otherwise.

Equally over-emphasised is the idea that the New Hollywood Lucas and his peers built across the 70s was somehow wiped out by Spielberg's *Close Encounters of the Third Kind* (1977) or *ET: The Extra-Terrestrial* (1980) or Lucas's *Star Wars*. The movement burnt itself out in a blizzard of cocaine, production excess and in-fighting after ten years of conspicuous artistic success. Blockbusters didn't replace the kind of films that Coppola and Scorsese made; they replaced the mindless westerns, overblown musicals, disaster movies and lushly sweeping melodramas that were also the cinematic staple of the 70s. Like for like, popcorn for popcorn, and they brought audiences back into cinemas in record numbers too. More money meant more films, more cinemas, more screens: more choice. Non-studio pictures have won the most prestigious Academy Awards in recent years, the ultimate vindication of Hollywood having to accept the strength and power of the independents.

Those who argue that Lucas's fantasy picture robbed the world of another decade of startlingly brilliant work from his peers choose to forget that almost all of the movie brats continue to work; and they ignore the fact that while Lucas's idea of a

personal project may have been the insipid *Willow*, Paul
Schrader's was *Cat People* (1983), John Milius's was *Red Dawn*
(1985) and William Friedkin's was *Sorcerer* (1977).

Time Magazine's Jay Cocks called *Star Wars* 'a combination' of
Flash Gordon, The Wizard of Oz, Errol Flynn swashbucklers,
westerns, the Hardy Boys, Sir Gawain and the Green Knight and
The Faerie Queen, and when he labelled it 'a subliminal history of
the movies, wrapped in a riveting tale of suspense and adventure',
he got closer to the truth of it than anyone before or since. It was a
view shared by other critics; years later Vincent Canby of the *New
York Times* – always an admirer of the film – called *Star Wars* 'a
knowing critique of various ancient myths and legends and the
written fiction [they] have given rise to'. This isn't to say that
Lucas has unthinkingly or ignorantly appropriated others'
techniques and archetypes – to call it plagiarism as some have done
is spectacularly misplaced. *Star Wars* is Lucas's personal summary
of culture: a blend of pop, literature and film that borrows brands
and motifs and tropes from wherever it chooses. It's one of the first
artefacts of cut-and-paste culture and – when it was made there
wasn't quite a way to express this through metaphor – it functions
like Internet hypertext. Click on a moment and it takes you
somewhere else in an instant. It has an abundance of moments and
glances, lines and shots, images and ideas that lead an attentive
viewer to seminal cornerstone works such as those listed above.

Star Wars is a beautiful film – technically exquisite, witty and
endlessly exciting. It's smarter than its critics too, its blending of
elements from wildly diverse sources an onscreen representation
of Lucas's own brand of pop-literate, eclectic intellectualism;
something that the list of films he made his crew watch before
filming (see **EXTERNAL REFERENCES**) proves beyond
question. Lucas's film has given more than one generation a
passion for cinema in all its forms, and led people to cinematic
experiences they would never otherwise have had. It's the reason
teenagers know who Akira Kurosawa is.

Star Wars didn't kill cinema; it's a primer *for* it, and to appreciate
how different it is from those films made in imitation of or
attempting to cash in on it, one only has to sit down and watch it.

AWARDS: The Academy Awards that covered the period of *Star
Wars'* release were presented on 29 March 1978. The ceremony
saw the picture nominated for nine Oscars – a substantial haul by

any standard. The nominations (an asterisk donates a nomination which went on to win) were as follows: Best Actor in a Supporting Role – Alec Guinness; Best Director – George Lucas; Best Picture – Producer Gary Kurtz, Executive Producer George Lucas; Best Screenplay Written Directly for the Screen – George Lucas; Best Art Direction, Set Decoration* – John Barry, Roger Christian, Leslie Dilley, Norman Reynolds; Best Costume Design* – John Mollo; Best Effects, Visual Effects* – Robert Blalack, John Dykstra, Richard Edlund, Grant McCune, John Stears; Best Film Editing* – Richard Chew, Paul Hirsch, Marcia Lucas; Best Music, Original Score* – John Williams; Best Sound* – Derek Ball, Don MacDougall, Bob Minkler, Ray West.

The picture would sweep the technical awards; fitting recognition that nothing physically like it had been produced before. Sound Designer Ben Burtt was even awarded a special achievement Oscar – no suitable category to recognize his work existed – for his contribution to the picture.

Where *Star Wars* lost out was with the more prestigious 'mainstream' awards, and Lucas himself won nothing despite being nominated in three categories. Alec Guinness's failure to win what would have been his second Oscar was presumably made up for by the Academy's presentation to him of a Special Award for a career 'Advancing the Art of Screen Acting' a year later. Lucas has still never won an Oscar for himself, and whilst Hollywood remains possessed of its (unconsciously) deeply ironic commercial self-loathing he is unlikely to. Lucas's loss was Woody Allen's gain, as that director's *Annie Hall* (rather ordinary by Allen's own remarkable standards, it must be said) took most of the awards *Star Wars* had also been up for.

At the Saturns, the awards ceremony of the American Academy of Science Fiction, Fantasy & Horror Films, the movie cleaned up, taking Best Actor (Mark Hamill), Best Actress (Carrie Fisher), Best Costumes (John Mollo), Best Make-Up (Rick Baker, Stuart Freeborn), Best Science Fiction Film, Best Special Effects (John Dykstra, John Stears), Best Supporting Actor (Alec Guinness) and Best Writing (George Lucas). Lucas also won a Best Director award, but he had to share it with Steven Spielberg who had garnered an equal number of votes for *Close Encounters of the Third Kind*. John Williams's award for Best Score was also tied with that for *Close Encounters* but as Williams had scored that film as well, he didn't have to share the award with anyone else.

The American Cinema Editors nominated co-editors Richard Chew, Paul Hirsch and Marcia Lucas for their Eddie and the British Society of Cinematographers nominated DOP Gil Taylor for Best Cinematography but none of them won.

At the 1979 BAFTAs the film won Best Sound (the entire sound team of twelve was named on the night). It was also nominated for Best Costume Design (John Mollo), Best Film, Best Film Editing (Paul Hirsch, Marcia Lucas, Richard Chew) and Best Production Design/Art Direction (John Barry).

At the Golden Globes Lucas was nominated for Best Director, the film for Best Motion Picture (Drama) and Alec Guinness for Best Motion Picture Actor in a Supporting Role.

The Los Angeles Critics Association gave *Star Wars* Best Picture and it won the Hugo for Best Dramatic Presentation. Lucas's screenplay was nominated by the Writer's Guild of the USA as Best Comedy Written Directly For The Screen. The People's Choice Awards gave the film Favourite Motion Picture.

John Williams's total number of awards for Star Wars was immense. As well as the Oscar he picked up the Anthony Asquith Award for Film Music at the BAFTAs, a Grammy, a Los Angeles Critics Association Award and a Golden Globe.

TRIVIA: The opening battle between the Star Destroyer and Princess Leia's ship (usually referred to as 'the Blockade Runner' or the *Tantive IV*) is one of the most famous film openings in movie history. Ironically, despite the Star Destroyer dwarfing the other ship in the scene as recorded, the Blockade Runner model was 194cm long and the Star Destroyer a mere 91cm, their relative sizes disguised by camera positioning and editing. The 'smaller' model was larger because of the greater amount of detail required by the design.

Sound Designer Ben Burtt created R2-D2's signature whistles by combining sounds of a baby gurgling with noises from an electronic keyboard, producing something that simultaneously had a live quality whilst seeming resolutely artificial in origin.

TITLE TATTLE: At the time of its release the film was entitled simply *STAR WARS*; the caption above the famous 'crawl' which reads *Episode IV* and, on the next line, *A New Hope*, were added for the 10 April 1981 theatrical rerelease, after the decision to produce a sequel (and implicitly prequels) had been made (see **The Empire Strikes Back**).

'I had to build up from scratch my own special-effects company'

Industrial Light and Magic was set up by George Lucas to provide the special effects for *Star Wars* (1977), and was initially headed by John Dykstra, who had worked on *The Andromeda Strain* (Robert Wise, 1971) and *Silent Running* (Douglas Trumbull, 1975). Dykstra later departed to set up his own effects company, but before leaving was instrumental in the development of motion-control cameras. Traditionally models moved and cameras were stationary. The creative leap forward that the fledging ILM was able to make was the realisation that if a camera's motions were precisely controlled by a computer then the camera could move around the model, giving the illusion that the model moved at the same time as the camera. For the first time special effects seemed to be taking place in three-dimensional space. The special effects for *Star Wars* were judged to be so much better than anything produced up to that point that one reviewer (Gary Arnold in the *Washington Post*) suggested that the previous year's Oscar for special effects should be revoked, as what had been achieved (on the De Laurentiis *King Kong*) was so inferior to what *Star Wars* had managed less than a year later.

ILM remains one of the principal innovators in the history of special effects, key in the development of optical compositing, go-motion, CGI (Computer Generated Imagery), morphing and film input scanning. The company has won nearly a dozen Oscars and many more nominations for its work on films as such as *ET: The Extra-Terrestrial* (Steven Spielberg, 1982), *Terminator 2: Judgment Day* (James Cameron, 1992), and *Forrest Gump* (Robert Zemeckis, 1994). It remains the effects house against which the work of all others is judged, and many of its staff, such as Dennis Muren and Phil Tippett, have become among the few 'backroom' filmmakers whose names are recognised outside the film industry.

EXPERT WITNESS: 'It's got an amazing shelf life, it never really died. There's never really been a time when it hasn't been popular; [people even make] trick-or-treat costumes of Luke and Leia. Obviously it's tough when you become a mythic figure . . . it's not for me to claim as my own in that sense.' Actor Mark Hamill (Luke Skywalker)

LUCAS ON STAR WARS: '. . . life sends us along funny paths. We think we know where we are going but we don't. I was really determined to be a documentary filmmaker and do *avant garde* things on the side.'

More American Graffiti (1979)

(110 minutes)

Universal
A Lucasfilm Ltd Production
Based on characters created by George Lucas and Willard
Huyck & Gloria Katz
Written by BWL Norton
Director of Cinematography: Caleb Deschanel
Art Director: Ray Storey
Produced by Howard Kazanjian
Executive Producer: George Lucas
Original music by Gene Finley
Edited by Tina Hirsch
Directed by BWL Norton

PRINCIPAL CAST: Paul Le Mat (*John Milner*), Candy Clark (*Debbie Dunham*), Ron Howard (*Steve Bolander*), Mackenzie Phillips (*Carol/Rainbow*), Bo Hopkins (*Joe Young*), Charles Martin Smith (*Terry Fields*), Cindy Williams (*Laurie Bolander*), Anna Bjorn (*Eva*), Richard Bradford (*Major Creech*), John Brent Ralph (*Club Owner*), Scott Glenn Newt (*Leader, Electric Haze Band*), James Houghton (*Chopper Pilot*), John Lansing (*Lance*), Manuel Padilla (*Carlos*), Ken Place (*Beckwith*), Mary Kay Place (*Teensa*), Tom Ruben (*Eric*), Doug Sahm (*Bobbie*),Will Seltze (*Andy Henderson*), Monica Tenner (*Moonflower*), Ralph Wilcox (*Felix*), Carol Ann Williams (*Vikki Townshend*), Rosanna Arquette (*Girl in Commune*), Tom Baker (*Cop #1*), Eric Barnes (*Sergeant James Dutton*), Becky Bedoy (*Girl in Bus*), Buzz Borelli (*The Freak*), Ben Bottoms (*Perry*), Patrick Burns (*Musician #1*), Tim Burrus (*Slick Eddie*), George Cantero (*Guard*), Chet Carter (*Race Starter*), Dion Chesse (*Delivery Man*), Gil Christner (*Ed*), Don Coughlin (*Cop #2*), Mark Courtney (*Kevin Bolander*), Michael Courtney (*Teddy Bolander*), Denny Delk (*Police Sergeant*), Frankie Di (*Trophy Girl*), Steve Evans (*Race Announcer*), Nancy Fish (*Police Matron*), Rocky Flintermann (*Neighbour*), Michael Frost (*Musician #2*), Jonathan Gries (*Ron*), Paul G Hensler (*Lieutenant*), Julie Anna Hicks (*Child in Commune*), Robert Hirschfeld (*Delivery Man*), Erik Holland (*Ole*), Jay Jacobs (*Congressman*), Naomi Judd (*Girl in Bus*), Leslie Gay Leace (*Girl in Bus*), Delroy Lindo (*Army Sergeant*), Dwight

Reber (*Pilot*), Sandra Rider (*Girl in Commune*), Kevin Rodney Sullivan (*Lieutenant*), Morgan Upton (*Rick Hunt*), John Vella (*Big Guy*), Dan Woodworth (*Student Leader*), Clay Wright (*Pilot*), Harrison Ford (*Bob Falfa*)

TAGLINE: Whatever became of the carefree, crazy kids you met in *American Graffiti*?

SUMMARY: New Year's Eve 1964. After a brief reunion with Steve and Laurie Bolander and Terry Fields and Debbie Dunham, John Milner struggles through a difficult day's drag racing (ultimately teaming with an old rival to triumph over a new one) and romances a beautiful Icelandic girl. Driving home, clutching his winner's trophy, he's killed by a drunk driver.

New Year's Eve 1965. On tour of duty in Vietnam Terry Fields survives the gung-ho attitude of his new immediate superior and the visit of a self-important senator, but the death of Joe, a friend from his old days in California, causes him to desert the army. After faking his own death he goes on the run to Europe.

New Year's Eve 1966. Debbie Dunham splits up with her boyfriend, dilettante Lance, and spends the day with the members of an exciting, but hardly famous, band. She then crashes a New Year's party at the Fillmore club.

New Year's Eve 1967. Steve and Laurie are planning their spectacular New Year's Eve party, when a row about Laurie's desire to get a job leads to her spending time with her younger brother Andy. This consequently gets her involved in an anti-Vietnam War demonstration. Steve follows her, and as the two try to work out their differences, they become increasingly politicised by the brutal way the establishment deals with those who do not share its views.

PRODUCTION: After the hugely successful post-*Star Wars* rerelease of *American Graffiti* Universal Pictures presented the sequel to their picture to George Lucas as a *fait accompli*. Contractually able to make a sequel with or without his consent, they nevertheless informed him that they were intending to produce one and asked if he would like to be involved. Despite his involvement in *The Empire Strikes Back* and *Raiders of the Lost Ark*, then heavily in pre-production, Lucas accepted the studio's overtures.

Although there was no question of him solo-writing and/or directing the film he was determined to be in charge of it. Taking the attitude that there was no point in making the picture at all unless they 'took risks' and that the most important thing to do was to make a film they could be proud of, Lucas began looking for a writer to work with on the screenplay.

Lucas had three conditions that anyone he would contemplate hiring would have to meet. They'd have to be roughly contemporary in age to him, they would have to be from the West Coast of America (the failure of Richard Walter's draft of the first movie had left him convinced that there was a distinctly West Coast ambience to the material that had to be adhered to) and finally they would have to be experienced in writing comedy.

Amongst those Lucas and designated producer Howard Kazanjian[1] interviewed was Bill Norton, a writer and one-time director who immediately asked Lucas if he could shoot as well as script the film. Lucas and Kazanjian asked Norton to write a script for their consideration, and made it clear that if the script was to their liking he would be first choice to direct.

Lucas spent a week in intensive meetings with Norton, and the two roughed out the shape and structure of the storyline. They decided that the film would be divided into four sections, each set in a different year and each dealing with the fate of a different character from *Graffiti*. As with the original film each section of *More* would take place over just one day. The film would then cut between the different years throughout its running time, flashing backwards and forwards continually.

Although the team were bound by the constraints of the epilogue to the original film (see **American Graffiti**), it was decided to utilise the audience's foreknowledge of characters' destinies to increase the impact of their screen time. Thus everything Milner does during the day is given added poignancy by the audience's certain knowledge of his death that night. Norton took Lucas's ideas away with him and completed a first draft of the script.

Lucas liked what he read, and hired Norton to write and direct the movie. The film was shot over 44 days, at a cost of $3 million, Norton's crew shooting virtually all of the film within California –

---

[1] Howard Kazanjian. Attended USC before becoming a highly regarded assistant director; films in this capacity include Alfred Hitchcock's *Family Plot* (1976). Moved into production at Hitchcock's suggestion and quickly acquired a reputation for efficiency.

even the sequences set in Vietnam, which were filmed near the Sacramento river. For these Vietnamese sequences, which were filmed in the manner that Lucas had intended to shoot *Apocalypse Now* when he was attached to that project as director, Lucas accepted a demotion to cameraman and worked under Norton's direction; this was his heaviest on-location involvement in the main production of the picture. He would be intimately involved – as he often is with movies he's producing – once the film reached the editing suite. 'Editing . . . that's his first love', commented Norton later. Lucas worked with credited editor Tina Hirsch (who prepared the first cut) as well as Lucasfilm's extremely talented Duwayne Dunham[1] and Marcia Lucas, who untangled the complex split-screen processing of the 1966 sequences (see **VISUAL INTERESTS**).

CASTING: In contacting Lucas about the film Universal made a wise decision, as almost all of *American Graffiti*'s original cast stated on being contacted that they'd never become involved in a sequel made without Lucas's explicit blessing. Of *American Graffiti*'s principals only Richard Dreyfuss was unwilling to take part. He had won an Oscar for his performance in *The Goodbye Girl* (Neil Simon, 1977) and was uninterested in returning to the role of Curt. The part was sensibly not recast and the character's absence referred to just once, briefly (during an argument with Laurie, Steve points out that Curt is in Canada). Presumably it was felt that the card at the end of the first film – to which this line is a reference – was explanation enough.

Ron Howard was – ironically– only available to work over the summer; he was busy the rest of the year shooting the *American Graffiti*-inspired TV series *Happy Days*. Cindy Williams, too, was occupied most of the year on a TV series (the *Happy Days* spin-off *Laverne and Shirley*). Mackenzie Philips was now a regular on TV show *One Day at a Time* (a sitcom with no obvious connections to *Happy Days*). The shooting of *More* was thus specifically arranged to take place in the summer 'off' season when TV actors aren't required by their respective shows.

Howard and Williams's TV fame gives an added textual frisson to their increased politicisation as their section of the movie

---

[1] Duwayne Dunham, co-editor *Return of the Jedi*, editor *Blue Velvet* (David Lynch, 1986), *Wild at Heart* (David Lynch, 1990) and the 90-minute *Twin Peaks* pilot episode (David Lynch, 1990). Director *Twin Peaks* episodes 1, 18 and 25.

progresses; Norton and Lucas took great delight in getting two 'white-bread Americans . . . TV heroes' to punch out a cop and rescue a bus load of draft-dodging Vietnam demonstrators. Norton argued that the police's indiscriminate attack on Steve ('But I voted Republican!' he snarls as they search him) and their clear lack of regard for the rights of the demonstrators was an effective illustration of how the Johnson and Nixon administrations had turned even their own supporters against them through their civil order methods.

Harrison Ford – whose career, like Dreyfuss's, had now moved into stratosphere – did agree to return to the role of Bob Falfa, albeit briefly. He did one day's filming and received no fee or credit for his work. The sequence featuring Falfa, once a drop-out jock and now a snarling police motorcyclist (badge no. 54362) who obviously gets off on busting hippies, is one of the movie's best scenes.

Anna Bjorn, hired by Norton to play the mono-lingual Icelander Eva, can speak perfect English.

QUOTES:
Terry's motto in Vietnam: 'Kick ass, take names and eat Cong for breakfast.'

Lance: 'You got nothing better to do than hassle long hair?'
Officer Falfa: 'It's my life, friend, I love my work.'

Laurie: 'You like living in squalor?'
Andy: 'I love it. Every little piece of trash and rancid dirt.'

Andy tries to justify his demo sign which reads 'Pigs eat shit': 'We have to communicate in a vernacular the police will understand.'

MUSICAL NOTES: Like *American Graffiti* itself, it was intended that the sequel would be a 'musical', albeit one in which none of the principals actually sings. One of Lucas's pieces of advice to Norton was to write scenes to represent and/or be underscored by specific songs. Again – as in the original film – music was used to character effect, although this time it had a more political or ironic bent. The use of Percy Sledge's 'When a Man Loves a Woman' over one of Steve and Laurie's marital arguments is very effective, and the sight of Vietnam jungles burning whilst Diana

Ross hollers 'Stop in the Name of Love' is exactly the kind of brutal juxtaposition favoured by late-90s/early-00s filmmakers.

RECURRING CONCERNS: The teasing of an audience which knows a character's final fate became *de rigueur* during the Republic trilogy.

VISUAL INTERESTS: A fascinating and radical visual experiment, *More American Graffiti* exploits the fact that it takes place simultaneously in four different times by using one of four totally different cinematic styles for each of its settings. The styles are so distinctive, and so clearly delineated, that only those viewers paying no attention at all could possibly be confused by it. The 1964 sequences are shot with Panavision 50mm lenses and use minimal camera movement – the effect is to make these scenes look like an early 60s Elvis movie. The Vietnam section is shot on slightly overexposed 4:3 16mm film and consequently looks like news footage of the time. The 1967 campus story was shot using long lenses and a 1:1.85 screen ratio, like many campus movies of the era; the most unorthodox section is the 1966 one, shot in widescreen and in a manner reminiscent of Michael Wadleigh's film of Woodstock. Boxed images move up, down and around the screen; scenes are shot from multiple angles and several of them are represented on-screen simultaneously. Characters flit from one box to another and back again. The effect is hallucinatory, disorienting and brilliant.

EXTERNAL REFERENCES: The use of the song 'The Green Berets' over the initial Vietnam scenes is clearly designed to evoke memories of the 1968 film of the same name (co-directed by Ray Kellogg and star John Wayne). A notoriously right-wing propaganda puff piece, and militantly pro the Vietnam War, it ends with Wayne and a Vietnamese child walking off hand in hand into the sunset.

RELEASE: Put out on 17 August 1979, *More American Graffiti* sank without trace almost immediately, despite Universal head Ned Tanen (who loudly professed to liking it more than the first picture) willingly splashing out on publicity for it. It ultimately didn't matter anyway; Universal had already pre-sold the film to television stations for more than it cost to produce. To date it has grossed around $8,100,000, just under three times its original cost.

CRITICISM: *Variety* was impressed by *More American Graffiti*'s conceptual and editorial conceits, but not with the finished picture. 'One of the most innovative and ambitious films of the last five years', it commented, before concluding that as a whole the film was 'daring but ultimately pointless'. The *New York Times*, on the other hand, took offence at the movie's tone, protesting at the 'trivialisation' of the Vietnam War and the 'comic' look at campus riots, despite the former being a charge answered within the film itself and the latter not really occurring in the picture at all. The review – which also somehow confused the characters of Andy and Curt – concluded that 'Wolfman Jack ... has long since outworn his welcome'. The film's reputation hadn't really shifted 21 years later when it received its belated UK video cassette premiere: 'all the coherence and drama is missing', felt one reviewer of the VHS, who admitted that he found the film's aims 'bewildering'. The permanent dismissal of Norton's film is rather a shame as the finished movie is both emotionally complex and a technical treat. The queasy farce of the Vietnam sequence is grim rather than funny, but this appears to be the intended effect; when deaths do occur they're so utterly horrific that it can't be fairly suggested that the film is trivialising the experiences of the men who fought the war. It's simply attacking the people who sent them to fight it.

The four strands are kept aesthetically separate whilst being thematically linked and all display wit and poignancy. The helicopter Mede-vac sequence, in which the audience is convinced Terry will die, is absolutely terrifying, and the final scene of Milner driving cheerfully to his death is heartbreaking. The drag racing is lush and exciting and the film makes valid political comments whilst illustrating how much America changed over just three years. The entire film is, moreover, subtly and brilliantly edited. The performances of all the actors, especially Le Mat, are superb, and Ron Howard again shows an ability to find levels of subtlety and even danger within his usual screen persona that isn't even hinted at in his more famous acting work. *More*'s total failure at the box office can be put down to three things. It's far too dislocated, ambitious and odd to appeal to mass audiences, its sequel status deprived it of the chance to be taken seriously by

'It's safe to say that *Star Wars* single-handedly created the film merchandising business' James Surowiecki, *Slate* magazine (29 December 1989)

The suggestion that *Star Wars* was the first film to be extensively merchandised before, during and after its release is either utterly disingenuous or wildly inaccurate depending on who's making it. To compare the film series – with its admittedly high number of spin-off products – to mid-80s cartoon series such as *Masters of the Universe* or *ThunderCats*, both of which were created purely to sell an extant toy range, is inappropriate. Whilst there have undoubtedly been a large number of *Star Wars* products produced since December 1976, the facts of the matter are substantially different to those routinely trotted out.

Ten years before *Star Wars*, Universal's *Dr Dolittle* had been released accompanied by a huge merchandising push. No fewer than three hundred separate items – including dolls, toys and clothing – were licensed by the studio, and whilst most sold poorly the intent to make money from the movie in stores as well as in box office rentals was clearly there. *Thunderball* (Terence Young, 1965), the fourth of Eon Pictures' James Bond series, was extensively merchandised by its production company; items available included vodka, clothing, men's cologne and an invisible-ink writing pen that also doubled as a whistle and a cap gun. Gilbert Toys produced two-inch cast metal figures of characters from the film and a twelve-inch Action Man/GI Joe-style doll of Bond. Further licensees created toy pistols, spy cameras, toy cars, jigsaw puzzles, watches, spy briefcases, games, lunchboxes, bedspreads, pillowcases and a Scalextric-style car-racing track to sate a public in the grip of Bond fever.

At the time of *Star Wars*' production the two biggest licences were for the Universal television series *The Six Million Dollar Man* and Fox's own collapsing movie franchise *Planet of the Apes*, both of which – particularly *Apes* – were heavily merchandised by their parent companies. *Apes* items included record/book adaptations of the films and a range of six-inch articulated 'action figures' (dolls for boys) that came out through Mego. Mego also produced similar figures under licence from Marvel Comics (creating a range based upon superheroes such as Spiderman and the Fantastic Four) and Paramount (*Star Trek* figures). There were plenty of licensed toys and other items in stores, and Fox were sufficiently aware of the potential value of this market that when Lucas asked for control of the merchandising rights for *Star Wars* rather than an increase in salary (when the success of *American Graffiti* made it possible for him to renegotiate the terms of his deal with Fox), the company was initially reluctant, and ultimately only granted him 60% of the rights. He acquired the remaining 40% over the next two years after another round of negotiations.

Neither is it accurate to suggest that vast amounts of *Star Wars* merchandise were available when the film was given its release by Fox, who were at the time convinced that the film would be a financial disaster. Lucas had begun writing a novelisation of the shooting draft, which he allowed to be completed by Alan Dean Foster, and it had been released with little fanfare in December 1976. It sold out of its initial print run but the publisher refused to reprint it, claiming the run had been set at exactly the level they knew it would sell. Aside from this, only a double LP of Williams's score (priced $8.90) was available in May 1977. Fox were then producing soundtrack LPs for all but a handful of their pictures and *Star Wars*' status as a disaster waiting to happen affected even that. Only 2,000 LPs were pressed for the initial run, a far smaller number than usual.

Extensive merchandising was never part of the *Star Wars* game plan for Lucas; if it had been there would have been products on the shelves in May 1977. He'd badgered Fox for the rights for an entirely different reasons: 'I thought I was getting the ability to promote the film using posters and T-shirts', he later explained. His reasoning was that Fox wouldn't promote the film themselves, and in a sense he was proved right: the distributor produced no posters, no T-shirts and only a single one-minute trailer to promote the film's original release. A desultory number of programmes were produced for and by Fox for the first run at Mann's Theater, but they were cheap and uninspired and sold out quickly once the film was actually released.

The right to produce toys, games and other products was granted only after the film had proved such a remarkable financial success in cinemas, and then only at the demand of potential licensees who wanted a piece of the action. 'It wasn't as though I said, "Let's create a Luke Skywalker action figure" ', Lucas later claimed, defending himself against the charge of having commercialised movie-making – 'It was someone else'. On another occasion he has stated that 'The licensing thing is something that grew spontaneously. It certainly wasn't something [I] predicted.'

Puzzles, jigsaws and other items that could be produced with relatively short lead times were just beginning to reach toy shops across America at Christmas 1977, but Kenner – who had purchased the right to create a range of four-and-a-half-inch plastic action figures of the *Star Wars* characters – had simply not had enough time to create their product. It became apparent to everyone at the company that they were going to miss Christmas.

Worried that by the time their products were available the *Star Wars* obsession of America's children would be over, the company devised the '*Star Wars* Early Bird Certificate Package'. This was a large envelope available in toy stores. It included a certificate which the recipient would post to Kenner, including their name and address. The recipients would then, as soon as they were produced – and before they were physically available in shops – receive the first four of Kenner's *Star Wars* action figures: Luke Skywalker, Princess Leia, R2-D2 and Chewbacca.

Also included in the envelope, presumably to keep any child occupied on Christmas morning, were a cardboard action-figure display stand/playset, a sticker sheet, a '*Star Wars* Space Club' membership card, and two colour photographs from the film. Sales were colossal, and no one had suspected how much children wanted *Star Wars* toys until they were offered them – it was then that the full extent of pre-teen enthusiasm for the movie became abundantly clear.

> The *Star Wars* action-figure range expanded to around a hundred items by the time of its eventual closing-down nearly a decade later. When challenged about the range, and the one that replaced it around ten years later, in time for the Special Editions, Lucas responded curtly but disarmingly, 'Letting kids have toys and use their imagination isn't an evil thing . . . I think play is a healthy thing.'

critics, and lastly its clear belief that the Vietnam War was a shameful, squalid conflict run by petty incompetents and supported only by the ignorant offended those middle Americans who did see it. In urgent need of radical reappraisal, *More American Graffiti* is a very good film.

EXPERT WITNESS: 'The idea was to make something that touched some of the major highpoints of the 60s; that really dealt with the 60s as a theme.' Writer/Director BWL Norton.

LUCAS ON MORE AMERICAN GRAFFITI: 'I did *More American Graffiti*, it made 10 cents, it failed *miserably.*'

Star Wars: Episode V – The Empire Strikes Back (1980)

(120 minutes original edition/122 minutes special edition)

Twentieth Century Fox
A Lucasfilm Production
Director of Photography: Peter Suschitzky, BSC
Screenplay by Leigh Brackett and Lawrence Kasdan
Story by George Lucas
Produced by Gary Kurtz
Special Edition Produced by Rick McCallum
Production Designer: Norman Reynolds
Music by John Williams
Executive Producer: George Lucas
Directed by Irvin Kershner

PRINCIPAL CAST: Mark Hamill (*Luke Skywalker*), Harrison Ford (*Han Solo*), Carrie Fisher (*Princess Leia*), Billy Dee Williams (*Lando Calrissian*), Anthony Daniels (*C-3PO*), David Prowse

(*Darth Vader*), James Earl Jones (*Voice of Darth Vader*), Peter Mayhew (*Chewbacca*), Kenny Baker (*R2-D2*), Frank Oz (*Yoda*), Jeremy Bulloch (*Boba Fett*), Kenneth Colley (*Admiral Piett*), Julian Glover (*General Veers*), Michael Sheard (*Admiral Ozzel*), John Hollis (*Lando's Aide*), John Ratzenberger (*Major Durlin*), Denis Lawson (*Wedge*)

TAGLINE: The Star Wars saga continues.

SUMMARY: A long time ago, in a galaxy far, far away, those rebels that survived the battle of Yavin (see **Star Wars**) have settled on the ice planet of Hoth, and are building a base from which to attack the Empire. Luke Skywalker, who now carries the military rank of commander, is with them – as is Han Solo, despite his need to pay the money he owes to Jabba the Hutt in order to have the vast price now on his head lifted by the crime lord.

Seriously injured by a creature native to the planet (a wampa) and dying in a snow blizzard, Luke is visited by the spectre of Obi-Wan Kenobi. Kenobi's ghost tells him to go to the planet Dagobah where he will learn from Yoda, a Jedi Master who was one of Kenobi's own teachers. Luke is rescued from certain death by Han, who has defied instructions and risked his own life to save that of his friend.

Shortly afterwards the Imperial Starfleet, led by Darth Vader, attacks Hoth and the rebels are forced to evacuate the planet. Vader's objective is not simply to crush the rebellion; he is also unapologetically obsessed with finding Luke, for reasons none of his officers seems to understand.

Luke goes to Dagobah – taking Artoo – where he meets Yoda and is instructed in the ways of the Jedi. There he also meets and talks to the spirit of Obi-Wan, and the two Jedi advise Luke on his future. Luke also suffers a hallucination where he fights and defeats Darth Vader only to discover that the Dark Lord has his face.

Han, Leia, Chewie and Threepio flee Hoth in the *Millennium Falcon*, and Vader, knowing that they are Luke's friends, pursues them obsessively. Prevented from rendezvousing with the rest of the rebel fleet, they instead head to a giant floating gas mine, Bespin Cloud City, which is run by Lando Calrissian, an old smuggling friend of Han's. During their pursuit from Vader, and later at Bespin, Han and Leia's combative, acerbic verbal relationship blossoms into a combative, acerbic romance.

Lando betrays Han and Leia to the Imperials. He insists he had no choice, citing his responsibilities to the people of Bespin, and explains that Vader and his troops, accompanied by bounty-hunter Boba Fett, arrived not long before the *Millennium Falcon* did. Leia and Han are to be the bait in a trap that Vader has set for Luke.

On Dagobah Luke receives visions that Han and Leia are in pain, and decides that he must go to help them. Yoda and Obi-Wan insist that Luke should stay with them and complete his training as a Jedi. In confronting Vader, they claim, Luke faces grave moral peril. He will be tempted by the dark side of the force and may – as Vader himself once did – find it impossible to resist. Promising to heed their warnings Luke flies to Bespin to rescue his friends. By the time he arrives Han has been frozen into a block of solid subzero carbonite so that he may be transported to Jabba more easily, and Vader plans to do the same to Luke so that he may be sent to the Emperor. Leia, Chewie and Threepio escape from Bespin in the *Millennium Falcon*, accompanied by Lando, whose change of heart has been in part influenced by his realisation that Vader cannot be trusted to keep his promise to return control of Bespin once Skywalker has been captured.

Vader and Luke fight a lightsaber duel in the carbon-freezing chamber, and despite Luke's obvious abilities Vader easily bests him, cutting off Luke's right hand. As Luke prepares to be killed Vader instead reaches out to him, saying that Luke has not yet begun to realise the extent of his powers. Vader asks Luke to join him. Together, he claims, they can end the civil war and restore order to the galaxy. Luke refuses.

Vader tells Luke that *he* is Luke's father, and again asks Luke to join him. Instead Luke throws himself off the gantry on which he has been hanging, choosing death rather than corruption.

Hanging from the underside of Bespin Luke calls out to Obi-Wan for help, but the old Jedi doesn't appear. He then calls out to Leia, who somehow hears his pleas, and the *Millennium Falcon* returns to Cloud City to rescue him. The *Falcon* escapes Vader's Star Destroyers and makes a rendezvous with the rest of the rebel fleet.

Shortly afterwards Lando and Chewie leave in the *Falcon*, aiming to rescue Han from Jabba the Hutt. Luke arranges to meet them once he's fit, and together he, Leia and the droids watch the *Falcon* leave for Jabba's base world of Tatooine.

SCREENPLAY: Once *Star Wars* became such a success a sequel was inevitable. Whilst contemporary interviews and later comments seem to suggest that Lucas was personally more interested in developing the backstory to his biggest success than following up its events, it was obvious that what the public wanted to see was a follow-up to the single most successful movie of all time. Some of the cast were contractually tied to any sequel (Hamill and Fisher, for example) if Lucas chose to use them, whilst others (Ford and Guinness) had no such obligations. Another contractual complication was that whilst Lucas owned the sequel rights to *Star Wars* they would revert to Fox if he didn't begin work on any such sequel within two years. It is entirely possible that Lucas only began work on the film that became *The Empire Strikes Back* because he wanted someday to work on something conceptually similar to *The Phantom Menace*.

Both the writing and directing of *Star Wars* had proved extremely trying for Lucas, and the final straw had been the heart-attack scare he'd suffered during the preparation of the final cut. At the time *Empire* began production he was convinced that he would never script or direct again. He was now in his own eyes an 'executive producer', albeit one of a different stripe to those who had run Hollywood for decades – he would develop his own projects, edit them, storyline them, fund them and even shoot second unit for them when he had to. He could make the movies he wanted to make via a role that would paradoxically allow him more control but greater freedom: he could supervise everything without going through the day-to-day trauma of shooting on a soundstage or endlessly and painfully redrafting screenplays. This mode of working would also allow him to work on more than one project at time (indeed, whilst developing *Empire* he would also work on *Raiders of the Lost Ark* and *More American Graffiti*).

Lucas wrote a story treatment for his *Star Wars* sequel, one reputedly based upon the abandoned second act of one of his earlier, excessively long *Star Wars* outlines and littered with ideas from earlier drafts and treatments.

To have the screenplay written he contacted Leigh Brackett. Brackett had written or co-written more than half a dozen films, mostly for Howard Hawks. These included acclaimed Raymond Chandler adaptation *The Big Sleep* (1946), John Wayne/Dean Martin western *Rio Bravo* (1959) and further Wayne westerns *El Dorado* (1967) and *Rio Lobo* (1970). In all of these she'd demonstrated a flair for dialogue and character interaction, although she had less grasp on plots and plotting (*The Big Sleep* simply does not make narrative sense, and the other three films all have the same storyline). As Lucas's outline was detailed with regard to structure and incident, the assignment played to her strengths whilst shoring up against her weaknesses.

Brackett was no stranger to pulp science fiction either: her novels included the luridly entitled *Queen of the Martian Catacombs* and *Black Amazon of Mars*, and she'd been a regular contributor to anthology magazine *Planet Stories*. These facts together rendered her, in Lucas's eyes, perfect for the assignment.

Brackett wrote a first draft from Lucas's outline and delivered the screenplay to him in March 1978. When, weeks later, Lucas got around to phoning her to discuss suggested rewrites, he was informed by her husband that she'd died a few days before.

Time pressures forced Lucas to rewrite Brackett's first draft himself whilst searching for another writer to complete the script. As he worked he listened – as he had done while writing *Star Wars* – to selections of classical music which he felt best summed up the mood he was trying to inject into the scene. This was a development of the technique he'd come up with of listening to classic rock'n'roll whilst writing *Graffiti*, and it made the writing process less unpleasant for him.

Young screenwriter Lawrence Kasdan was already on the Lucasfilm payroll, writing the screenplay for the projected Lucas/Spielberg collaboration *Raiders of the Lost Ark*, the first draft of which he was shortly due to deliver. As much of a movie buff as Lucas or Spielberg, Kasdan had a thorough knowledge of Hollywood history and a love for Warner Bros gangster films of the kind that Brackett herself had written. During his later career he carved a unique niche as a man who could take the archetypes of 40s cinema and imbue them with wit and depth in a contemporary setting.

When Kasdan arrived in person at Lucas's home to hand the *Raiders* screenplay over to him, the producer immediately offered him the job of scripting *Empire*. Kasdan was flattered but, since Lucas hadn't yet read *Raiders*, he was also concerned about what would happen if Lucas hated the screenplay. Lucas told Kasdan that he would read the *Raiders* script that night and if he didn't like it he'd call the next day and cancel the offer. He didn't, however, consider it likely: 'I get a feeling about people,' he told the screenwriter. When Lucas didn't call, Kasdan began work.

Including Brackett's script and Lucas's own rewrite of it, the screenplay went through five major drafts. Unlike *Star Wars*, which changed radically from outline to outline and draft to draft, *Empire* altered little in spirit, tone or structure throughout the rewriting process. Set pieces changed position in the script (the flight through the asteroid field originally took place after the rebels' escape from Bespin), character and place names changed (Yoda was 'Minch Yoda' in the outline, and simply 'Minch' in Brackett's script, while Bespin was initially called Katbrae and then Kettlebrae), but in essence the story remained the same. It always began with the fall of a rebel stronghold and ended with Vader asking Luke to join him. Among the changes made during the writing was the addition of the spectral Obi-Wan Kenobi, factored in when it became clear that Guinness was not averse in principle to a cameo appearance. In the Brackett/Lucas drafts Luke heads for Dagobah not because of cryptic advice from Kenobi, but because he's discovered the co-ordinates for the mysterious system on a talisman that had once belonged to the late Jedi. In later drafts Artoo-Detoo deduces the co-ordinates from information encoded on a crystal Luke finds hidden inside the lightsaber Kenobi gave him in the previous film.

A 'fight' between Obi-Wan's spirit and Yoda, in which the two Jedi demonstrate to Luke their respective skills with a lightsaber, was written in and then cut, presumably when the decision to make Yoda a puppet was made (see **Attack of the Clones**).

It was not until the second draft that Han was encased in carbonite at the film's climax. Earlier versions had him escape with Leia and Chewie, and in the film's final scene leave his friends behind in order to reacquaint himself with his stepfather – an influential figure in their home system – and ask him to lead his people into the rebel alliance.

Luke's ordeal with a phantom Vader on Dagobah changed over time; originally Luke hallucinated a debate between himself and Vader in which the Dark Lord told Luke that only Solo stood between him and the love of the Princess Leia, and that if Luke came over to the dark side then Vader would see to it that the princess became his.

In the finished screenplay/film Luke and Han's rivalry over Leia – a comic subplot in *Star Wars* – is reduced to a minimum. Leia kisses Luke on Hoth, but seems to do it principally to annoy Solo, with whom she is already sparring in a manner similar to the Bogart/Bacall-style archetypal sparring lovers that Kasdan adored and that Brackett had helped define. The rivalry disappears entirely in the next film, where it is revealed to both Luke and Leia (and the audience) that they are siblings separated at birth. This suggests – as *Star Wars* and *Empire* producer Gary Kurtz has since intimated – that Lucas did not originally intend Luke and Leia to be related, and that perhaps he was playing with another mythically archetypal situation. One of the few mythic tropes not touched anywhere across the *Star Wars* project is the equivalent of Arthur's Queen Guinevere becoming the lover of Arthur's most senior knight Lancelot, an action that ultimately leads to the collapse of the new golden age they have built together. Can we for Arthur read Luke, and for Guinevere and Lancelot read Leia and Han?

An alternative explanation would be that, as Lawrence Kasdan has suggested, Lucas intended to imply that Luke and Leia were drawn to one another *because of* their blood relationship and mutual affinity with the force ('Somehow, I've always known', Leia says in *Jedi* after being told), and that while they both misconstrued their subconscious recognition of this as romantic attraction, this recognition also stopped either of them from ever acting on it. They are, after all, said to be not merely brother and sister but twins in *Jedi*, and in mythological terms twins are often depicted as having intuitive or psychic rapports similar to the one Luke and Leia demonstrate in the finished version of *Empire*. It is also possible that Lucas at one point intended to push this incest-tinged romantic rivalry subplot a little further, in a manner that would make the films retroactively less than suitable for children, before shying away from the subject matter. It has been further suggested by some commentators that the hint of incest was included in *Empire* by Lucas to increase the film's already numerous resonances to Shakespeare's *Hamlet* (see **EXTERNAL REFERENCES**). When asked about the extent of his own foreknowledge, Kasdan made it clear that he was only aware of Luke and Leia's familial relationship when he was handed the outline/first draft for *Return of the Jedi*. As for Lucas, however, Kasdan was frank: 'I don't know when *he* knew that . . . I don't know if that was [always] part of the scheme. It's about family, this saga. It makes sense – this is how the [Han/Luke/Leia love] triangle is going to be solved.'

Other alterations made to the film's plot included the removal of an entire race of aliens (the Whatnots) who occupied another of the planets in Bespin's system. They would meet Han and Leia before the rebels' visit to Cloud City, and would later help Luke fight against the Empire on his arrival. They were dropped for representing simply one subplot too many.

Also simplified was the middle section of Vader's plotline. In the Lucas/Brackett drafts Vader retreated to a castle (probably on the Imperial capital world, not yet named as Coruscant [see **The Phantom Menace**]) to ponder on the pursuit of the *Millennium Falcon*. In the film he merely retreats into a meditation chamber on his Star Destroyer. In the first draft the Emperor talks to him via a viewing screen rather than appearing as a giant hologram, while in the second the Emperor himself does not appear at all, his vizier Sate Molock visiting Vader instead. In all versions the essence of the message relayed to Vader is the same.

Another interesting aspect of the script is that no version of it contains the moment where Vader reveals to Luke that he is Luke's father. The scene where he offers the young Jedi half of the galaxy if Luke will become a servant of evil is always there, from as far back as Lucas's initial outline, but the line itself doesn't appear in *any* script. Even the shooting draft had the line 'Obi-Wan is your father' instead. Director Irvin Kershner and Lucas famously took Hamill aside, swore him to secrecy and then told him what line of dialogue James Earl Jones (who voiced Vader) would actually be dubbing over so that the actor could tailor his reactions to what would be said in the film rather than what Prowse said on set. It has been estimated that as few as five people (Lucas, Kasdan, Hamill, Jones and director Irvin Kershner) knew the truth before the film was released (Kershner later described the deception as 'the perfect crime' and noted with glee that 'no one knew').

This controversy however raises the idea that, much as with the Luke/Leia relationship, Vader's exact relationship to Luke had not been defined during production. Yet this seems unlikely. For the villain to be the hero's father is a classic motif, and one that features in some of Lucas's many outlines produced for the original *Star Wars*. If the issue was not set in stone during the making of *Star Wars* (which is more than possible) it was certainly so by the time *Empire* began filming in 1979. Any other possible ending for the shooting draft simply lacks sufficient impact to produce Luke's anguished reaction and subsequent suicide attempt; 'Obi-Wan is your father', for instance, translates in story terms as 'the dead father you revere is actually another dead man you revere', which is neither shocking nor dramatic. The only other real possibility – 'The Emperor is your father' – lacks impact due to the Emperor's own lack of screen time in the films made thus far, and is supported by far less internal evidence and foreshadowing than the line used in the completed film.

The screenplay for *Empire* is full of wit and darkness and, cunningly, chooses to pair off characters who had little screen time together in the previous film (i.e. Artoo and Threepio, who spend *Star Wars* side by side, are split up early on, Leia here spends most of her time with Han rather than Luke, and Threepio barely speaks to Han in *Star Wars* but the two are paired off here), thus creating new character situations and partnerships not really suggested by the *Star Wars* script.

Kasdan's first major draft was completed by November 1978, and Lucas sent a copy to Alan Ladd Jr at Fox with a note that read 'Best read listening to the *Star Wars* album'.

CASTING: For the most part the cast of *The Empire Strikes Back* were, like the crew, returning members of the *Star Wars* company. The one major human role that needed to be cast was Lando Calrissian; for this Lucas turned to Billy Dee Williams, a charismatic screen actor who'd been in the business since childhood. A native New Yorker, Williams is also an acclaimed oil painter whose work is widely exhibited. His movie roles have included parts in *The Out of Towners* (Neil Simon, 1970) and *Lady Sings the Blues* (Sidney J Furie, 1972), opposite Diana Ross.

Of the other roles that needed to be cast none could be called major and all were cast out of Lucasfilm's London office. Perhaps the most significant (and even the actor involved would be hidden behind a mask and have his lines redubbed by another artiste) was the bounty hunter Boba Fett. The role went to Jeremy Bulloch, a smiling, charming actor much on British television who had been in Cliff Richard's *Summer Holiday* (Peter Yates, 1962).

The imperial officers seen taking flak from Darth Vader were played by Julian Glover, Michael Sheard and Kenneth Colley respectively. Sheard, although vastly experienced, had not yet gained the role that would make him a British TV legend – Mr Bronson in *Grange Hill*. Julian Glover's work was principally on the stage, although he would become the Bond series' most low-key villain ever, Aristotle Kristatos in *For Your Eyes Only*, the following year. Both Sheard and Glover would be thought of by Lucas again ten years later for roles (see *Indiana Jones and the Last Crusade*).

A job that nestled somewhere between performer, actor, puppeteer and technical crew was that of 'performing Yoda', as the end credits had it. 'When I created Yoda I said I want him to be really, really small,' Lucas later explained. 'I decided to do it as a puppet.' This puppet was designed by Stuart Freeborn using aspects of his own face and that of Albert Einstein, and the job of realising and portraying the three-foot high green Jedi master was offered to Jim Henson, creator of the Muppets. Henson was too busy, but suggested Frank Oz, a performer/puppeteer who had arguably had almost as much impact on the evolution of the Muppets as Henson himself. Oz played Miss Piggie and Fozzie Bear, amongst other characters, and was frequently referred to by Henson as 'the other half of me'. The range of subtleties that Oz wrings out of the Yoda puppet in the finished film is extraordinary.

PRODUCTION: To direct the film Lucas selected Irvin Kershner, an independent filmmaker who had been one of his teachers at USC. Before Kershner left for London to shoot the film Lucas gave him two pieces of advice: the first was 'Remember, nothing will work, so you've got to improvise', and the second was 'Don't be intimidated by what they tell you can't be done'. Gary Kurtz would again produce and when first-choice production designer John Barry chose to take the opportunity to direct the movie *Saturn 3* instead, the job of realising the look of the film went to his former assistant Norman Reynolds. John Mollo returned to take charge of the costumes. There was no question of rehiring *Star Wars*' director of photography Gilbert Taylor (see **Star Wars**), and instead Lucas and Kershner hired Peter Suschitzky. Suschitzky was a member of the team behind the remarkable pseudo-documentary *It Happened Here* (Kevin Brownlow, Andrew Rollo, 1963), set in a Nazi-occupied Britain, and he had since worked on *Leo the Last* (John Boorman, 1969) and *Lisztomania!* (Ken Russell, 1975). Following *Empire* he would become David Cronenberg's favoured DOP, shooting for him *Dead Ringers* (1988), *Naked Lunch* (1991), *M Butterfly* (1993) and *Crash* (1996).

Fox, the studio that had paid for *Star Wars*, would also be distributing the *Star Wars* sequel for Lucasfilm, although Lucas had decided that – when it came to film production – he should put his money where his mouth was. *Empire* would be funded out of his own personal resources, using his own wealth as collateral for the kind of extended line of credit studios acquired from banks in order to fund the production of films. Even if it stayed well within the budget parameters set by Lucas and Kurtz it would be the most expensive independent film ever made. Aware of the potential financial danger of this enterprise to him personally, Lucas set up a new company to deal with the making of *Empire* and with self-mocking irony named it 'Chapter 11', after the section of American law that dealt with bankruptcy.

As well as sharing much of *Star Wars*' crew *Empire* would also occupy the same soundstages at EMI Elstree studios outside London. For Reynolds's set for the planet Dagobah, home of Jedi Master Yoda, however, there was no stage at Elstree big enough, so Lucasfilm decided to build one; a new, huge (albeit unsoundproofed) stage was constructed on the studio's backlot. Kurtz planned to begin building the sets in February 1979, shortly after the bulk of the studio's stages were due to be empty following completion of a Stanley Kubrick adaptation of Stephen King's *The Shining*.

On 24 January 1979 an accidental fire started on Kubrick's set, ravaging Stage 3 and damaging others. Never known for completing a picture quickly, Kubrick now had a legitimate reason for being behind schedule. Once the stage was repaired and his sets rebuilt, Kubrick went back to work. By April he was still occupying the studio space.

The first scenes shot for *Empire* were undertaken in March 1979 (Kershner's team arrived on the 3rd) in Norway. Finise, the crew's base for the shoot, was a tiny community with a population of 75. The temperature was minus 10, with a wind-chill factor that pushed it down to minus 30 at times. It was a difficult place to shoot, and the problems and dangers of filming in an area only accessible by helicopter were fully appreciated by Kershner. Whilst scouting the area in November the previous year the 56-year-old director had become stranded in the snow thanks to a helicopter malfunction and had walked alone for four miles across a glacier and around a frozen lake before reaching the safety of a hotel.

The fall of the rebel base on Hoth was captured over three 11-hour days spent shooting atop a 6,000-foot high glacier in almost impossible conditions. As he was filling Lucas's shoes Kershner thought it sensible to replicate some of his approach: 'consider it as . . . shooting a documentary,' he told his crew. It was so cold on the glacier that the film stock itself became brittle and on one occasion snapped in the camera.

Whilst in Norway Kershner decided that a sequence he had originally intended to shoot in the studio, Han's rescue of Luke, would be better accomplished on location. Harrison Ford was summoned to Finise. The actor flew from London to Oslo, and then boarded a train for Finise. When blizzards and fifty-foot snowdrifts prevented the train travelling any further Ford travelled seven miles in two separate taxis and then completed his journey huddled in the engine compartment of a snow clearance vehicle which happened to be passing close to his intended destination. He arrived at midnight on 7 March 1979 and began filming the next day.

After Norway Kershner's crew moved to London, where Kurtz had moved the production to the smaller Lee International Studios in Wembley in deference to the fact that Kubrick was obviously not going to finish soon, and it was there that production began, moving to Elstree as the space became available.

John Barry, one of *Star Wars'* Oscar-winners, returned to the production unexpectedly soon afterwards. He'd started directing *Saturn 3*, but had quarrelled with producer Stanley Donen and actor Kirk Douglas. Fired by the producer, he was contacted by Kurtz who told him *Empire* was now behind schedule. As he knew the cast, crew and characters Kurtz wondered if Barry would come and shoot second unit to help them make up time. Barry agreed.

On 6 June, Barry was talking to associate producer Robert Watts – the practical producer who worked as Lucasfilm's head of London operations – about the production in his office when he collapsed. He was rushed to hospital and was diagnosed with meningitis. He died at 2 a.m. the next day.

This tragedy was one crisis too many for Lucas, who saw the film sliding into disaster, and flew to London with Marcia. Paul Hirsch had prepared a rough cut of the film for the executive producer, but it didn't meet with his approval. He recut it himself and then after consultation with Hirsch recut it again. Lucas took over the second unit himself and began shooting scenes he felt had been missed or mishandled. London-based American filmmaker Harley Cokeliss[1] called by to see crew members he knew and was offered the job of shooting yet another unit.

By this time Elstree was filled with *Empire*'s sets as the multiple units worked simultaneously. The rebels' command post was on Stage 1 and the Star Destroyer *Executor* on Stage 5. The interiors of Yoda's hut were shot on the tiny Stage 9 (photographs of Lucas directing these scenes exist) and Bespin Cloud City occupied the larger Stages 2 and 5, once the *Executor* scenes were done. The fight between Luke and Vader took place on Stage 4, a dangerous raised set rendered more difficult to use by the dry-ice smoke obscuring the edges from which incautious cast or crew could easily fall (although no one did).

Kubrick returned to Elstree for further reshoots on *The Shining*. In their few free moments Lucas and Kubrick chatted amiably about the traumas suffered by their respective films. Lucas recommended *Eraserhead* (David Lynch, 1980) to Kubrick, telling him it almost redefined the term 'timeless'.

Empire was now so over budget that Lucas negotiated a loan with the First National Bank of Boston to allow him to finish it; the bank were only prepared to pay him the money if Fox guaranteed the loan. Fox were willing, but only for 15 % of the profits of *Empire*, a sizeable increase on the terms of their original deal. A compromise was struck whereby Fox would get some increase (although not such a substantial one) on *Empire* and the same on the next *Star Wars* film, which Lucas was already talking of as the final part in a trilogy.

Empire's wrap party – supposedly a symbolic occasion to mark the end of filming – was on 31 August 1979. Shooting didn't actually finish for another month. On 5 September 1979 Sir Alec Guinness arrived by private car to reprise his role as Obi-Wan. He shot all of his scenes in under six hours, and had left the studio long before the day's recording ended. Reshoots and pick-ups continued until the last shot (Han cutting open a Tauntaun's belly with Luke's lightsaber on Hoth) was done on the 24 September. *Empire* had been expected to take around 100 shooting days (*Star Wars* had taken 82 including re-shoots); it ultimately took 175 and cost Lucas $35 million of his own money.

---

[1] Harley Cokeliss, director *The Battle of Billy's Pond* (1976), *Glitterball* (1977), *That Summer* (1979), *Of Muppets and Men* (1981), *Hercules and the Lost Kingdom* (1994).

ALTERNATIVE VERSIONS: Irvin Kershner was involved on all levels in the Special Edition version of *Empire* issued in 1997. A few years before the director had publicly mused on 'things I would like to change' in the film, and while he and Lucas would make several alterations to *Empire* it would be subject to fewer alterations than either its predecessor or its sequel. The wampa costume for the film had failed on location, and instead Phil Tippet had constructed the hand puppet used for the creature's brief appearance. For the Special Edition a new wampa costume was created and cutaways to it inserted into the scene of Luke trying to escape its cave.

Aside from this some new special-effects shots were added to the *Millennium Falcon*'s approach to Cloud City and windows digitally added to the walls of the city itself, opening Bespin up and making it seem larger. Some new cutaways to extras walking around a digitally created Bespin landscape were added for similar reasons, and during Leia and Lando's escape from the city some walls were digitally deleted so they seemed to be running along a balcony rather than in a corridor.

The only other scene added is a brief one of Vader walking down a corridor after Luke's suicide attempt, saying 'Alert my Star Destroyer to prepare for my arrival', followed by an effects shot of an Imperial shuttle and a brief sequence of Vader exiting the shuttle in a hangar bay. This last element was unused footage shot along with the opening scene of *Return of the Jedi*.

CUT SCENES: In the shooting draft the Hoth scenes featured the rebel base coming under attack from numerous marauding wampas which have found their way in. Lucas found the scenes as shot deeply unconvincing and they were removed. Traces of the subplot remain in the film as released. Someone speaks of 'one of those creatures' during the rebel briefing early on, and signs bearing a graphic which essentially means 'beware of the wampas' can be seen on some doors inside the base (one is very visible as Threepio flees towards the *Millennium Falcon*); a dead tauntaun is also visible in the background in some sequences, having been slaughtered by the wampas.

QUOTES:
Han: 'Scoundrel? Scoundrel? I like the sound of that. I think you like me because I'm a scoundrel. You haven't had enough scoundrels in your life.'

Leia: 'I happen to like nice men.'
Han: '*I'm* nice men.'

Leia: 'I love you.'
Han: 'I know.'

Vader: 'Obi-Wan never told you what happened to your father.'
Luke: 'He told me enough. He told me you killed him.'
Vader: 'No. *I* am your father.'

Yoda: 'Try not. Do or do not. There is no try.'

Yoda: 'Excitement? Adventure? A Jedi craves not these things.'

Yoda: 'If you choose the quick and easy path, as Vader did, you will become a servant of evil.'

Vader: 'The force is with you, young Skywalker, but you are not a Jedi yet.'

MUSICAL NOTES: When cutting *Empire* Lucas initially noted where he wanted the Williams score to go; later it became obvious that it would be easier to note where there shouldn't be music rather than where there should. New themes Williams introduced to the *Star Wars* universe in this film include the hectic 'Asteroid field' and – most famously – 'The Imperial March', often referred to as 'Darth Vader's Theme'. A bombastic, martial refrain full of suspended notes and malevolence, it is – after the opening theme – the series' most familiar piece of music. Also new is 'Han Solo and the Princess' – a lush romantic melody most noticeably used during the quieter scenes on the *Millennium Falcon* during the flight from Hoth – and a warm, woodwind-heavy theme for Yoda which segues easily into 'The Force Theme' from *Star Wars*. Williams utilises all these themes, as well as those others left over from *Star Wars*, to weave an elaborate musical tapestry that tells the story on its own. From the insistent strides of 'The Force Theme' as Luke flies to Bespin to begin what he thinks is a date with destiny, to the rumbling, harsh insistence of 'The Imperial March' as he lies injured in the *Falcon*, tempted by the darkness, Williams's score matches the dramatic and character content of the film perfectly.

The 20th Century Fox fanfare used to open all of the *Star Wars* films was written by Alfred Newman in 1933, the year that 20th Century films merged with Fox Movietone. After many years of inconsistent use of multiple arrangements in various versions, both stereo and mono, *Star Wars* had returned the original version of the fanfare to mainstream cinema audiences. For *Empire* Williams chose to rerecord Newman's theme; in doing so he created the new standard version of the theme. It was the first recording of one of cinema's most familiar refrains for 25 years.

RECURRING CONCERNS: *Empire* is the first of the *Star Wars* films to really begin to tackle the idea of 'turning to the dark side'; both Obi-Wan and Yoda warn Luke against using his powers for personal gain as this will lead him down Vader's path. In plot terms the implication is that the force, when used for selfish reasons, somehow physically and mentally corrupts those who use it, making them evil regardless of their intentions. In realistic terms this is simply a metaphor through which Lucas tries to make the basic point that to do the wrong thing, even for the right reasons, is morally harmful to the individual. This idea is given its greatest grandstanding moment at the very end of the film, where Luke is given a straightforward choice: reunion with the father he has always idolised and opportunities for power, or almost certain death. He's in a situation where to do the right thing is not simply personally disadvantageous but fatal. Death or dishonour. It's an old dilemma, superbly handled. Luke chooses the literal fall over the metaphorical one.

VISUAL INTERESTS: In terms of colour schemes *Empire* is a journey from blue (Hoth) to red (Bespin). What makes this relevant is that these are the colours of the lightsabers seen so far in the series: red = corruption and blue = purity. Thus Kenobi's lightsaber is blue and Vader's is red; indeed by the end of the film we understand that Vader himself is Luke's father, and therefore the blue lightsaber Obi-Wan gave Luke in *Star Wars* becomes less an object bequeathed by a dying man to his son than an object a corrupted man had to (metaphorically) give up when he became too debased for it.

Luke's journey from Hoth to Bespin can be seen as both a physical and moral/emotional one; the story begins with much hope, but ultimately descends into tragedy. Luke's costuming is initially rendered in whites and blues, but by the time he reaches Cloud City he is clad in deep muddy beiges and reds. Emblematic of this keen colour sense is the moment when the viewer first glimpses Vader in the carbon freeze chamber on Bespin. Vader is in silhouette, all we can see is a shadow, and tiny lights both blue and red flicker on his chest plating. The top of the picture is a searing light blue and the bottom a deep, dark red. Symbolically, morally and literally the higher ground on Bespin is blue; most of the fight, which is an angry and brutal affair, takes place in the red. Later, Luke loses his blue lightsaber (it drops into a pit from where it is never recovered) moments before he is informed of the truth about his parentage. Thus the loss of the symbol of innocence, and the shattering of Luke's assumptions, come almost simultaneously. Luke is a far more reserved and contemplative figure in the next picture (see **Return of the Jedi**) and the audience never see him (or indeed anyone else) carry a blue lightsaber again.

This theme carries over into almost every other character's costuming – Lando wears a blue shirt, but his blue cape hides a red lining, a symbol of his duplicity. When he changes sides and throws his lot in with Leia and Chewie he discards the cape and is afterwards clad entirely in blue.

FORWARDS/BACKWARDS: Story purists may like to note that arguably the most important moment in the entire six-film story (when Vader realizes that the man who destroyed the Death Star was his son) occurs off screen. Vader's motivations in *Empire* are particularly interesting. At the beginning of the film he is already searching for 'Skywalker', and all of his officers are aware of this fact. Yet later, when the Emperor contacts him, he informs Vader that 'we have a new enemy, Luke Skywalker' and Vader reacts as if this is a new piece of information to him. Vader appears to be deceiving the Emperor over something. This, combined with his suggestion to Luke that his son has the power to 'destroy the Emperor', and his offer to share power with the younger Skywalker so they can 'rule the galaxy as father and son', suggests that Vader, whilst clearly in thrall to the Emperor, does have his own agenda, and has contemplated the possibility of usurping his master's place.

The moment where the audience discovers that Vader is Luke's father is remarkable filmmaking for one very simple reason; it's not the actual revelation that shocks the audience, it's the gap between Vader's 'no' and 'I' – the split-second gap where something that's not been particularly foreshadowed or suggested, where something that's completely implausible, something that makes no narrative sense at that point, goes from being all of the above to being terribly, crushingly *inevitable*. The audience work it out before Vader says it; and that's the moment the *Star Wars* series changes from being about space-ships and swordfights and becomes, instead, about who we are.

EXTERNAL REFERENCES: With a visual style more appropriated from the film it's a sequel to than anything else, *Empire* is less visually eclectic than *Star Wars* but there are still textual and thematic resonances with external works. As pointed out by Simon Guerrier in *Film Review*, most of the individual plot points of *Empire* come from the conventions of revenge tragedy, as best represented by *Hamlet*. There's a ghost who counsels and a young man intent on achieving revenge for his father's murder but trapped between his need to do so and an ethical viewpoint that demands he forswear proactive violence. One of the heroes travels to a foreign land which should be a safe haven but is instead betrayed, and all the time armies are on the move in the background. The central characters are caught up in world-shaking events, but are often too traumatised by their implications to act heroically. The end of the drama comes after a protracted swordfight, during which startling revelations are made. What makes this especially clever is that the film contrives to throw it all away: Luke can't revenge his father by killing his father. Vader's revelation turns the whole impetus of the drama on its head. This is a different story to the one the audience thinks it's watching; crushed by this reversal of dramatic logic the characters can only run away.

Joseph Campbell makes his influence felt as always, but there is something of the Native American or Aboriginal in Yoda's ability to see the future through clouded visions, and Luke's hallucinated encounter with Vader on Dagobah combines this with touches of Freud (this is, after all, a conflict between father and son).

With Brackett and Kasdan on board the debt to the Warner Brothers gangster films of the 40s is immediately obvious and felt in almost all the dialogue, but it also affects Solo's character. Here he becomes less the cowboy, more the reluctant hero: a Chandleresque man who walks down mean streets but avoids being mean himself. In *Empire* Han's talk is of gambling and odds, scams and staying on the right side of the law; in *Star Wars* he was a cowboy who talked of smuggling and speed.

RELEASE: *The Empire Strikes Back* was released on 21 May 1980, the third anniversary of *Star Wars'* own release. Lucasfilm estimated that it would do roughly a third of its predecessor's business. In Hollywood *Empire* opened at Mann's Egyptian Theater, rather than the smaller Chinese at which *Star Wars* had been unveiled to the public. For the first 24 hours of its release *Empire* played non-stop on a loop. In a phenomenon then unprecedented yet much repeated since, the lines around the block began three days before the film's release. Despite the dreadful production overruns *Empire* was in profit inside three months.

CRITICISM: Reviews of *Empire* went against the grain of those normally given for sequels, assessing it on its own merits rather than dismissing it simply as a follow-up to another movie; comparing it to *Star Wars* but taking it seriously in the process. 'Grainier and grimier . . . and considerably more violent', was the *New York Times'* Janet Maslin's view, praising Harrison Ford for 'steal[ing] the show' with a 'comicbook conversational style' and a final 'great show of nobility' that brought 'a real air of tragedy' as he went to what may or not have been his doom for his friends. The film as a whole offered 'hints and clues and riddles that may take eons to unravel', while Yoda, the asteroid field and Bespin were among the film's 'great marvels'.

In the *New Yorker* Pauline Kael was impressed: 'There is no sense that this saga is running thin on imagination or that it has begun to depend excessively on special effects'. She also enjoyed the 'neo-Sophoclian overtones' of the film's final revelation – although in common with all other reviewers at the time she kept Vader's true identify a secret. The *Los Angeles Herald-Examiner*'s Michael Sagrow claimed the movie's epic intentions would 'do Homer proud'.

Empire is thin on plot, the thinnest of all of the *Star Wars* films in this regard, in fact, but it compensates for this by combining an awkward, dark beauty with raw human emotions. Regarded by many as the most 'grown-up' of the Imperial trilogy, its startling visual consistency and intensity are all the more remarkable given the torturous production process.

What make it such a good filmic sequel, though, are two separate but complementary things. The first is the way it avoids repeating *Star Wars*. The only location from the previous film the audience sees again is the *Millennium Falcon* – and that's not a place, it's a vehicle. From ice wharfs like nothing ever put on film before to cloud cities like nothing that has ever existed, *Empire* pushes Lucas's 'used future' further and further.

The second is the confidence with which the movie approaches its audience – the sheer amount of risks, both creatively and financially, that Lucas was willing to take. The knowledge that people would see *Empire*, and that they already cared for its characters, seems to inform every scene. A sequel to the most successful film of all time seemed guaranteed vast financial rewards, and Lucas and his collaborators took full advantage of that; they made a blockbuster that, for all the adolescent pontificating of later efforts like *The Crow* (Alex Proyas, 1994), remains genuinely the darkest popcorn film yet committed to celluloid. What is most extraordinary is that the production process continued in this vein even after *More American Graffiti* did so badly critically and financially. A viewing experience as emotionally battering as it is visually exhilarating – one with a deferred ending and a subsequent denial of catharsis – *The Empire Strikes Back* pushes the audience not simply into enjoying the characters' adventures, nor simply into caring about what happens to them, but into *feeling* for them. *Star Wars* may well be one of cinema's all-time great comfort movies; *Empire* isn't ever going to make anyone feel safe.

TRIVIA: The Emperor as seen in this film is actually an elderly woman, hired by ILM and then photographed wearing white make-up and a robe. The eyes of a chimpanzee were then superimposed over her own in post-production to make the Emperor's face more sinister, and the dialogue was dubbed over by British actor Clive Revill.

EXPERT WITNESS: 'I like Yoda, he's smaller than me.' Actress Carrie Fisher (Princess Leia)

'It's the second movement of a symphony, which is slower . . . it was my job to generate a certain amount of emotion with the characters . . . so that you cared about them.' Director Irvin Kershner

LUCAS ON THE EMPIRE STRIKES BACK: 'It's the middle act of a three-act play . . . it is a darker film [but] you don't have an exuberant happy second act . . . that's drama.'

Raiders of the Lost Ark (1981)

(111 minutes)

Paramount
A Lucasfilm Ltd Production
Screenplay by Lawrence Kasdan
Story by George Lucas and Philip Kaufman
Director of Photography: Douglas Slocombe
Production Designer: Norman Reynolds
Produced by Frank Marshall
Associate Producer: Robert Watts
Executive Producers: George Lucas, Howard Kazanjian
Music: John Williams
Edited by Michael Kahn
Directed by Steven Spielberg

PRINCIPAL CAST: Harrison Ford (*Dr Henry 'Indiana' Jones Junior*), Karen Allen (*Marion Ravenwood*), Paul Freeman (*Dr Rene Belloq*), Ronald Lacey (*Toht*), John Rhys-Davies (*Sallah*), Alfred Molina (*Sapito*), Denholm Elliott (*Dr Marcus Brody*), Wolf Kahler (*Dietrich*), Anthony Higgins (*Gobler*), Vic Tablian (*Barranca/Monkey Man*), Don Fellows (*Colonel Musgrove*), William Hootkins (*Major Eaton*), Pat Roach (*Giant Sherpa/1st Mechanic*), Christopher Frederick (*Otto*), Tutte Lemkow (*Imam*), Ishaq Bux (*Omar*), Kiran Shah (*Abu*), Souad Messaoudi (*Fayah*), Terry Richards (*Arab Swordsman*), Steve Hanson (*German Agent*), Martin Kreidt (*Young Soldier*), George Harris (*Captain Katanga*)

TAGLINES: Indiana Jones – the new hero from the creators of *JAWS* and *STAR WARS*.

The return of the great adventure.

SUMMARY: 1936. After having been frustrated in his attempts to acquire a valuable golden godhead idol by long-time rival Belloq, Indy returns to the university where he teaches. Here he is contacted by representatives of the US government. They are convinced that the German government is currently obsessed with recovering the Lost Ark of the Covenant and are close to finding it thanks to a dig outside Cairo. They have contacted Indy for two reasons: firstly his slightly dubious reputation as a recoverer of rare artefacts ('no questions asked', as his colleague Marcus Brody puts it) and secondly because an old lecturer of Indy's from his days at the University of Chicago – Abner Ravenwood – is mentioned in Nazi despatches concerning it. Indy deduces that the Nazis are looking for the headpiece of the staff of Ra, an item which will enable them to divine the ark's location, and heads out to find Abner. Instead he discovers Abner's daughter – and Indy's old flame – Marion, and is told that his friend is dead. Marion – after some argument – lets Indy have the headpiece and declares herself his 'goddamn partner'. They travel to Cairo, where they find that the head of the Nazis' expedition is Belloq. Indy recovers the ark, but the Nazis take it from him. He recovers it and he and Marion book themselves onto a pirate steamer headed for England. The Nazis arrive in a U-boat, take the ark back again and head for an unidentified Greek island. Indy and Marion are captured, and Belloq opens the ark. The wrath of God emerges from the chest and scours the area, killing everyone except Marion and Indy. Indy transports the ark to America, where the government confiscate it, locking it in a crate and storing it in a warehouse with thousands of similar boxes, each presumably containing an ancient treasure.

SCREENPLAY: *Raiders of the Lost Ark* was essentially born during the most significant sandcastle construction in movie history; during May 1977 Lucas, Spielberg and their respective partners were vacationing together. Lucas wanted to escape the number-crunching that he felt would accompany the opening of *Star Wars* and so he and Marcia had flown out to Hawaii earlier in the month to spend time with Willard Huyck and Gloria Katz and Steven Spielberg and Amy Irving.

By this point Lucas and Spielberg had known each other for about ten years. Descriptions of their first meeting vary; some accounts suggest that Spielberg's short film *Amblin* (1968) was shown at USC whilst Lucas was a postgraduate student. Spielberg introduced the picture at a screening at which Lucas was present, they met after the film – which Lucas disliked – and Spielberg (who went to UCLB) became one of the 'hangers-on' of the USC crowd. Other reports suggest that the two first crossed paths at a student film festival held at UCLA. Lucas was showing *THX 1138 4EB*, which Spielberg greatly admired.

Regardless of the circumstances of their initial meeting the two men became – and remain – good friends. Spielberg has publicly referred to Lucas as 'my best friend' and Lucas has reciprocated the comment. Lucas showing a childishly delighted Spielberg around the Naboo sets at Leavesden Studios, with neither man seemingly giving a thought for the camera following them, remains one of the highlights of the *Star Wars: Episode I – The Phantom Menace* DVD.

After a while the Huycks departed – they had work to do back in America – but the other two couples stayed. One morning, after the fabulous success of *Star Wars* became clear, Spielberg found Lucas out on the beach, intensely making sandcastles. Spielberg had recently expressed his desire to direct a James Bond movie, but that morning Lucas told him that he had a better idea. Pretty soon Lucas was explaining a project he thought they should work on together, a series of stories he'd been developing on and off for years. They were about a playboy/archaeologist/college professor, who would have adventures reminiscent of old cinema serials: a 'serial adventure hero [who went on] supernatural treasure hunts'.

The screenplay to *Raiders* was written by Lawrence Kasdan. Kasdan had been submitting speculative scripts in Hollywood for several years with limited success – one screenplay he wrote during this period was a projected Steve McQueen vehicle entitled *The Bodyguard*. It wasn't made until 1992, when it starred the rather less iconic Kevin Costner. One sale Kasdan *had* made was the script for *Continental Divide* (Michael Apted, 1981), which caught the attention of Spielberg. *Raiders*' prospective director passed it on to Lucas to read. Equally impressed, Lucas contacted Kasdan and asked him to work on the movie.

Initially the three men worked together in intensive script conferences, creating a first draft out of Lucas's folder of Indiana Jones-related ideas. The central plot strand they alighted on was one Lucas had long ago worked on with friend and fellow California filmmaker Philip Kaufman[1] – the search for the Lost Ark of the Covenant, the box that contained the actual tablets upon which the Ten Commandments had been written. Kaufman had as a child known a man who was obsessed with the search for

[1] Philip Kaufman, co-writer *The Outlaw Josey Wales* (Clint Eastwood, 1975), writer/director *The Right Stuff* (1983), *Henry and June* (1990), *Quills* (1999) and *The Unbearable Lightness of Being* (1988), for which he received an Oscar nomination.

the ark, an enthusiasm Kaufman had picked up and then passed on to Lucas. Kaufman initially agreed to receive a percentage of the film's profits in lieu of credit, but his agent later pushed for on-screen attribution as well, which Lucasfilm granted.

Once this process was over, Kasdan went away and wrote the screenplay, which he delivered to Lucas by hand (see **The Empire Strikes Back**). During the writing he took as his models any great adventure movie he could think of and later mentioned *The Crimson Pirate* (Robert Siodmak, 1952), *The Adventures of Robin Hood* (Michael Curtiz, 1938), *The Great Escape* (John Sturges, 1963) and *The Gunfight at the O.K. Corral* (John Sturges, 1957) as particular inspirations. He was however equally fired up by the producer and director's enthusiasm for silent movies. Although Kasdan would gain a reputation as a fine writer of dialogue he later noted with some pride, '*Raiders*, you can turn off the sound and follow the story without any problem'.

Although much visual play and occasional dialogue would be improvised during the film's arduous shoot much of the pace and structure of *Raiders* is Kasdan's and his contribution cannot be overstated.

CASTING: Lucas and Spielberg initially agreed that an unknown was required to play their hero; 'I wanted to have a fresh face to play the character', Lucas later explained. It was much the same feeling that had led him to want to have no one from *Graffiti* in *Star Wars*, although ironically the final choice to play Indy turned out to be the only actor who'd appeared in both of those films.

After much deliberation Spielberg and Lucas decided on Tom Selleck, then known as a model rather than actor – he was the *Marlboro* cigarette man – but fate intervened. Selleck had made a TV pilot for a series called *Magnum PI*, and the company that produced it had, in the event of their deciding to make the series, first call on his services. The series was picked up and Selleck dropped out. Instead Lucas went to Harrison Ford. The role would push Ford from being a movie star into the status of full-blown icon. The interest of the role for Ford was that 'the fact that he behaves heroically is a part of his nature but it isn't a description of his character', and he was amused by the ongoing question as to whether Indy was a college professor who pretended to be an action hero or an action hero who pretended to be a professor. Across all of the Indy films he would do as many of his own stunts as he was allowed to; 'I try to do as much as I can; [it's] important for an audience to have continuity of character in these physical moments,' he later observed.

For Indy's leading lady – a character modelled on the kind of tough-talking, deeply attractive women who populate director Howard Hawks' films – Spielberg initially thought of his girlfriend Amy Irving, but that ceased to be possible when the relationship broke up. Karen Allen was respected for stage work and known to two entirely different persuasions of filmgoers for the light, funny and stupid *National Lampoon's Animal House* (John Landis, 1978) and William Friedkin's debased, unpleasant and complex *Cruising* (1980). Spielberg had seen the former, and cast her on the strength of it.

After TV star Danny DeVito (*Taxi*) turned down the role of Indy's friend, Sallah, Welsh actor John Rhys Davies was offered the role. A confident actor who would make a career out of secondary parts in big movies, he would later appear in *The Living Daylights* (John Glen, 1987) and *The Lord of the Rings: The Fellowship of the Ring* (Peter Jackson, 2001). Rhys Davies was once described by Spielberg as 'a brilliant Shakespearean actor [with] a Pavarotti spirit', whose performance in the Indiana Jones films 'made you wanna hug the guy'.

Lucas initially wanted crooner Jacques Dutronc to play villainous archaeologist Belloq (this is the reason the character is French) but eventually decided on British actor Paul Freeman. Again more a stage and television actor than a film star, Freeman's only significant movie role to date was in *The Long Good Friday* (John MacKenzie, 1980). Freeman's performance as Belloq is *fantastic*; he is a charismatic, intelligent, charming villain who gets a large share of the film's best lines *and* whose protestations that he's little different to the picture's hero have more than a little truth to them.

PRODUCTION: By 1977 Lucas and Spielberg were the richest, most successful and most eminently bankable of the creators to emerge from the movie-brats generation; a collaboration between them was a cinema-owner's dream, but it was also the most plausible way of eradicating their need to depend on studio money once and for all.

First they enraged opinion by negotiating with every studio simultaneously, the height of crassness in the eyes of Old

Hollywood. The terms set out in those negotiations were also the subject of raised eyebrows. Traditionally the amount of money taken at a film's box office (termed 'rentals') was split 50/50 between the theatre owners and the studio. 30% of the US domestic, 33% of the UK and 40% of all overseas markets went directly into studio coffers, with the remaining share of the studio's 50% covering costs, taking care of expenses etc. Lucas and Spielberg demanded – and got – a totally different kind of deal. They wanted $20 million up front from the studio, in essence the price of the right to distribute the movie. Of this $4 million would go to Lucas directly as executive producer/creator and $1.5 would go straight to Spielberg. In addition, the studio's cut of rentals was to be divided with Lucas and Spielberg from the first dollar down (traditionally even when owning a part of a movie, the production company would have to make its own investment back first, before it began distributing money to filmmakers). Instead of the 50% that was normally theirs, the studio would get only 20%. The rest would belong to Spielberg and Lucas. The cost of prints, publicity and advertising would be absorbed by the studio. The two movie brats would retain enough of a proportion of sequel, licensing and merchandise rights to control them. Most studios were unable to agree to these terms in any form, despite their keenness to acquire the picture. Michael Eisner at Paramount saw things differently; he would accept the deal in principle with a few caveats. Most important among them was that Lucas was contractually obliged to be involved in any future *Jones* films. Lucas demurred. He would be involved in sequels, but he wasn't to be contractually tied to them. He asked Eisner to trust him.

After sleepless nights (a metaphor which Eisner insists, in this case, should be taken literally) Eisner buckled and agreed to Lucas and Spielberg's demands. The nature of Hollywood contracts had fundamentally changed.

Shooting began at London Elstree in March 1980 before moving on to to La Rochelle, France, then Kuai, Hawaii and Tunisia. Lucas, who had remained in America during much of the shoot, flew out to Tunisia to join the production, which utilised several locations he had originally scouted for *Star Wars*. Famously the valley where Indy threatens to destroy the ark with a bazooka is the same place where Jawas attacked R2-D2 in the earlier film. The producer and director had agreed with

Paramount that the film would be completed within 85 days, but with the critical commercial disasters of *More American Graffiti* and Spielberg's *1941* (1979) (not to mention the overlong and over-budget shooting of the latter film) casting shadows over their respective careers, both men wanted to re-establish their reputations for efficiency. Lucas shot the second unit, famously capturing the shot of the small monkey giving a Hitler salute (described by Spielberg 'nuts . . . just so nuts, my favourite moment in the picture'), and production overall moved at a startling pace. Some actors report Spielberg shouting instructions for retakes and pick-ups to actors and crew whilst the camera was still turning, a breach of traditional etiquette which nevertheless enabled shooting to proceed quickly. The film wrapped eleven days ahead of schedule and under budget.

Months later one extra scene was shot for the picture – that of Marion and Indy walking off arm in arm for 'a drink'. It was Marcia Lucas's suggestion – she felt the end of the picture lacked emotional resonance, and that the audience would want to know what had happened to Marion.

CUT SCENES: Much of Indy and Marion's opening conversation in the bar was trimmed, to screenwriter Lawrence Kasdan's dismay. A lengthy scene in which a smoking German soldier deliberates whether or not to execute Sallah was cut because it slowed the story down.

QUOTES:

Marcus: 'The Bible speaks of the ark levelling mountains and laying waste to entire regions. An army which carries the ark before it is invincible.'

Belloq: 'Jones, do you realise what the ark is? It's a transmitter. It's a radio for speaking to God.'

Belloq: 'You and I are very much alike; archaeology is our religion. Yet we have both fallen from the pure faith . . . It would take only a nudge to make you like me . . . you know it's true.'

Belloq: 'Indiana, we are simply passing through history. This [the ark], this *is* history.'

Indy: 'I'm making this up as I go.'

MUSICAL NOTES: John Williams's award-winning score is another fine piece of work from the man regarded by many as the God of modern film scoring. Williams approached his music in 'balletic terms' and set out to create moods through a series of changing tempos. 'The Raiders March' (more popularly thought of as Indiana Jones's theme) is now one of the most recognisable pieces of movie music in the world; the audience first hears it in a comical version as Indy swings on a vine towards Chuck's plane and then falls off. Elsewhere in the score there's the love theme (played on a flute and reminiscent of Williams's romantic themes for *The Empire Strikes Back*), some superbly amusing 'monkey music' for the treacherous Nazi simian, and the *pizzicato* strings of the chase in the opening South America sequence. Perhaps most impressive are the chords of 'Ark Theme' – oppressive, yet beautiful in the minor mode.

RECURRING CONCERNS: There's an undeniable similarity between the characters of Indy and Karen and John and Carol from *American Graffiti*, and even a physical resemblance between the respective actors. *More American Graffiti*, made at the same time, shows how Carol spent the 60s looking for a substitute for John (someone notes she 'goes for those 50s guys' as she snuggles with a Le Mat clone in the 1966 section), and although John and Carol's relationship was never romantic their acerbic, affectionate banter is continued – in spirit – here.

FORWARDS/BACKWARDS: Indy and Marion's prior relationship is much discussed in the picture's first half-hour. Marcus is aware of it, and seems to understand that it was awkward. It's also explicitly the reason that Abner Ravenwood and Indy fell out. Marion has some bitterness towards Indiana, telling him that 'what you did was wrong' and referring to herself as 'a child' and 'in love' when they first knew each other; he contemptuously replies, 'You knew what you were doing.' Elsewhere it's stated that Indy is as old as the century, so he's 36 during this movie, and 26 'ten years' before. Karen Allen was 30 during filming, suggesting that Marion was 20 or younger during their previous relationship. Steven Spielberg has repeatedly said he wanted Indy to be a flawed hero, and here they come dangerously close to suggesting that Marion was dubiously – perhaps illegally – young when they first became lovers. It would certainly explain the severity of Abner and Indiana's quarrel.

Indy claims he doesn't believe in 'magic . . . hocus pocus' despite having experienced the events of *Indiana Jones and the Temple of Doom* (made after, but set earlier) and the *Young Indiana Jones* episode 'Masks of Evil' already.

The viewer sees the fictional origin of Indy's look in *Indiana Jones and the Last Crusade* (1989), but in fact Lucas and Spielberg took the silhouette from Humphrey Bogart's Fred C Dobbs in *The Treasure of the Sierra Madre* (John Huston, 1948). Also explained in the third *Indiana Jones* film are Indy's skill with a whip – actually borrowed from *Lash La Rue, Man with the Steel Whip* (1937) – and his fear of snakes.

EXTERNAL REFERENCES: The initial action sequence in Peru is derived from an issue of Disney's *Uncle $crooge Comics*, the work of the legendary 'Duckman' Carl Barks, whose vibrant, fast-paced and witty style is a declared influence on many contemporary filmmakers. 'The Prize of Pizarro' in *Uncle $crooge* #26 (June–August 1959) features Scrooge, Donald, Huey, Dewey and Louie Ducks exploring a temple. Donald Duck, his nephews, and Uncle Scrooge McDuck evade a succession of booby traps, including flying darts, a decapitating blade, a huge boulder and a tunnel flooded with a torrent of gushing water (see **Indiana Jones and the Temple of Doom**).

As Indy gets on the plane to Nepal, the Nazi agent (played by special-effects man Dennis Muren) is reading *Life* magazine vol. 1, no. 2 (30 November 1936). Pages 42 and 43 of this issue are an article dedicated to Adolf Hitler's alternative career as a painter.

This is a Steven Spielberg film, however, as well as a George Lucas production, and the majority of external references are therefore to other movies. The opening Paramount logo (a mountain as per normal) dissolves into film of a real mountain shot in Hawaii; the dissolve is almost imperceptible.

In the map room Indy is essentially dressed as Peter O'Toole playing TE Lawrence in *Lawrence of Arabia* (David Lean, 1962), one of Spielberg's favourite movies (see also *Young Indiana Jones*).

Indy being chased through a jungle by natives was inspired by Clark Gable in *Too Hot to Handle* (Jack Conway, 1938).

The use of a Flying Wing (the circular Nazi aircraft) came from the serials *Fighting Devil Dogs* (1938) and *King of the Mounties* (1942), and the truck/horse chase that Lucas remembers being in 'practically every episode' of every serial he saw as a child appears to have originated in Episode 8 of *Zorro's Fighting Legion*.

At one point Indy utters what many collaborators have labelled Lucas's catchphrase, 'Trust Me'.

Sallah twice sings songs by light operetta duo Gilbert & Sullivan.

It is worth pointing out that *Raiders* has perhaps the first literal *deus ex machina* ending in cinema history – a cunning, comic playing with theories of drama. They open the box, God comes out, the film ends.

RELEASE: *Raiders* came out on 21 June 1981 in the USA, and grossed $81 million in just three days. By the end of the year it had grossed $241 million – the year's best-selling movie by far. In the UK it had to put up with second place, grossing a little less than *For Your Eyes Only* (John Glen, 1981), Eon Pictures' twelfth James Bond film. Clearly the established homegrown adventurer was slightly preferable to this new imported upstart in the eyes of British cinemagoers, and suggested that they disagreed with critic Dilys Powell's assessment that Indy 'Out-Bonds Bond'.

CRITICISM: The *New York Times* called *Raiders* an 'instant classic' and suggested that comparisons with the chapter plays that had inspired it were misplaced. *Raiders* did recall those serials, but 'in a manner that was forever beyond the artistic and economic reach of the people who made them'; it was the chapter plays 'as they have lived in our imagination', not as they actually were. *Variety* was happy too, calling the picture a 'smashing adventure' and 'exhilarating escapist entertainment' which had the decency to 'cheerfully wear its improbabilities on its sleeve'. The characters were 'delightfully etched' and the movie one of 'the best crafted' of recent times. 'One leaves *Lost Ark* feeling, like the best films of childhood, it will take up permanent residence in the memory', concurred Richard Schickel in *Time* magazine. 'When the flood of cheap *Raiders* imitations arrive we . . . are going to know the difference', pointed out one commentator in response to the suggestion that *Raiders* was neither a complex blend of elements nor a difficult film to make. Bearing in mind the quality of those imitations – among the better of them are Spielberg protégé Robert Zemeckis's uninspiring *Romancing The Stone* (1984) and its sequel *The Jewel in the Nile* (1985), among the worst are the limp adaptations of H Rider Haggard's Allan

Quartermain novels, *King Solomon's Mines* (J Lee Thompson, 1985) and *Allan Quatermain and the Lost City of Gold* (Gary Nelson, 1987) – the point becomes inarguable.

Raiders of the Lost Ark blends chapter play and Warner Bros movies with a post-*Star Wars* sensibility based on a combination of sheer exhilaration, wit and underlying air of self-confident intelligence and integrity. Funny, fast and smart, it's one of the best ways to spend two hours in front of a television that anyone has ever come up with; its *joie de vivre* is palpable. To say this has become a cliché, but it remains the gold standard by which action movies should be judged.

AWARDS: At the March 1982 Academy Awards ceremony the movie regarded by many as the New Hollywood popcorn dream ticket was nominated for eight Oscars. As was typical of both Spielberg and Lucas films of the period it won most of the technical awards it was up for (Art Direction, Editing, Visual Effects and Sound, but not Original Score or Cinematography) but missed out on the more prestigious awards for which it had been nominated (Best Picture, Best Director). Ben Burtt and Richard L Anderson were also given a special achievement award for their innovative Sound Effects Editing. The American Cinema Editors bestowed their own award – highly prized by those in the industry – on the film, giving Michael Kahn the 'Eddie' for Best Edited Feature Film. Norman Reynolds' production design picked up a BAFTA too, the only one of seven British Academy nominations to be converted into a trophy. In France the *César* Awards nominated Spielberg for the *Meilleur film étranger* (Best Foreign Film) but it didn't win. Spielberg's DGA nomination for Outstanding Directorial Achievement in Motion Pictures didn't translate into a win on the night and neither did Lucas/Kasdan/Kaufman's WGA nomination for Best Comedy Written Directly for the Screen, but the film did pick up the Hugo Award for Best Dramatic Presentation while John Williams's score garnered the composer a Grammy for Best Album of Original Score Written for a Motion Picture or Television Special. Unsurprisingly *Raiders* also got the People's Choice Award for Favourite Motion Picture of 1981.

TRIVIA: The building used for one of the exterior shots of the university is the music department of the University of the Pacific, Stockton, California, close to the locations used for *American Graffiti*.

'The audience is listening'

The standards of projection and sound in cinemas always appalled George Lucas. Especially in America where most theatres belong in some sense to film studios, there was simply no excuse for allowing cinemas to degrade and refusing to spend a portion of rentals on making sure that the cinematic experience was of as high a technical quality as possible for the moviegoer. In 1983 Lucasfilm launched the THX Theater Alignment Program (usually abbreviated to TAP). Its declared aim was to become the film industry's most comprehensive quality assurance program; audiences would know which cinemas were offering quality picture and sound because they would be THX TAP-certified. To these ends the program reviews prints before they are sent out in order to make sure they achieve certain standards of image and soundtrack quality, and vets cinemas to make sure they meet certain technical standards pertaining to projection (a list of THX-certified theatres is available to filmmakers). It also sends out literature to cinemas for each film it guarantees, explaining the exact technical details of the print and the precise equipment alignment required to screen the film to maximum advantage.

Films are furthermore withheld from cinemas which do not meet the standards set by the film's creators, and TAP employees conduct random 'mystery customer' tests on THX-certified theatres to make sure that standards are maintained. The company maintains a website and a toll-free number for consumers to report any conditions that distracted from their enjoyment of a certified film. All measures are designed to encourage studios and theatre chains to invest in cinemas to the advantage of audiences.

Amongst the first to sign up for the then fledging TAP was an enthusiastic Stanley Kubrick, as much a believer in the quality cinematic experience as Lucas. Kubrick had operated an informal version of such a system himself throughout the 70s, famously sending precisely cut masking apertures out to every single cinema which was to exhibit his 1975 film *Barry Lyndon* (the picture was made in an unusual, perhaps unique aspect ratio of 1.59:1).

In order to further encourage THX TAP take-up Lucas specifically barred any non-TAP-certified cinemas from screening *Star Wars: Episode I – The Phantom Menace*, with the result that the film opened on just under 2,000 screens across America and *Attack of the Clones* consequently debuted on around 5,000 (a comparable, although non-TAP-certified film, the Sam Raimi-directed *Spiderman*, opened on nearer 8,000 a few weeks before *Clones*).

A company that acts like a consumer group, THX TAP is perhaps Lucas's most significant contribution to cinema. It protects the rights of consumers and filmmakers of all stripes. Certainly it has improved technical conditions in movie theatres beyond measure and has been adjudged by industry watchdogs as 'to the obvious advantage of any neutral party'.

TITLE TATTLE: Although the publicity for, and the cover of, the VHS rerelease of 2000 insist the film is called *Indiana Jones and the Raiders of the Lost Ark* (it isn't) the prints of the film weren't altered to take into account this revisionism; they still just call it *Raiders of the Lost Ark*.

LUCAS ON RAIDERS OF THE LOST ARK: 'Most of the films I've made, I've had no idea whether the audience is going to relate to them or not, but I was so convinced that this was going to be a crowd pleaser.'

Star Wars: Episode VI – Return of the Jedi (1983)

(132 minutes original edition/130 minutes special edition)

A Lucasfilm Limited Production
Screenplay by Lawrence Kasdan and George Lucas
Story by George Lucas
Director of Photography: Alan Hume, BSC
Production Designer: Norman Reynolds
Producer: Howard Kazanjian
Special Edition Produced by Rick McCallum
Executive Producer: George Lucas
Music by John Williams
Edited by TM Christopher (Special Edition only), Sean
Barton, Duwayne Dunham, Marcia Lucas
Directed by Richard Marquand

PRINCIPAL CAST: Mark Hamill (*Luke Skywalker*), Harrison Ford (*Han Solo*), Carrie Fisher (*Princess Leia*), Billy Dee Williams (*Lando Calrissian*), Anthony Daniels (*C-3PO*), Peter Mayhew (*Chewbacca*), Sebastian Shaw (*Anakin Skywalker*), Ian McDiarmid (*The Emperor*), Frank Oz (*Yoda*), James Earl Jones (*Voice of Darth Vader*), David Prowse (*Darth Vader*), Alec Guinness (*Ben [Obi-Wan] Kenobi*), Kenny Baker (*R2-D2/Paploo*), Michael Pennington (*Moff Jerjerrod*), Kenneth Colley (*Admiral Piett*), Michael Carter (*Bib Fortuna*), Denis Lawson (*Wedge*), Timothy M Rose (*Admiral Ackbar*), Dermot Crowley (*General Madine*), Caroline Blakiston (*Mon Mothma*), Warwick Davis (*Wicket*), Jeremy Bulloch (*Boba Fett*), Femi Taylor (*Oola*), Annie Arbogast (*Sy Snootles*), Claire Davenport (*Fat Dancer*), Jack Purvis (*Teebo*), Mike Edmonds (*Logray/Jabba Puppeteer*), Jane Busby (*Chief Chirpa*)

TAGLINE: Return to a galaxy . . . far, far away.

SUMMARY: A long time ago, in a galaxy far, far away, construction on a second, more powerful Death Star is nearly complete. This Death Star is in orbit around the forest moon of Endor, protected by an energy field created by a shield-generator on the moon itself. It is impossible to get to or from either the station itself or the generator without a passcode. In the last stage of the station's construction both Darth Vader and the Emperor arrive in quick succession; they are so determined that the battle station will be completed on schedule that they intend to supervise the construction themselves.

Luke Skywalker, along with Lando Calrissian, Princess Leia, Artoo, Threepio and Chewbacca, stages an elaborate rescue of Han Solo from Jabba the Hutt's palace, to which Solo has been taken by Boba Fett following events at Bespin Cloud City (see **The Empire Strikes Back**). Luke gives Jabba three chances to free his friend or face destruction, but Jabba refuses them all and the Hutt and many of his minions are duly killed during the rescue. Following this Luke goes to meet Yoda, and the others rendezvous with the rest of the rebel fleet.

On Dagobah a dying Yoda reluctantly confirms to Luke that Vader is indeed his father, but insists that as the last of the Jedi it is his duty to kill Vader anyway. Yoda dies, and Luke converses with the spirit of Obi-Wan Kenobi, who is also convinced that Vader is irredeemable and that the only hope for the galaxy is for Luke to kill him. Obi-Wan tells Luke that Vader has another child, Luke's twin sister – Leia. Luke leaves and meets up with the others.

The rebels have learned of the second Death Star and are about to launch an all-out attack on both the station and its shield generator. Lando volunteers to lead the assault, and Han agrees to take command of the strike team who will destroy the shield generator. Luke, Leia, Artoo, Threepio and Chewbacca are to go with him. Using a stolen Imperial code they land on the moon where they befriend small furry bear-like creatures called Ewoks who agree to help the rebels destroy the shield generator.

Luke abandons his friends and surrenders to the Empire, determined to meet and talk to his father, convinced there is still good within him. Vader delivers Luke to the Emperor on board the Death Star. There the ruler of the Empire explains to Luke that he has only constructed this Death Star so that the rebels will put all their resources into a single assault on it, and he will be able to wipe them out in one day. This Death Star, although it looks incomplete, is now fully operational. It was the Emperor himself who leaked the shield generator code to the rebellion. It's a trap. The Emperor tells Luke that the rebellion will fail; Luke must join Vader at his side. Luke refuses, and the Emperor mocks and manipulates Luke into trying to kill him, knowing that if young Skywalker gives in to his hatred he too will cross to the dark side of the force and become a servant of evil. Vader defends his master, and fights Luke. Angry and afraid, Luke bests his aged father, cutting off the Dark Lord's hand just as Vader did to him on Cloud City. Shocked out of his anger by the injuries he has given to his father, Luke refuses to kill Vader and instead throws his lightsaber aside. He would rather die than turn to the dark side. As on Bespin, faced with the choice between doing the right thing and surviving he chooses integrity and death. The Emperor then begins to torture Luke, but rather than watch his master kill his son Vader attacks the Emperor; the tyrant is killed but Vader is mortally wounded defending his child.

Han's party and the Ewoks destroy the shield generator, and Lando destroys the Death Star. Luke escapes, carrying Vader's body, in a stolen shuttle moments before the explosion. Returning to Endor, Luke burns Vader's corpse on a huge funeral pyre. As everyone else celebrates Luke stands alone watched by three spectral figures: Obi-Wan Kenobi, Yoda and Anakin Skywalker, redeemed by his final sacrifice and returned to the light.

SCREENPLAY: In constructing the script for what would be the last *Star Wars* film made for some considerable time, Lucas turned to the third act of his 1976 synopsis. Working from this he created a rough draft which he revised once, before *Empire* and *Raiders* screenwriter Lawrence Kasdan was invited to co-write the actual screenplay with Lucas. Despite being at a stage in his career where he only wanted to write screenplays to direct himself, Kasdan accepted, considering co-writing the final *Star Wars* film with Lucas 'a favour' to the producer who had been instrumental in his career success.

During the writing process, Lucas and producer Howard Kazanjian began looking for directors for the project. Initially Lucas offered the film to David Lynch to direct. Whilst Lynch seems, in retrospect, an odd choice, he had at this point not yet made the career-defining *Blue Velvet*, and was best known for the brilliant, yet orthodox *The Elephant Man* (1980). It was Lynch's earlier, stranger *Eraserhead* (1976), however, which interested Lucas. Lynch turned the project down, reportedly because he didn't want to do either a science fiction film or a film where he wouldn't have complete creative control (ironically his next project was to be Dino De Laurentiis's adaptation of Frank Herbert's first *Dune* novel, which the producer was making as a direct rival to *Star Wars*).

After this setback, Steven Spielberg offered to direct *Jedi* but Lucas turned him down. 'I understand why George won't let me do one,' Spielberg commented when asked in 2002 about this perhaps surprising rejection. 'I wanted to do one fifteen years ago and he didn't want me to do it – *Star Wars* is George's baby,' he went on to explain. 'George is my best friend and . . . I am his, but we *are* all competitive. This is George's . . . fingerprints.'

Various other directors were considered by Lucas before he selected Welsh-born, Oxford-educated Richard Marquand, whose *Eye of the Needle* he saw a rough cut of and with which he declared himself 'very, very impressed'. The atmospheric and emotionally complex wartime thriller appealed to Lucas, who contacted the director on the strength of it. After several interviews Marquand convinced the producer he was the man for the job.

Once Marquand was on board Kasdan and Lucas held story conferences with him, and rewrote the screenplay to incorporate details and ideas from the director; these included suggestions made during discussions Marquand held with returning actors: 'I said [to each of them] "You know this character. Tell me how you feel about his character. Tell me how you feel this character is going, what this character's got to offer . . . I discovered some . . . nice things about the characters, which we were able to inject into the film"'.

Carrie Fisher was bored of Leia being such a tomboy but simultaneously wanted her to have more action scenes. It was felt that Leia's independence in the previous pictures had consisted of giving orders and being spiky and so rewrites obliged her by giving her a lot of shooting to do and by putting her into a costume that would become so famous it'd later have an entire episode of the sitcom *Friends* devoted to its effect on the psyche of adolescent males. 'She's a very sexy lady and in this film we [the audience] get to find that out,' Marquand teased reporters before the film's release. Marquand's contributions to the screenplay also included the suggestion that Luke's party would penetrate Jabba's palace in varying disguises. Although Kasdan saw it as part of his remit as primary screenwriter to be 'very responsive to Richard Marquand's desires for the film', he was also insistent that 'he and I are in the service of George', and later made it clear that his role as he saw it was 'to serve the needs of the saga'.

That said, the screenplay discussions were sufficiently open that Kasdan felt able to suggest radical alterations to the ending (Lucas's handwritten first draft ends, as the film does, with Vader dying saving his son from the Emperor). These included showing Luke succumbing to the dark side of the force and becoming the Emperor's new enforcer, letting Luke die as a result of his injuries and Luke using the Death Star's weapons to destroy the Imperial capital. All of these were rejected by Lucas who felt very strongly that the ending as planned was the core of the film and should not be discarded.

At one point the screenplay was going so well, and was so to Lucas's liking, that he seriously contemplated directing the film himself. Whether this was before or after Marquand signed on has never been confirmed, but given Marquand's input into the evolution of the script the latter seems far more likely. Lucas's stated reason for deciding not to direct the movie at this stage was that 'I took one look at the amount of work and thought, "My God, my life is complicated enough"'. Had Lucas chosen differently Marquand's role would have been a difficult contractual puzzle to solve.

PRODUCTION: To shoot the film Marquand brought with him Alan Hume, his cinematographer on *Eye of the Needle*. Hume had been DOP on *Carry On Girls* (Gerald Thomas, 1973) one of the weakest and blandest of the long-running series of deeply unfunny British 'sex comedies', although he had gone on to bigger things by becoming the cinematographer on the James Bond movie *For Your Eyes Only* (John Glen, 1981). After *Jedi* he would shoot two further James Bond films, *Octopussy* and *A View to a Kill* (both for Glen, 1983/1985) and two top-notch comedies, *A Fish Called Wanda* (Charles Crichton, 1988) and *Without a Clue* (Thom Eberhardt, 1988).

Jedi occupied all nine sound stages at EMI Elstree Studios for 78 days. Stage 6, aka 'the *Star Wars* soundstage' (actually built for

The Empire Strikes Back), housed the gateway to Jabba's palace and later the Death Star's docking bay within its cavernous internal dimensions of one and a half million cubic feet. The docking bay set, which alone cost $800,000, was 248 feet long, 120 feet wide and 45 feet high, and contained within it the full-size Imperial shuttle model which weighed nearly six tonnes.

Later still the stage was turned over to the vast Ewok village set, built 20 feet off the ground and surrounded by a 360-degree cyclorama. Stage 4 held the Emperor's throne room, constructed with its own internal elevator system, and Stage 5 held the rebels' briefing room aboard their mobile headquarters. Stage 8 held Jabba's vast throne room; sequences shot there required a crew of 90, plus 9 mime artistes, 42 extras and 19 puppeteers. During shooting director Marquand read out Jabba's lines himself (they would later be dubbed by a linguist speaking Quechua, the language of the Incas also spoken by Greedo – an employee of Jabba's – in *Star Wars*).

Following this the cast and crew spent eight weeks on location. Tatooine was represented not by Tunisia as in *Star Wars* but by the surely ironically named, sandblasted expanse of Buttercup Valley, Arizona, not far from the Colorado river and the border with California. This was the only place in America which satisfied Lucas's desire for sand dunes 'as far as the eye could see' and filming took place across April 1981. Whilst there the crew were effectively undercover; all call sheets bore the fictitious title *Blue Harvest*, and cast and crew wore TV shirts and baseball caps bearing a logo for such a film and carrying the slogan 'Horror beyond your imagination'. The actors were given codenames and it was these that were used on call sheets. Anyone phoning Lucasfilm to enquire about the new *Star Wars* was informed that it was shooting in Germany and that cast and crew were incommunicado.

Once Tatooine was over and done with it was the turn of the redwood forests of Marin County, California to stand in for an alien world, in this case the forest moon of Endor, site of the final battle between rebels and Imperial forces.

Perhaps because of the problems on *Empire* Lucas was present for much of the shoot; officially only as executive producer (a designation which for Lucas always seems to include uncredited second-unit direction anyway), but it has often been implied by many commentators that Lucas second-guessed Marquand during much of the shoot, offering suggestions and becoming in essence a 'back-seat driver'. Others have gone further and suggested that much of *Jedi* was ultimately directed by Lucas himself despite Marquand's presence on set. Marquand always strenuously denied such suggestions. Generally speaking Marquand's fondness for close-ups and a roving camera style seem visually very different to Lucas's approach on *Star Wars* (and indeed the prequels), although there are a few shots here and there which do look as if they were framed by George Lucas.

The last scene recorded for the Imperial trilogy was the cremation of Darth Vader, shot by Lucas himself near Skywalker Ranch long after principal photography was completed.

ALTERNATIVE VERSIONS: The Special Edition of 14 March 1997 had the most alterations to it of any of the three Imperial trilogy *Star Wars* films. Extensive reshooting was undertaken by Lucas and this material was mostly added to the first forty minutes of the film during the sequences on Tatooine. Lucas had never been satisfied with the dance sequence in Jabba's palace. It was a late addition to the screenplay, and had replaced a sequence in which Jabba 'held court' with a variety of lowlifes begging favours from the Hutt. It served the same plot function, even including the first instance of someone who has displeased Jabba being thrown to his pet rancor. Lucas took this out and substituted the song-and-dance number instead because he thought 'it would be funny to have a song-and-dance number in the middle of a *Star Wars* movie'. The scene as shot, however, never lived up to its full potential, with the strangely immobile singer/dancer Sy Snootles failing to impress. The reshoots encompassed the addition of three new backing singers (two alien, one human) to Sy's band, more instrument-playing aliens (including two extras beating a six-foot-high drum) and new footage of bounty-hunter Boba Fett; these were then cut into the film in place of the 1982 footage. Sy herself was redone as a CGI puppet and given another alien singer – a 'yuzzum' – to duet with. For this re-shooting the actress who had played dancing girl Oola (Femi Taylor) was re-hired for pick-up shots for her character thirteen years after she originally wrapped. John Williams also wrote a new song to cover the sequence, referred to on the CD soundtrack reissue as 'Jedi Rocks'.

The replacement sequence is faster, funnier and more opulent, and far better achieves Lucas's original intentions. The general coverage of the scene is better, with appropriate cutaways at the right moments, and includes a brief new shot of Oola waiting in fear to be attacked after she has fallen into the rancor pit.

It is worth noting that *Indiana Jones and the Temple of Doom*, Lucas's very next project, also features an amusingly incongruous song-and-dance sequence, suggesting Lucas still hadn't got the desire to play around with such scenes out of his system.

The failure to shoot scenes with a bantha (a large pachyderm native to Tatooine) during the *Star Wars* March 1976 shoot in Tunisia caused Lucas to indulge in his first ever period of reshooting for the *Star Wars* series in January 1977. Even then only being able to show one of the beasts close up left him unsatisfied. Presumably because of this a short CGI special-effects shot of a herd of bantha crossing the desert was inserted into *Return of the Jedi* immediately before the arrival of Jabba's party at the Sarlaac pit.

The pit itself was substantially redone for the reissue, with tentacles and a gaping beak-like mouth added to the existing footage to change the nature of the monster and make it more fearsome.

Perhaps the most inexplicable alteration is a single line of dialogue. When Han Solo is trying to shoot the Sarlaac's tentacle to stop Lando being dragged in, he says 'I can see a lot better now', instead of (as in the theatrical cut) 'It's alright. Trust me'.

One of the more subtle, but perhaps important, alterations was made near the end of the movie; as Vader attacks the Emperor to protect Luke from him, he now lets out a tortured scream as he does so. This sound effect – which does much to humanise Vader and adds desperation to his action – was added during sound work for the Special Edition. To achieve the effect the sound of James Earl Jones screaming was mixed with screeching tire noises recorded by Skywalker Sound's Ben Burtt.

The panning shots across planets in the Empire which were added to the first few moments after Darth Vader's funeral were done using computer models created for the Special Editions of *Star Wars* (Tatooine) and *Empire* (Bespin). The final planet shown, however, was the Imperial capital of Coruscant, which had not yet been seen in a *Star Wars* film. Lucas wanted to feature Coruscant because he was already aware that the planet would be a major location throughout the prequel trilogy. The brief shots of the city were achieved using a mix of models, matte paintings and

CGI by George Hull and Doug Chiang at ILM. They worked from designs completed by Ralph McQuarrie during the original planning period for *Jedi*, and despite the sequence's brevity it took two and half months to complete. Probably the most noticeable change made to the film is the replacement of the Ewok campfire song at the film's finale with a new piece of music, 'Victory Celebration', written in 1996 and recorded by Williams and an orchestra over 26–27 November that year. A melancholic variation on 'The Force Theme' (see **Star Wars**), it's a far more fitting, tonally ambiguous ending for the film than the jocular tribal music of the previous version.

Less noticeably, but perhaps more importantly, *Return of the Jedi* also appears to have been re-edited from top to tail; almost every single scene transition is subtly different, taking place fractionally sooner or later and with – in some places – slightly different takes of scenes appearing to have been substituted for those in the original theatrical edition. One of the more obvious of these differences occurs in the very final moments; when Luke arrives in the Ewok city he greets all of his friends one by one. In the Special Edition, this group includes Wedge, whom Luke seeks out amongst the dancing rebel pilots and embraces. This shot is not in the earlier version of the film. Generally speaking, and in particular regard to the film editing, the *Return of the Jedi* Special Edition is a much better film than its forebear.

CUT SCENES: The very first scene shot for *Return of the Jedi*, and the only one in the picture to feature the full-size *Millennium Falcon* mock-up built for the original *Star Wars*, was cut during editing. Also on the stage were full-size mock-ups of Luke's X-wing and a Y-wing fighter (presumably the ship with which Threepio and Leia arrived on Tatooine). The scene featured Luke and his friends having difficulty reaching their ships because of a sandstorm. Shooting took place on 11 January 1982 on Stage 2 at Elstree and took nine hours. Lucas cut it because he felt that after the chaos of the Sarlaac sequence a moment of calm was required, and so he elected to jump straight to the shot of the ships leaving the planet's orbit (the full-size X-wing prop was left in place on the stage for when Tatooine was transformed into Dagobah to shoot scenes set on the swamp planet.

Immediately before the scene which begins with the Emperor telling Vader that he told Vader to remain on the command ship, there was a brief sequence of the Emperor's red-robed guards attempting to deny Vader access to their master's throne room; as they attempt to stop him Vader chokes the guards using the force, and they reluctantly let him through. This was removed after discussions about how the 'gag' of Vader being able to strangle people simply by using the force had been perhaps overplayed in *Empire*, where Vader disposes of several inept subordinates in such a manner.

Also cut very late (so late that Williams scored it – the music is included on the 1997 CD issue of his soundtrack) was a scene which had survived in some form since the rough draft. Coming between Vader's arrival on the Death Star and the sequence of Artoo and Threepio moving towards Jabba's palace, this featured Luke on Tatooine, being telepathically contacted by his father who tells him, as at the end of *The Empire Strikes Back*, that it is useless to resist, and that it is his destiny to turn to the dark side of the force.

QUOTES:

Vader: 'Sister. So you have a twin sister. Obi-Wan was wise to hide her from me. His failure is now complete. If *you* will not turn to the dark side then perhaps *she* will.'

The Emperor: 'I can feel the hate flowing through you. Give in to your hatred and your journey towards the dark side shall be complete.'

Yoda: 'Do not underestimate the power of the Emperor, or suffer your father's fate you will.'

Luke: 'Do you remember your mother. Your real mother?'
Leia: 'It's just images really. Feelings. She was very beautiful. Very kind, yet somehow sad. Why do you ask?'
Luke: 'I have no memory of my mother.'

Officer: 'You rebel scum!'

Han: 'I love you.'
Leia: 'I know.'

MUSICAL NOTES: Williams's *Jedi* score builds on those of the previous films in the trilogy, and adds three major new themes – 'Luke and Leia' is a sweeping melody used to back scenes about the twins, and there's a jaunty, rhythmic tune for the Ewoks, but most impressive is the dark, wordless choral chanting which accompanies the Emperor. Williams would return to this melody sixteen years later for *The Phantom Menace*.

RECURRING CONCERNS: If Lucas's talk of the *Star Wars* series as a conscious modern mythology – of its desire to pass on values and ideas to young people via epic storytelling – is to be given any weight, then now is the point to look at what the Imperial trilogy seems to say. Lucas himself never made any claims beyond the obvious for the series, saying that it was about living 'a compassionate life' – that the characters and situations demonstrated the value of selflessness over selfishness, and that this was the job of a certain kind of story. In the films the equation of worth with the selfless extends as far as apparently minor actions such as Han allowing Lando to use his beloved *Millennium Falcon* in the attack on the Death Star because it's for the greater good.

Indeed Han Solo's journey from smuggler to rebel general, although not overstated, is a nicely realised statement of Lucas's basic point. He is motivated by money in *Star Wars*, and told by an angry Leia that if money is all that he loves then that's all he'll receive. When he returns during the Battle of Yavin and saves Luke he prioritises the life of his friend not only over the fortune he has made, but also over his own life. He does this again when he risks himself to save Luke on Hoth, and the bravery with which he allows himself to be carbon-frozen in *Empire* is one of the trilogy's stand-out scenes. There's also Han's declared willingness to 'not get in the way' between Luke and Leia when Luke returns from the Death Star (he doesn't know about Luke and Leia's blood relationship), giving up the love he has found for the sake of his friend. It is this unselfishness that causes Leia to return his love: money isn't all that he loves, so it's far from all he receives.

Jedi, though, is more Luke's film than Han's, and its finest moment is when Luke proves that he is the man his father failed to become, and again chooses death rather corruption – 'Never, I'll never turn to the dark side. You've failed, your Highness. I am a Jedi, like my father before me'. This is all the more impressive in character terms because it's the second time he's had to make this choice. Lucas is repeating the idea that death is preferable to dishonour, and making it clear that to do the right thing even when it's personally disadvantageous – even fatal – is the highest form of heroism. This is what Vader's final sacrifice is about: he was unable to save his mother (see **Attack of the Clones**), and whatever may have happened to him since, whatever he may have done, he is incapable of watching someone harm his child. What would have happened had Vader let the Emperor kill Luke? Nothing would have changed. Vader would have continued to act as the Emperor's right-hand man; his enforcer, with the power and opportunity to do as he wished across an entire galaxy. This perfect selfless, suicidal act is enough to redeem him.

EXTERNAL REFERENCES: Jabba is briefly seen smoking a huge pipe, mentioned in the script as an allusion to the smoking caterpillar of Lewis Carroll's *Alice in Wonderland*.

In earlier drafts of the screenplay Leia kisses the unconscious Solo, waking him up and reversing the traditional roles of Sleeping Beauty and Prince Charming. This neat reference was dropped in favour of more dialogue between the two characters.

RELEASE: Released on 25 May 1983, *Jedi* broke the opening weekend box office record set by Spielberg's *ET: The Extra-Terrestrial* two years before, making $45.3 million.

CRITICISM: Reviews of *Jedi* were indulgent but weary. '. . . a visual treat throughout', noted *Variety*, with 'enough menacing monsters to populate a dozen horror pictures, [yet it] suffers in comparison to [*Star Wars*] when all was fresh'. The *New York Times*'s critic found themselves 'thinking fondly toward the Ewoks . . .' and readily praised a 'quite wonderful chase sequence' (on the speeder bikes), but felt that on the whole *Star Wars* films had been 'too often imitated to hold our imaginations the way they once did', Lucas's success robbing him and his series of the adulation that had been felt at first. 'The force is with them but the magic is gone', the reviewer finished regretfully.

Regarded as the runt of the *Star Wars* litter until the prequel trilogy caused a general shift in critical perception of all three films, *Jedi* has much to recommend it. It has the best screenplay of any *Star Wars* film, one in which Lucas's intuitive understanding of pace and structure perfectly matches Kasdan's ability to write heightened but witty dialogue. Their script pauses for breath only when the audience wants it to, and when it does it gives centre stage to its characters. Luke and Leia's scene in the Ewok city is rather wonderful, and all of the sequences on Dagobah are rich in character impact yet never descend into Disneyfied sentimentality. Mark Hamill, much criticised in some quarters, is superb throughout, and Vader turning from the dark side provides a moment of real catharsis.

AWARDS: At the 1984 Academy Awards *Return of the Jedi* was given a solitary Oscar – a special achievement award for its groundbreaking visual effects. Richard Edlund, Dennis Muren, Ken Ralston and Phil Tippett picked up the statuettes. Production designer Norman Reynolds and his team (Fred Hole, James L Schoppe and Michael Ford) were nominated for Best Art Direction, but didn't go on to win it. Neither did Ben Burtt (nominated twice, once for Best Effects, Sound Effects Editing and once for Best Sound) or John Williams. That Williams, Reynolds and Burtt had all previously received Oscars for their work on *Star Wars* films probably had something to do with the Academy deciding that that year's Oscars should go elsewhere.

It was much the same at the BAFTA Awards, where the special effects team won, whilst the Norman Reynolds team missed out as did Burtt and his team. Also nominated yet disappointed were make-up artists Phil Tippett and Stuart Freeborn.

At the all-science fiction Saturn Awards Mark Hamill picked up another Best Actor award and the movie got Best Film. The effects team were honoured again, and Aggie Guerard Rodgers' costume department and Tippett's make-up crew also received awards. Inevitably the final film in the trilogy that had revitalised and re-popularised screen science fiction won the Hugo Award for Best Dramatic Presentation and the People's Choice Award for Favourite Motion Picture, both of which were decided by open votes rather than by an electoral college.

TRIVIA: The faintly disquieting undertone of Jabba the Hutt's voice was created by miking the sound of someone running their hands through a cheese casserole and then mixing it with Jabba's pre-recorded dialogue.

TITLE TATTLE: The title of *Star Wars: Episode VI* was originally released to the press as *Revenge of the Jedi* and was changed very late in the day to *Return*. The reason given at the time was that Lucas had realised that the noble Jedi would not take revenge, although it has since been intimated that the real reason behind the late change was to trick bootleg merchandisers who were subsequently left with items bearing the false title.

Regardless, *Return* makes more sense as a title for the movie that was made. The film isn't about the return of the Jedi in the sense that it is about the restoration of the Jedi order; it's about the return of one particular Jedi, Anakin Skywalker. If the title were *Revenge* it would suggest that his killing of the Emperor was in some way selfish, which defeats the point of the action's plot function.

EXPERT WITNESS: 'One thing George wanted was a director who wasn't going to be rowing with him all the time. You can't make movies on that basis, it isn't possible . . . I had partly prepared myself for [being given a script and told to get on with it]. But it didn't happen, which was wonderful. The attitude all along was "You're the director!" I just had to get chapter and verse right. I had to understand the rules of *Star Wars*, the givens, which are very rigid.' Director Richard Marquand

LUCAS ON RETURN OF THE JEDI: 'This one was grim for me, just as bad as directing . . . *Jedi* almost killed everybody, every department. Everything was very, very hard on everybody.'

Indiana Jones and the Temple of Doom (1984)

(118 minutes US edition/113 minutes UK edition)

Paramount
A Lucasfilm Limited Production
Screenplay by Willard Huyck & Gloria Katz
Story by George Lucas
Director of Photography: Douglas Slocombe
Production Designer: Elliot Scott
Produced by Robert Watts
Executive Producers: George Lucas, Frank Marshall
Music: John Williams
Editor: Michael Kahn
Directed by Steven Spielberg

PRINCIPAL CAST: Harrison Ford (*Dr Henry 'Indiana' Jones Junior*), Kate Capshaw (*Willie Scott*), Amrish Puri (*Mola Ram*), Roshan Seth (*Chattar Lal*), Philip Stone (*Captain Blumburtt*), Roy Chiao (*Lao Che*), Ke Huy Quan (*Short Round*), David Yip (*Wu Han*), Ric Young (*Kao Kan*), Chua Kah (*Joo Chen*), Rex Ngui (*Maitre d'*), Philip Tan (*Chief Henchman*), Dan Aykroyd (*Weber*), Akio Mitamura (*Chinese Pilot*), Michael Yama (*Chinese Co-Pilot*), D R Nanayakkara (*Shaman*), Dharmadasa Kuruppu (*Chieftain*), Stany De Silva (*Sajnu*), Raj Singh (*Maharaja Zalim Singh*), Pat Roach (*Chief Guard*)

TAGLINES: If adventure has a name it must be Indiana Jones.

The hero is back!

Trust him.

The man in the hat is back ...

SUMMARY: 1935. After a run-in with a gangster and a car chase through Shanghai, Indiana Jones – accompanied by his child sidekick Short Round and wannabe chanteuse Willie Scott – crashes down in India where he stumbles onto a village blighted by famine. All the village's children have been kidnapped and a holy Sankara stone – which guarantees prosperity and good harvests for the region – has been stolen. Indy traces the thieves to Pankot Palace, underneath which lurks a cult worshipping the Thuggee goddess Kali. The children are being used as a slave labour force, digging for the final two Sankara stones – there are five in total, and the Thuggees already have two in addition to the one they took from the village. After much unpleasantness and several action sequences, Indy frees the children by leading a slave revolt and the Thuggee leader Molar Ram is killed. Indy returns the stone to the village.

SCREENPLAY: Once it had been decided that there would be another Indiana Jones film and that Lucas, Ford and Spielberg would all return for it, attention turned to the unused outlines in Lucas's folder of Indiana Jones stories. After Lawrence Kasdan turned down the opportunity to script the feature, *American Graffiti* screenwriters Willard Huyck and Gloria Katz were offered the chance to develop an outline of Lucas's tentatively

GEORGE LUCAS Indiana Jones and the Temple of Doom

entitled *The Temple of Death*; after a week of story meetings with Lucas and Spielberg the husband/wife writing team put together an initial draft in six weeks.

The *Temple* outline had been selected, according to Spielberg, because Lucas wanted 'a darkness . . . to kind of push the envelope' and aimed to create something that would be to *Raiders* what *The Empire Strikes Back* had been to *Star Wars*: a film darker, weirder and harder than its predecessor that nevertheless contained many of the same elements and had much the same appeal. Lucas was adamant that the second film 'demand a lot more of its audience than *Raiders* had'. To balance out this increasing darkness it was agreed that Indy himself should become warmer, and more of a traditional hero figure; Spielberg came up with the idea of the adventurer having a kid sidekick in order to achieve this. The casting of Indy in a paternal role makes it all the more shocking when he is enslaved by Kali towards the end of the film. Harrison Ford was in broad agreement with these intentions, feeling that the only reason to revive or reprise a movie character was to allow an audience to see different aspects – and achieve a more complex understanding – of them.

Katz and Huyck wrote a further two drafts; ideas they were given to play with included the image of Indy hiding from gunfire behind a rolling gong, an escape from a plane using a rubber raft and a chase along an underground railroad in a mine car. All of these had been discussed and dismissed (for budgetary or practical reasons) during the production of *Raiders of the Lost Ark*, and all found their way into the new film. Another old idea dusted off and used was Lucas's original plan for Indy to appear occasionally as an evening dress-wearing, champagne-swilling frequenter of hot nightspots and society parties. Once the Huycks had finished their work, John Milius[1] did an uncredited dialogue polish and the movie began shooting on 18 April 1983.

CASTING: In creating a new leading lady for their *Indiana Jones* prequel Lucas and Spielberg were very cautious not simply to create a carbon copy of *Raiders*' heroine, Karen Allen's Marion Ravenwood, described by Spielberg on many occasions as a

---

[1] John Milius, a Lucas contemporary at USC; co-screenwriter *Apocalypse Now* (Francis Ford Coppola, 1979), *Clear and Present Danger* (Philip Noyce, 1994) and *Magnum Force* (1973); writer/director *The Wind and the Lion* (1975); co-writer/director *Conan the Barbarian* (1992) and *Red Dawn* (1984).

'two-fisted hellraiser'. '[Marion] is very tough, very strong . . . independent,' commented Lucas later. 'We wanted to not repeat this character over again.' Instead the diametrically opposite approach was taken. Unfortunately the creation of cabaret prima donna and unwilling adventuress Willie Scott as a reaction to Marion almost by necessity meant creating a character that embodied those very traits against which Marion herself had been such an impressive reaction. Lucas was insistent that the character be blonde, 'like Jean Harlow', and acquiesced to the casting of Spielberg's choice, brunette Kate Capshaw – whom he conceded was ideal on all other counts – on the condition that she be prepared to bleach her hair for the shoot. A former model, albeit one with a Master's degree from the University of Missouri, Capshaw had appeared in TV soap opera *Edge of Night* and been the female lead in infidelity comedy *A Little Sex* (Bruce Paltrow, 1982) before auditioning for the role of Willie. Nearly a decade after production on *Temple of Doom* finished she married its director.

Ke Huy Quan, cast as Indy's pre-teen sidekick Short Round, was found at an open casting call (an event where anyone who is of the right age can attend regardless of their acting experience). Lucas saw Quan as 'a perfect find . . . bright, capable [and] funny'. Spielberg concurred, considering Quan by far the best of the children he interviewed. Quan's performance is delightful, assisted by a script which gives him most of the best lines.

The travelogue nature of the plot meant that almost none of the roles other than the above two and Jones himself were much more than cameos. The more substantial of these included two major Indian actors. Roshan Seth (Chattar Lal) had come to Western attention following his strong performance as Nehru in *Gandhi* (Richard Attenborough, 1982), whereas Amrish Puri (playing principal villain Molar Ram) had also been in *Gandhi* but sadly neither his appearance there nor here – his only two performances in mainstream Western films – come close to suggesting the charismatic versatility he has demonstrated over a 30-year career in Hindi cinema.

Philip Stone, here playing British army Captain Blumburrt, was at the time a frequent collaborator with director Stanley Kubrick, having played Malcolm McDowell's father in *A Clockwork Orange* (1971), Graham in *Barry Lyndon* (1975) and Delby Grady in *The Shining* (1980).

In the scene where *Saturday Night Live* star Dan Aykroyd, latterly known for his role in *Ghostbusters* (Harold Ramis, 1985), makes an amusing cameo at the end of the opening sequence as airport man Weber, you can see – just behind him – a group of harassed travellers played by producers Frank Marshall and George Lucas and director Steven Spielberg. Marshall is the one pulling the rickshaw.

PRODUCTION: Lucasfilm were denied permission to film in Rajasthan's Rose Palace of Jaipur (the government disliked the screenplay) and so the India sequences were shot near Kandy in Sri Lanka. Second-unit photography took place simultaneously in Shanghai before both units made their way to Elstree for studio shooting on Elliot Scott's enormous and elaborate sets.

During shooting Harrison Ford injured his back and Lucas shut down the production for a few weeks to give the actor time to heal. Ford's injury proved inoperable and so doctors injected his spine with a derivative of green papaya (often used as a meat tenderiser), following which he was fit to return to work within six weeks. Once filming resumed it was on a reworked and tightened schedule designed to bring the film in as close to its originally planned finishing date as possible.

Pick-ups and the final confrontation on the rope bridge were the last sequences of the movie to be shot; they were lensed in California. Spielberg, who admitted to a fear of heights, found himself unable to cross the rope bridge, and instead had to drive a three-mile round trip every time he wanted to move from one side of the gorge to the other. The film finished shooting on 8 September, only a few days behind schedule.

Spielberg's regular editor Michael Kahn cut the movie, working with Lucas, whose approach was to aim for maximum pace and audience disorientation in the underground sequences, an approach he later described as 'an experiment . . . to see how far we could push the genre'.

ALTERNATIVE VERSIONS: The UK 2000 VHS release (rated PG – earlier editions had been 15) is butchered beyond all comprehension, losing so many shots 'for violence' that at times – especially in the second half of the picture – it totally loses visual coherence, whilst a badly relaid soundtrack makes nonsense of some sequences' pace. At a full five minutes shorter than the US theatrical version the cuts to this edition are far too many to list, but inevitably include the infamous shot of Molar Ram pulling out a sacrificial victim's heart with his hand. A classic example of censors seemingly misunderstanding the sensibilities of audiences, it remains the only version of the film commercially available in the UK, but should nevertheless be avoided at all costs. Hopefully any future DVD release will be better; it could hardly be worse.

QUOTES:
Short Round: 'Hey Dr Jones, no time for love!'

Short Round: 'You call him Dr Jones, doll!'

Indy: 'Fortune and glory, kid, fortune and glory.'

Lal: 'Dr Jones the eminent archaeologist?'
Willie: 'Hard to believe, isn't it?'

MUSICAL NOTES: The opening musical number is Cole Porter's 'Anything Goes', sung in Cantonese by Kate Capshaw in character as Willie Scott. It's *glorious*. The use of phrases from this song in the score for the immediately succeeding chaotic fight sequence is inspired, as is the exact synchronisation of a scored cymbal noise with Indy's use of a cymbal to hit a henchman in the face. New themes include a chirping tune using oriental scales for Short Round, but for much of the time Williams seems to be content to play with the 'Raiders March' (used most effectively as Indy regains his personality after his possession), a sharp contrast to the approach he'd adopt five years later in *Last Crusade*. Once we're inside the eponymous temple he really lets rip, using discordant choral chanting and repeating, escalating drumbeats to complement Spielberg's red-flooded photography perfectly, creating an almost unbearably oppressive atmosphere.

RECURRING CONCERNS: The travelogue structure is pure Lucas, as are ideas such as corrupt or ineffectual monarchical figures manipulated by advisers. Lucas's interest in comparative religion is indicated by the way this picture treats Hinduism and its mysticism as being (for plot purposes) literally, factually true – much as *Raiders* accepted Judaism as fact (and indeed as *Last Crusade* embraces a sort of Gnostic Christian mysticism). This acceptance of Hinduism (Indy is enraged that Molar Ram has betrayed the beneficent god Shiva, whose power is shown to be very real) is in stark contrast to the film's condemnation of Thuggee worship as 'an abomination'. Across the three films three separate, mutually exclusive religions are shown to be entirely 'correct'. There is something of Joseph Conrad's *Heart of Darkness* about the descent into the *Temple of Doom* itself (see **Other Projects**).

VISUAL INTERESTS: Spielberg told *American Cinematographer* magazine that the movie's visual style – of tight angles, deep colours and low-level ersatz natural light – sprang into his brain during Lucas's initial relation of the plot. 'I heard Kali cult . . . thuggees . . . *Temple of Doom*, black magic, voodoo and human sacrifice. What came to mind . . . was torchlight and shadows and red lava light . . . [the story] dictated the visual style of the movie.' The lavish travel sequences seem indebted to the Merchant Ivory school of filmmaking (such as *A Room With a View*, James Ivory, 1986), albeit with a touch of Hammer Horror – the swooping bats seem straight out of *Dracula, Prince of Darkness* (Terence Fisher, 1966).

FORWARDS/BACKWARDS: *Temple of Doom* was Lucas's first prequel, and turns the clock back to the year before *Raiders of the Lost Ark*. When asked why, the writer/producer confessed he was 'not quite sure' why he had decided to do it, but suggested that a desire to avoid a wartime setting and more Nazis played a part. One of *Temple of Doom*'s most famous sequences comes when Indy – confronted with two sword-wielding guards – immediately goes for his gun, planning to shoot them as he had in a similar sequence in *Raiders*. Although the scene inevitably gets a good reaction from audiences, it defies story logic due to the movie's prequel status. Not that it matters.

The 1935 setting prompted Harrison Ford to observe that as he had been too old for the part anyway (in *Raiders* Indy is 36, while during filming Ford was 38), going back in time a year three years after the first movie merely compounded an existing problem. When Willie claims that she's 'hard to handle' and Indy replies he's had worse, the implication is that he's talking about Marion Ravenwood (although, on the other hand, see much of **Young Indiana Jones**).

EXTERNAL REFERENCES: As just about everybody who has ever seen the movie knows, the club in the opening sequence is called Obiwan (with no space), after the *Star Wars* sequence's most famous Jedi Knight. Less commented upon is the resemblance between the Thuggee make-up and *The Phantom Menace*'s Darth Maul. In said club Indy wears a white tuxedo and tucks his left hand into his pocket, which gives more than a hint of Humphrey Bogart's Rick from *Casablanca* (Michael Curtiz, 1942). The opening shot allows the Paramount mountain logo to dissolve into a shot of a very similar mountain carved onto a gong. This gong is then struck by a muscular servant in clear imitation of the logo of the Rank film organisation. This is in itself, however, a pastiche of the opening of *Gunga Din* (George Stevens, 1939), which also parodied the Rank logo *and* was itself a movie which featured a battle with a Thuggee sect, an underground temple and the worship of Kali. Thus this is an opening sequence which incorporates one studio's logo into another's whilst parodying *both* logos and an earlier film that previously parodied one of the logos – a film which is itself a major influence on this film (phew!).

'Dr Jones, I presume,' asks Captain Blumburrt, a clear reference to Stanley's famous question to Dr Livingstone.

Indiana Jones is famously named after the Lucas family dog, and this approach is extended to the other characters here. Willis is named after Spielberg's dog, and Short Round after the Huycks' – although there is also a character called Short Round in *The Steel Helmet* (Sam Fuller, 1951).

Saturday morning serials specifically referenced in *Temple of Doom* include 1944's *Tiger Woman* (victims lowered into boiling lava in a cage), 1942's *The Perils of Nyoka* (the spikes moving down from the ceiling), 1940's *The Drums of Fu Manchu* (abandoning the hero in a pilotless plane), and many, many more. Most serials made by the Republic studios had at least one mine car chase; the studio had a standing mine railroad set and was loath to let it go to waste.

RELEASE: Put out on 23 May 1984 in the USA, *Temple of Doom* created the new PG-13 certificate. Spielberg was fully aware that the film he had made did not fit into the PG category, but was unwilling to accept an R for what was still, after all, a popcorn picture. He suggested to Jack Valenti – then Chairman and CEO of the Motion Picture Association of America – that maybe it was time for a new certification between PG and R, designed for films just like *Temple of Doom* (which Lucas has since described as not 'really strong enough to be an R'). Valenti acquiesced to Spielberg's suggestion and the PG-13 was born. The movie made $180 million at the USA box office, a figure it wouldn't have touched had it garnered an R rating.

CRITICISM: Pauline Kael, who had been none too kind to either *Raiders* or *Jedi*, found much to like in the movie and labelled it 'one of the most sheerly pleasurable comedies ever made'. Her fellow *New Yorker* reviewer David Denby, however, was appalled – 'that Spielberg should devote himself to anything so debased . . . is almost unbearably depressing'. *Variety* found itself more in line with Denby than Kael, muttering that 'Spielberg is such a talented director it's a shame to see him lose all sense of subtlety and nuance'. That said, the trade paper also noted the 'stunning display of design, lensing and editing' the film constituted even whilst reviling its 'vulgarity and senseless excess'. In the *New York Times* Vincent Canby demonstrated an understanding of the feature seemingly beyond most reviewers – that its grotesque carnival of delights would trouble adults far more than the children they were 'protecting' from it: 'The children . . . find it all delicious fun, though any adults in the vicinity will probably feel sick'.

One of the earliest British reviews was in SF magazine *Starburst*, whose reviewer asked the question he thought was on everybody's lips: 'Is it as good as *Raiders of the Lost Ark*?' His answer? 'Yes. [It's] a fantastic roller-coaster ride', with 'an opening credits sequence [which is] delirious in a way totally different to anything you've seen before'. The *Guardian*'s Derek Malcolm was unhappy with the popcorn picture he'd been forced to watch, complaining of a 'sore bum [and] a numb brain' after sitting through the picture.

A film that divides audiences as much as it divided critics, *Temple of Doom* is as visually astounding as it is unrelenting. For some the visceral pleasures, the extreme switches of mood and tone (it is both very funny and really quite disturbing) and the hypnotic brutality of it all render the film at least the equal of the others in the series and indeed rank it amongst both Lucas and Spielberg's finest work. For others, the slipshod – and occasionally incoherent – narrative, firmly episodic structure, overlong travelogue sequences and failure to inspire emotional involvement override the feature's admirable technical achievements.

The *New York Times'* Vincent Canby was very much in the former camp, arguing that *Temple of Doom*'s structure was entirely deliberate. 'Old-time fifteen-part movie serials didn't have shape, they just went on and on, which is what [*Indiana Jones and the Temple of Doom*] does, with humour and technical invention'; it's a valid angle, and one with which this author finds himself in firm agreement. *Temple of Doom* is one of the few Lucas/Spielberg projects that seems to justify the charge often (and usually unfairly) levelled at both men – that they produce films that are little more than strings of set-pieces linked by the faintest breath of narrative. In this case it's hard to argue with, but here each of those set-pieces is put together with such skill, wit and precision that it seems churlish to criticise them for doing it, especially if – as seems likely this time round – it isn't so much a fault, as *the point*, although that's obviously little compensation to those who just don't get the joke.

Film is a visual medium as well as a narrative one, and it is in the realm of the purely visual that *Temple of Doom* most clearly triumphs. It also remains the perfect film to show to those who think that Lucas has only ever had one idea, or that Spielberg is an unremittingly sentimental filmmaker.

Incidentally for a perfect and entirely loving parody of this movie see the fifth episode of the Kevin Smith-produced *Clerks* television cartoon series, made in 2000 and available on DVD.

AWARDS: *Temple of Doom* was nominated for two Academy Awards: one for John Williams's magnificent score and a second for Best Visual Effects (Dennis Muren, George Gibbs, Michael J McAllister, Lorne Peterson), the latter of which it won. The effects crew also won a British Academy Award.

TRIVIA: The onscreen credits actually read 'Harrison Ford starring in' before the name of the feature comes up, a measure of Ford's increased popularity and box office power since the production of *Raiders*.

The Ewok Adventure (TVM 1984)

(88 minutes)

Lucasfilm Limited/Korty Films
Teleplay by Bob Carrau
Story by George Lucas
Cinematography by John Korty
Production Designer: Joe Johnston
Producer: Thomas G Smith
Executive Producer: George Lucas
Music by Peter Bernstein
Directed by John Korty

PRINCIPAL CAST: Eric Walker (*Mace Towani*), Warwick Davis (*Wicket*), Aubree Miller (*Cindel Towani*), Fionnula Flanagan (*Catarine Towani*), Guy Boyd (*Jeremitt Towani*), Burl Ives (*Narrator*), Daniel Frishman (*Deej*), Debbie Lee Carrington (*Weechee*), Tony Cox (*Widdle*), Kevin Thompson (*Chukha-Trok*), Margarita Fernández (*Kaink*), Pam Grizz (*Shodu*), Bobby Bell (*Logray*), Tiffany Brissette (*Voice*)

TAGLINE: You'll live the adventure . . . You'll love its heroes.

SUMMARY: A starcruiser occupied by the Towani family – mother Catarine, father Jeremitt and children Mace (fifteen) and Cindel (four) – has recently crashed on the Endor forest moon. When their parents go missing the children reluctantly team up with a group of Ewoks to find them. It transpires that the parents have been kidnapped by the Giant Gorax. Embarking on a long trek, they eventually rescue them, but at the cost of the Ewok warrior Chukha-Trok's life.

PRODUCTION: ABC approached Lucasfilm about a TV special from the company for Thanksgiving 1984. Lucas was intrigued by the suggestion, and decided to use the opportunity to revisit the world of *Return of the Jedi*'s most controversial creations – the Ewoks. There was a certain amount of logic in returning to the world of the Ewoks. Although sneered at by older *Star Wars* fans, the creatures were popular with younger audiences – and, crucially, with young Amanda Lucas – and many props and costumes from

Jedi were still in storage and available to use. Perhaps most importantly the location used for filming scenes set on the forest moon of Endor was in Marin County, practically in Lucas's back garden. This would allow him to exercise considerable control over the project from the ranch. Initially planned as a one-hour special, the scope of the TVM expanded as Lucas's enthusiasm for the project increased. Designated writer Bob Carrau had been working as George Lucas's assistant; Lucas felt that the young man (still in his early twenties) had demonstrated some writing talent and should be given a break. He was commissioned to work Lucas's outline into a full 88-minute teleplay. *The Ewok Adventure* was planned to be shot in six weeks, with an additional two weeks allowed for overdubbing; Lucas hired independent Oscar-winning filmmaker John Korty[1] to direct the film, and gave him full autonomy in hiring his own cast and crew. Korty chose to be his own cinematographer, manning the camera himself.

After viewing the completed footage in his capacity as executive producer Lucas sanctioned an extra week of shooting, and as John Korty was by then busy on another project Lucas directed it himself. The reshooting chiefly involved revisions to the end of the film, as well as the scene where Mace's hand is nearly eaten by a carnivorous plant and another where the teenager verbally abuses a rock. Lucas also supervised the editing, and during the reshooting rewrote scenes and dialogue until they pleased him. Actor Eric Walker remembers Lucas handing him handwritten pages of retooled dialogue during shooting, and still has a call sheet for the reshoot week which names Lucas as the project's director. Total production time on the TVM, which with its 75 or so matte, blue-screen and other FX shots was extraordinarily ambitious for television, was around nine months (as opposed to the three years it had taken to make *Return of the Jedi*). Lucas supervised the final cut of the special himself although unlike, say, *Willow*, it doesn't make great use of his signature eccentric wipes and dissolves to move between scenes.

TRAILER: ABC produced a specially shot promo trailer which remains unaired. This featured Mace, Cindel and the Ewok Kaink

---

[1] John Korty, independent writer/director/cinematographer/editor and native of Lafayette, Indiana USA. Oscar-nominated for his anti-smoking short *Breaking the Habit* (1964), and won Best Documentary Film Oscar for *And Where Did They Get 19 Kids?* (1977). Other awards include Best Director Emmy for *The Autobiography of Miss Jane Pittman* (1974).

walking into a 50s-style American diner; they order sodas and someone recognises the Ewok, and then Mace turns to the camera and reminds everyone to watch 'George Lucas's first film for television'. Although he had granted ABC permission to use his cast and props to make the trailer, Lucas had not been provided with a script for it beforehand. Once he saw the finished commercial he objected to the placing of his *Star Wars* universe characters in a recognisable, near-contemporary setting, and vetoed its use for that reason.

CASTING: Open auditions were held for the pivotal role of Cindel, as there were so few three-to-five-year-old actresses available. Calls were held in Los Angeles and San Francisco before Aubree Miller, who had never acted before, was selected. Eric Walker was more experienced, having guested on popular TV show *Webster* and appeared in the movie *Having it All* (Edward Zwick, 1982) with Cary Grant's former wife Dyan Cannon. Walker and returning Ewok Warwick Davis – his participation was regarded by Lucas as the most important aspect of the production – bonded during production, shooting a video documentary about the making of the TVM. This also featured skits and outtakes performed by the cast and interviews. Copies were presented to the crew, including Lucas, after completion of the shoot.

ALTERNATIVE VERSIONS: The TVM was shot in 16:9 widescreen, but transmitted in 4:3 (the aspect ratio of most contemporary television). The foreign markets cinema version was in 16:9, but all VHS releases have been in 4:3. Contrary to fan speculation the US and foreign markets versions have the same running time.

QUOTES:
Cindel: 'That's not a starcruiser, that's a horse.'

MUSICAL NOTES: Composer John Bernstein was the son of the more famous Elmer; his chirpy string-based score makes liberal use of themes written by John Williams for *Return of the Jedi*, albeit without crediting Williams. It was recorded by an 80-piece orchestra. The TVM's music and effects were mixed in stereo as though it were a theatrical release, despite the scheduled television transmission inevitably being in mono, stereo television transmissions then being unheard of. Lucas struck a deal with various FM radio stations to transmit the full soundtrack, and asked that viewers watched *The Ewok Adventure* with their TV sound turned off and their radios on and tuned to the appropriate local station instead. Thus they got the film's soundtrack mixed in stereo as the producer intended.

RECURRING CONCERNS: Like *Star Wars* some of the plot is about someone trying to rescue their sister. Like much of Lucas's work the plot structure is that of a journey. The gradual acceptance of one culture by another to mutual advantage, despite manifest differences, has also been explored before, although the point is slightly blunted by being expressed in exactly the same way as in *Return of the Jedi*. There's also a great sequence where the medicine man Logray performs a dancing 'vision' ritual in order to ascertain someone's whereabouts; Logray is a typical Lucas figure, a shaman/mystic hero with precognitive abilities. Mace, a whining adolescent who becomes a hero as a result of traumatic events, cannot help but remind the viewer of Luke Skywalker, and his forename is reused for a pre-eminent character in the Republic trilogy – Mace Windu.

VISUAL INTERESTS: The lengthy hanglider sequence remains impressively shot and well edited. The emergence of the Giant Gorax from the fog during the pre-credits sequence is an effective shock moment. In some sense the entire special is a typical Lucas world-building exercise, in which the viewer sees far more of the Ewoks' own world than in *Return of the Jedi*, including encounters with various exotic animals and references to the creatures' own mysticism and religion. The audience also sees parts of Endor which are not forest, as the characters pass through desert on their way to the mountain range, giving the feeling (rare in SF films) that this is a world with multiple climates and geographical areas.

EXTERNAL REFERENCES: Narrator Burl Ives was well known for performing the same function for many other family-oriented holiday specials, including *Rudolph the Red-Nosed Reindeer* (1964) and *The First Easter Bunny* (1976); the use of him here places *The Ewok Adventure* firmly in that heart-warming, family-friendly heritage. He was also the recording artist responsible for legendary children's record 'I know an old lady who swallowed a fly', and won a Best Supporting Actor Oscar for his performance in western *The Big Country* (William Wyler, 1958). Ironically *Starlog* magazine's preview of *The Ewok Adventure* contains a sarcastic observation that despite the Thanksgiving transmission the special is unlikely to feature 'Burl Ives warbling about the holidays'. Ooops.

The minute female fireflies are obviously reminiscent of Tinkerbell from JM Barrie's *Peter Pan*. Mace and Chukha-Trok's axe-throwing competition is reminiscent of the archery competition used in most versions of the Robin Hood story.

RELEASE: Although it was always intended as a television special *The Ewok Adventure* received a limited theatrical release outside the United States, including in Great Britain. The international theatrical prints carry the more evocative, less self-explanatory title *Caravan of Courage*, although posters refer to it as *Caravan of Courage: An Ewok Adventure* to make it clear what the film is about. In the US the TVM was shown on 25 November 1984 on ABC between 8 and 10 p.m. (US commercial television at that time averaged sixteen minutes of commercials in an hour of programming). It garnered a 40 % share of the ratings for its timeslot, better than any of the competing channels. ABC were immediately interested in either a sequel or (better yet) a regular weekly TV series spinning off from the TVM, but Lucas was uninterested in the latter prospect. Discussions were however, held about a second TV movie (see **Ewoks: The Battle for Endor**).

CRITICISM: When *The Ewok Adventure* appeared in British movie theatres UK critic John Brosnan's scorn was so great that he felt moved to create a new award for the picture, 'Worst George Lucas TV movie masquerading as a feature'. US critics – most whom were invited to preview the special in a theatrical setting – weren't much kinder. 'Passable juvenile fantasy', commented *Films and Filming*, which went on to condemn the 'prosaic, cut-price nature of this whole silly spin-off'. Interestingly they articulated much of the appeal and contradiction of Lucas's work, commenting that despite the excessive cuteness of some sequences children were nonetheless likely to be 'scared out of their wits by half of it'. *Cinefantastique* went further, condemning the special as 'Hansel and Gretel in space, an embarrassment for Lucasfilm'. This review is interesting insofar as it later goes on to advance the theory that the special is simply an attempt by Lucasfilm to effectively buy cut-price advertising for *Star Wars* merchandise. Although not borne out by the facts (the impetus for the TV movie came from ABC, not Lucasfilm; the special cost $4.5 million to make and actually lost Lucasfilm money, as ABC had agreed in advance to pay the company only around $2 million for it), the theory is interesting in that it indicates the increasing shift in critical opinion of Lucas: away from perceptions of him as a filmmaker and rather perceiving everything he is involved in as being purely a business venture. Of all the reviews only that in the *Hollywood Reporter* was essentially positive about the TVM, calling it 'enchanting fare for children' and making no bones about it being 'more specifically [for] young children than the *Star Wars* trilogy of films'. Much praise was reserved for the way Aubree Miller's Cindel (described as 'impeccably precious') 'steals the picture'. Only a year later *Variety* labelled the special 'an evergreen family favourite' which it expected to be reshown nearly every holiday season in the same manner as other family-oriented specials.

   The Ewok Adventure is technically superb, but suffers from being both overly sentimental and strangely charmless. It does feel like a Lucas production – thanks to the aforementioned combination of sweetness and brutality that often occurs in his work – but it feels forced and watered-down; Lucas-pastiche, rather than the real thing. The screenwriter's inexperience shows with regard to the shambling episodic structure, and ultimately the special is – a few key moments aside – only going to hold the attention of the very young.

AWARDS: *The Ewok Adventure* won an Emmy award for Special Visual Effects. Given how much better it looks than almost any other television programme of the 1980s, this seems perfectly fair.

TRIVIA: Continuity error: Mace hurts his right hand whilst out looking for medicine, but for the rest of the TVM he has an injured left hand.

EXPERT WITNESS: 'George said, "It's just an hour special . . . we'll do it in eight or ten days", then the [budget] went right up the ladder and it took over 40 . . . post-production dragged on for months.' Director John Korty

'Warwick [Davis] has a very distinctive way of moving and you can spot him among all the other Ewoks. When you see him on screen there's a certain magic. He's a marvellous actor. Three feet tall, but filled with energy and charm and a sense of humour and a marvellous talent for pantomime.' Producer Thomas G Smith

LUCAS ON THE EWOK ADVENTURE: (Responding to ideas that he tried to cash in on the teddy bear) 'There are lots of teddy bears marketed [already]; you don't have anything . . . unique. If I were designing something original as a market item, I could probably do a lot better.'

Ewoks – The Battle for Endor (TVM 1985)

(88 minutes)

Lucasfilm Limited
Teleplay by Jim Wheat & Ken Wheat
Story by George Lucas
Cinematography by Isidore Mankofsky
Production Designer: Joe Johnston
Producer: Thomas G Smith
Executive Producer: George Lucas
Music by Peter Bernstein
Directed by Jim Wheat & Ken Wheat

PRINCIPAL CAST: Wilford Brimley (*Noa*), Warwick Davis (*Wicket*), Aubree Miller (*Cindel Towani*), Siân Phillips (*Queen Charal*), Carel Struycken (*King Terak*), Niki Botelho (*Teek*), Paul Gleason (*Jeremitt Towani*), Eric Walker (*Mace Towani*), Marianne Horine (*Young Witch*), Daniel Frishman (*Deej*), Tony Cox (*Willy*), Pam Grizz (*Shodu*), Roger Johnson (*Lieutenant*), Michael Pritchard (*Card Player #1*), Johnny Weissmuller Jr (*Card Player #2*)

SUMMARY: An army of Marauders led by the brutal King Terak attacks the Ewoks; the Towani family (see **The Ewok Adventure**) are all killed except their young daughter Cindel, who escapes with the help of the Ewok Wicket. Together they encounter grumpy old man Noa – who has also crashed his ship on Endor – and his furry companion Teek, an Ewok-like animal who can run at extraordinary speeds. Terak sends the sorceress Charal to capture Cindel and bring her to him, as he believes that she will understand how to activate a power cell he has acquired. Wicket, Noa and Teek rescue Cindel and take the power cell (which will work Noa's ship) but the Marauders give chase. After a final confrontation Terak is killed and Noa and Cindel leave Endor in his spaceship.

PRODUCTION: The ratings success of the Emmy-award-winning *The Ewok Adventure* prompted ABC to ask Lucasfilm for a sequel more or less immediately, and a second adventure was commissioned with the intention of it being shown in a similar slot the following year. This time Lucas hired the sibling team of Ken and Jim Wheat to write and direct the special, for which he would again be credited as having provided the 'story' and which would again be shot in the redwood forests of Marin County and at ILM. The Wheats would go on to gain greater fame for their screenplay for horror SF film *Pitch Black* (David Twohy, 2000) than for their involvement in the least interesting part of the *Star Wars* franchise.

Lucas's personal involvement in the project was significantly less than his contribution to *The Ewok Adventure*; he had meetings with the Wheats early on as they roughed out the story, and made periodic visits to the set – on one occasion he was accompanied by pop star Michael Jackson who was meeting Lucas to discuss a joint project for Disney's theme parks.

The special was shot in seven weeks starting on 11 May 1985. After a two-week break, a small period of pick-up shooting commenced but was over quickly.

CASTING: Siân Philips, the former wife of actor Peter O'Toole, had mostly worked on the stage rather than in films or television. Notable exceptions include her astonishing performance as Livia in *I, Claudius*, writer Jack Pulman and director Herbert Wise's 1976 transformation of poet Robert Graves's novel/pseudo-autobiography into a bloody soap opera set in Roman times which stands as perhaps the greatest dramatic achievement of British television. In *Ewoks – The Battle for Endor* she plays the witch Charal.

Wilford Brimley, cast as Noa, had made a career of playing rough-edged old men with hearts of gold, a character type he'd made his own before he was out of his forties. His memorable appearances in this kind of role include the strangely Arthurian baseball comedy-drama *The Natural* (Barry Levinson, 1984), crusties-in-love tearjerker *Cocoon* (Rob Howard, 1985) and latterly hit comedy *In & Out* (Frank Oz, 1997), in which he was Kevin Kline's downtrodden father. Brimley is perfectly cast here and his performance provides most of the project's few highlights.

RECURRING CONCERNS: A witch, an army, a ragtag group of unlikely heroes, a shape-shifting scene, an attack on a castle, a hunt for a child. *Ewoks – The Battle for Endor* is a dry run for *Willow* with less visual invention, a tenth of the budget and half the charm; an uneasy compromise between something that is unashamedly fantasy and something that is trying to cash in on *Star Wars*. The Marauders look as if they should be hanging around in the background at Jabba's palace.

VISUAL INTERESTS: The contrast between the very tall Marauders and the tiny Ewoks is occasionally used effectively; the appearance of dinosaur-like riding beasts ('Blurgs' in the script) recalls the failed experiment with 'dewbacks' in the original *Star Wars*, and their use here suggests Lucas was already using his company's projects as backdoor research and development reels for the potential *Star Wars* revival. The Ewoks vs Marauders battle sequence which takes up most of the last twenty minutes seems quite impressive until you remember the one that ended *Return of the Jedi*.

RELEASE: *The Battle for Endor* was screened on ABC between 8 and 10 p.m. on Sunday 24 November 1985.

CRITICISM: Many commentators picked up on the attempt to make this Ewok adventure tougher than the last one, with the *Hollywood Reporter* describing it as 'more intense' than its predecessor. As with Lucas's other recent projects the point was made that the special was 'confused about what audience it was made to please', featuring as it did an 'overdose of adorability' and a parental discretion advisory warning against letting very young children see the feature. Although feeling the effects work was praiseworthy the *Reporter* hit a note of caution: 'effects just don't have the same impact on the tube as they do on a large screen'. *Variety* was far more positive, calling *The Battle for Endor* 'a worthy entrant in the *Star Wars* canon', albeit one cursed with 'repetitiveness and cuteness (sic)'. Nevertheless it was 'an enjoyable change of pace from standard telefare' with 'numerous theatrical-film touches'. Siân Phillips's sorceress was praised, as was the costuming of Carel Struckyen's King Terak, but an important point was raised. Given that *The Ewok Adventure* was about the rescue of Cindel's parents, was the killing of these characters in the first act of *The Battle for Endor* a wise move? Would the commercial afterlife of the first special now collapse because nobody would want to see something about the rescue of characters they knew would later be arbitrarily disposed of?

Even more than its predecessor, the second Ewok TVM is episodic, slackly paced and rather dull, with events seeming to happen at random across its duration. It is, however, technically very impressive given when it was made and the fact that it's television, and has a few genuinely endearing moments courtesy of Warwick Davis's ever-watchable Wicket. Whereas *The Ewok Adventure* was unashamedly childish, childlike and intended for pre-teens, *The Battle for Endor* had pretensions towards being an action movie, and whilst its occasional bursts of action and reliance on laser guns to create excitement may impress the more self-consciously tough twelve-year-old, it's going to leave everyone else cold.

Among Lucas's original recommendations for the project were to concentrate on the youngest character Cindel (apparently because she had been young Amanda Lucas's favourite character in *The Ewok Adventure*). It is arguably this decision that hamstrung *The Battle for Endor* from the start; the early slaughter of the Towani family is ill judged and somehow both deeply unpleasant and strangely emotion-free. Their surviving daughter seems to mourn them little, and quickly finds replacement characters to serve as a substitute family. It all seems a little pointless.

'My Yoda' George Lucas's description of Joseph Campbell

Born in 1904, the Irish American son of a New York trader, Joseph Campbell developed an interest in Native American mythology as a child, reputedly after having been taken to see Buffalo Bill Cody's Wild West Road Show, and became interested in how different mythologies compared, contrasted and interacted. An excellent student, he attended Columbia University where, as well as becoming an enthusiastic admirer of then young, contemporary writers such as James Joyce, he was also a star athlete, setting a new college record for running the half mile that stood for many years.

His Master's thesis was written on Arthurian myths and the literature derived from them, and after completing it he headed to Europe to research for his PhD; he spent time at Paris University, studying mediaeval French, and in Munich, researching Sanskrit. It is here that he began developing and expanding his thesis that all of humanity's mythologies had a common origin in the unconscious of the human race; that there were ideas and concepts that evolved in parallel with languages and in some sense pre-dated them. In his theory all heroes have a common root.

In 1934 Campbell began teaching at Sarah Lawrence, a women's college. He remained on the staff for 38 years, and there he wrote his most famous book, *The Hero with a Thousand Faces*, in which he set out his contention that every human culture had developed and expressed its own version of the 'vision quest'. He divided the heroic story into five chapters – The Origin, The Call, The Wilderness, The Gift and The Triumph – and again demonstrated how this basic narrative structure applies to many human mythologies.

Campbell was a massive influence on Lucas, who first read his work in the early 70s while researching *Star Wars*. Lucas has repeatedly said since then that encountering Campbell's work was the only thing which it made it possible for him to understand the ideas he was formulating as he wrote and rewrote the many drafts of what eventually became *Star Wars*; that Campbell's theories confirmed what he already knew subconsciously and that he began to feed them into his own work conciously.

Campbell was pleased with the *Star Wars* films, which he described as the ideas he had identified in 'my books, but rendered in terms of the modern . . . which is man and machine'. 'I admire what he has done immensely, immensely', he said of Lucas, and described his protégé as a mythmaker for the end of the twentieth century.

Joseph Campbell died in 1987.

AWARDS: *Ewoks – The Battle for Endor* was nominated for three Emmy Awards: Outstanding Special Visual Effects (Michael J McAlister), Outstanding Children's Program (George Lucas, Thomas G Smith) and Outstanding Sound Mixing for a Miniseries or a Special (Tom Johnson, Randy Thom). It converted only the first of these three into an actual trophy.

TRIVIA: Primary Ewok Wicket appears to have learned how to speak English between the events of *The Ewok Adventure* and this TVM.

EXPERT WITNESS: Warwick Davis on the Ewok costumes – 'You wear pyjamas underneath. Then, there's padding to give it shape. And fur goes on top ... this costume ... makes you move like that, because it's so bulky and heavy.'

Willow (1988)

(120 minutes)

Metro Goldwyn Mayer
A Lucasfilm Ltd Production
Story by George Lucas
Screenplay by Bob Dolman
Director of Photography: Adrian Biddle, BSC
Production Designer: Allan Cameron
Associate Producer: Joe Johnston
Producer: Nigel Wooll
Executive Producer: George Lucas
Music by James Horner
Edited by David Hadley and Michael Hill
Directed by Ron Howard

PRINCIPAL CAST: Val Kilmer (*Madmartigan*), Joanne Whalley (*Sorsha*), Warwick Davis (*Willow Ufgood*), Jean Marsh (*Queen Bavmorda*), Patricia Hayes (*Fin Raziel*), Billy Barty (*High Aldwin*), Pat Roach (*General Kael*), Gavan O'Herlihy (*Airk Thaughbaer*), David Steinberg (*Meegosh*), Phil Fondacaro (*Vohnkar*), Tony Cox (*Vohnkar Warrior*), Robert Gillibrand (*Vohnkar Warrior*), Mark Northover (*Burglekutt*), Kevin Pollak (*Rool*), Rick Overton (*Franjean*), Maria Holvoe (*Cherlindrea*), Julie Peters (*Kaiya Ufgood*), Mark Vande Brake (*Ranon Ufgood*), Dawn Downing (*Mims Ufgood*), Michael Cotterill (*Druid*), Zulema Dene (*Ethna*), Joanna Dickens (*Barmaid*), Jennifer Guy

(*The Wench*), Ron Tarr (*Llug*), Sallyanne Law (*Mother*), Ruth & Kate Greenfield (*The Elora Danan*)

TAGLINES: Heroes come in all sizes, but adventure doesn't come any bigger than this.

The next great adventure.

SUMMARY: Willow Ufgood, a Nelwyn (or dwarf) with ambitions to be a sorcerer, happens upon a Daikine (human) baby girl, who he later discovers is the Elora Danan, a child who will bring about the end of the rule of the wicked Queen Bavmorda. Accompanied by mercenary Madmartigan and Bavmorda's turncoat daughter Sorsha, Willow sets out on a long journey, protecting the child from her enemies as he tries either to get her to safety or team up with someone who will be powerful enough to protect her. Others join their quest, including Madmartigan's old comrade Arik (who conveniently brings with him an army) and two 'brownies', six-inch fairies called Franjeen and Rool. A final confrontation takes place at Bavmorda's castle of Nockmaar, where Willow discovers his own magical abilities and tricks Bavmorda into banishing herself into another reality, never to return. Madmartigan and Sorsha promise to care for the baby, and Willow returns to his family confident of his destiny as a sorcerer, and is greeted by his village in a manner that befits a hero.

TRAILERS: It may well be the case that a lot of the bad press received by *Willow* stems from the astounding pomposity of its initial trailer. Against a background of swirling red clouds and loud electronic chords (which are unfortunately reminiscent of the work of Giorgio Moroder[1]), a ponderous voice-over intones 'You know what is real and what is not. You know what is light and what is dark. You know what is good and what is evil, now forget all you know – or think you know'. After namechecks for Lucas and Howard, the audience finally sees the film's logo in yellowing white, but still has little idea what it's about. The effect is alienating and disorienting, and leads the viewer to expect

---

[1] Giorgio Moroder: influential synth-pop pioneer who inspires love and hate in equal measure; scored *Scarface* (Brian De Palma, 1983) and *Electric Dreams* (Steve Barron, 1984) but is perhaps best known for producing Donna Summer's hit 'I Feel Love'.

something of the epochal nature of *2001: A Space Odyssey* (Stanley Kubrick, 1969) rather than an unashamed kids' movie.

The second trailer is a little better; running at around a minute it features quite raw footage from the film's shoot (some of it seems to have not been colour-corrected) and dollops of James Horner's score. The logo is now blue. The third trailer is much the same, a mix of action and jokes which sadly spoils most of the film's best stunts and lines in the manner common for trailers for popcorn pictures.

SCREENPLAY: During the film's release producer/creator Lucas claimed that he'd had the *Willow* storyline in mind for around fifteen years. Whilst this is impossible to verify, what is certain is that he mentioned the project to actor Warwick Davis during shooting for *Return of the Jedi* in 1981. Lucas saw in the then eleven-year-old Davis – who was playing significant Ewok Wicket – a potentially perfect lead for his planned fantasy epic. *Willow*, produced during 1987, was to be Lucas's first 'hands-on' production job following a two-year sabbatical away from involvement in the direct affairs of Lucasfilm.

Ron Howard appears to have been Lucas's first choice as director. Howard had been in Lucas's *American Graffiti* films and had starred in several seasons of the thematically similar TV series *Happy Days* before moving behind the camera. Initially a television director, he'd latterly had some success theatrically. His films as director then included *Splash!* (1984), a hit-and-miss albeit lucrative comedy starring future serial Oscar-winner Tom Hanks, and *Cocoon* (1984), a schmaltzy tale of elderly people meeting aliens who reinvigorate their ailing bodies. Executive producer Lucas had, it seems, sentimental reasons for hiring the director, telling reporters, 'I remember on *American Graffiti* [Ron] had an 8mm camera and was always running around . . . taking movies of us and saying how he was going to go to film school and become a director.'

Lucas and Howard's favoured screenwriter Bob Dolman (who had limited experience, having to date only written one episode of the TV series *WKRP in Cincinnati*) worked through Lucas's storyline with the producer and director, writing and rewriting each other. Dolman then wrote the actual screenplay, which was further altered by the director and producer as they saw fit. 'The three of us would throw hundreds of ideas into the hopper. When we would agree on one thing Bob would go off and write it', explained Howard when asked to describe the writing process. A clear indication of the collaborative nature of the writing is given by the name of the character of Cherlindrea. This beautiful, ethereal female was named after Cheryl, Ron Howard's wife; Andrea, Bob Dolman's wife; and singer/songwriter Linda Ronstadt, with whom Lucas had been seen socially on several occasions since his divorce, and with whom more than one reporter had linked him romantically.

From this script the budget for the picture was set at $34 million, a sum forwarded by Lucas's old *Star Wars* collaborator Alan Ladd Jr, who was now at MGM Pictures. Ladd underwrote the costs for the movie by pre-selling the potentially lucrative home video rights to RCA/Columbia.

CASTING: Ron Howard was initially uncertain about casting Warwick Davis. By now seventeen Davis was, in Howard's eyes, still too young to convince as the character the story portrayed as an experienced farmer, husband and father perhaps approaching middle age. Consequently other actors were screen-tested as well. Davis was only told the part was definitely his after a lengthy period in California during which he screen-tested against various actors auditioning for the role of Madmartigan. The obvious chemistry between Davis and Kilmer won Howard over, and the director agreed with Lucas's assessment that this was the right pairing of actors for their film's two heroic leads.

Before shooting commenced the leads were involved in a lengthy rehearsal and skill-acquisition period, supervised by Howard. Warwick Davis underwent two weeks of horse-training, which helped him overcome a fear of horses dating back to a childhood accident, and was trained to perform various magic tricks by master magician David Berglas. He was also given lessons from dialect coach David Sibley to enable him to speak in a more mid-Atlantic accent, as Howard felt (perhaps bizarrely) that mainstream America would be unable to understand Davis's Epsom accent. As part of this process Howard advised Davis to study the films of James Stewart. Howard regarded Stewart as perhaps the ultimate naturalistic actor – and he hoped Davis could replicate his approach in *Willow*. Davis was very keen to do as many of his own actions and stunts as he could, and agreed to be doubled by stuntman Peter Bonner as infrequently as possible.

Excluding Kilmer, the cast of *Willow* was predominately British. Jean Marsh had previously played an evil sorceress in *Return to Oz* (Walter Murch, 1986), a film in which Lucas had had some small involvement. She was, indeed remains, best known to television audiences for her role in the popular period drama *Upstairs, Downstairs* (October 1971–December 1975) which she devised as well as appearing in. Pat Roach, cast as General Kael, was a former wrestler, stuntman and actor with roles in all three *Indiana Jones* films. He too played a recurring role in a long-running British television series, that of Brian 'Bomber' Beckenbridge in *Auf Wiedersehen, Pet* (November 1983–May 1986, June 2002 to date), a series devised by *Quadrophenia* (1980) director and *Masterchef* creator Franc Roddam.

Joanne Whalley had also impressed on British television, as the ghostly daughter in *Edge of Darkness* (1985) and as the nurse on the receiving end of Michael Gambon's fantasies in Dennis Potter's *The Singing Detective* (1986).

Warwick Davis was thrilled to be able to work with Billy Barty, who was cast as the village headman. A personal idol of Davis', Barty was then perhaps the most experienced, famous and versatile little actor in the world.

PRODUCTION: Filming for the scenes set at the Nelwyns' village took place at Brocket Hall, a house with a wooded area outside London. Here Howard's crew constructed an exterior village set which still stands – albeit a little weatherworn – to this day.

225 short actors were hired to play Nelwyns, and crowd scenes were shot across the first week of June 1987. Little people had been drafted in from all over the world, and Warwick Davis estimates that there were at least thirteen different languages spoken on set during this one week of filming. One of the extras was Davis's future wife Samantha, although neither of them could have known it at the time as the two met only briefly during filming. Further location shooting was then undertaken in Epping Forest before the scenes set at Queen Bavmorda's castle were shot in Snowdonia, Wales. For the final storming sequence 150 horses and 200 pigs were required. With this many pigs – both male and female – in such a small space the animals frequently took it upon themselves to copulate during takes and had to be forcibly separated using buckets of cold water. The shoot took three days and two nights to complete.

The film's principal sets were constructed – a process that began seven months before shooting – at Elstree, some of them on the giant '*Star Wars* stage'. Three units worked simultaneously, one manned by Lucas and another by Howard. The third covered in-camera FX works and pick-ups and was usually overseen by associate producer Joe Johnston. Work was also done at various other UK studios, including Shepperton and Pinewood. 'I think we worked at every studio in England on *Willow*', commented Davis later.

The director and producer used video playback on set. This simple system essentially involves recording the day's action onto video cassette as well as film plates, enabling crew to watch (albeit lower quality) images of a take instantaneously on its completion, rather than waiting for film rushes to be developed – a process that takes several hours. This was clearly useful to Lucas; some behind-the-scenes footage still extant shows a lengthy discussion about shot continuity being solved by reference to the video copy.

The cast and crew then decamped to New Zealand, for four weeks' shooting near Queenstown and Mount Cardrona. The crew, ferried to their location by helicopters, worked through four feet of snow to complete several shots, including the film's most memorable moment, Madmartigan and Willow's sledging off the top of a mountain. Davis admits to experiencing 'real fear' during the stunt, which he performed around a dozen times to allow Howard's crew to achieve sufficient coverage. Another area of New Zealand the production visited was Milfourd Sound, in the very south of the country, an area which – at the time – consisted of a hotel, wild locations and little else. Warwick Davis recalls the place as being 'very, very strange'. Other sequences shot in New Zealand included the initial meeting between Willow and Madmartigan, the filming of which required Val Kilmer to spend several days trapped in a metal cage swinging from a tree. The actor amused himself by attempting to corpse Davis during the younger actor's many close-ups. It was during this period of shooting that Kilmer injured himself when a prop cage fell onto his right foot. Overly attentive viewers will note that the Madmartigan character had a slight limp – a result of this injury which some commentators labelled a subtle character affectation on Kilmer's part.

Towards the end of filming Howard elected to reshoot a small number of scenes featuring Val Kilmer and Joanne Whalley. The two actors had (famously) begun a relationship during the long shoot, and would marry soon afterwards. Howard felt that various romantic scenes between the characters could be improved now that the performers themselves were romantically involved.

Also shot during this period were 'trekking' sequences of the Nelwyn characters travelling in the first half-hour or so of the movie. Howard concluded that extra non-dialogue scenes here would give the movie's journeys a more epic feel. Almost the final work to be done on the film was the many 'reaction' close-ups of the Elora Danan. During shooting nearly twenty separate infants had stood in for the child at one point or another. 'The baby is three months old in a film that took six months to make', observed director Howard later. 'They grow real fast at that age.' Also utilised had been the prop that Davis quickly named 'the moto-baby', a thirteen-pound dummy which could move its head up and down and from side to side seemingly at random, and which – when dressed in swaddling clothes and held at the right angle – gave the impression that Davis was holding a real child. This was especially useful in sequences involving action in which it would be prohibitively dangerous to involve a real infant. 'The actual performance was completed towards the end of shooting when we knew what reactions we wanted and where. We brought in the twins, Ruth and Kate Greenfield. We were all very surprised by the number of subtle, interesting reactions we got. In a way each baby was improvising, and a true performance was achieved – not in a manipulative way but really in the honest expressions of those babies,' Howard later explained.

The exact level of Lucas's involvement in the filming of *Willow* is – as with many of his projects – uncertain. 'I'm not directly involved on the set', was how he explained his production role to reporters in late 1987, whilst conceding that he had more of a presence on *Willow* than on other then recent Lucasfilm projects simply because of the way his technical expertise made him a useful presence. Ron Howard insisted that having 'George Lucas to turn to on the set' was 'an unbelievable luxury', and that Lucas was at all times 'very respectful' of his position as director. Star Warwick Davis also remembers that 'Lucas was always available' while Val Kilmer was also impressed by Lucas's contribution to the film, declaring, 'George Lucas is like Zorro. He comes and goes on the set. And he leaves his mark when he's gone!' Certainly behind-the-scenes photographs and footage indicate a more or less constant presence from the executive producer. By the end of the shoot Howard was commenting, only half-jokingly, that 'Sometimes I don't feel like the director of this movie, I feel more like the vice president in charge of cinematic affairs for Lucasfilm'.

Like screenwriter Bob Dolman, editors David Hadley and Michael Hill were selected by director Ron Howard. They had previously worked with him on both *Cocoon* and *Splash*, and have gone on to cut practically all of his films since, including the Oscar-winning *A Beautiful Mind* (2001). Bob Dolman has only written two films since *Willow*, *Far and Away* (1992), also for director Howard, and *The Banger Sisters* (2002), which he directed himself. With a few exceptions the crew was – like the cast – predominately hired in Britain. One notable name continuing his association with Lucasfilm on the production was former ILM designer Joe Johnston (here credited as associate producer), who had been production designer on the Ewok TV movies for Lucas and would go on to direct movie hits *Jumanji* (1995) and *Jurassic Park III* (2001). This production's designer, Allan Cameron, had previously worked on acclaimed TV mini-series *Edward & Mrs Simpson* and *The Naked Civil Servant* as well as the 1984 film version of George Orwell's *Nineteen Eighty-Four*. His work since *Willow* includes *Showgirls* (1995) and *Starship Troopers* (1997), both for director Paul Verhoeven, and the James Bond movie *Tomorrow Never Dies* (Roger Spottiswode, 1997).

CUT SCENES: Shepperton studios was the location for the shooting of a lengthy deleted sequence in which Willow – travelling by boat to visit Fin Raziel – is attacked by a variety of sea monsters and a magical storm, all sent by Bavmorda to frustrate him. Warwick Davis remembers the process of shooting these scenes, which featured eight-foot waves engulfing the actor, as 'really, really gruelling'. Ultimately his efforts were wasted, as the footage failed to make it into the final cut of the film.

The UK release of the film was initially trimmed for violence. Two sequences, the death of a woman in the devil-dog attack pre-credits, and Madmartigan's cathartic killing of the brutal General Kael, were edited down to ensure a PG certificate. The 2002 UK DVD release, however, is uncut.

QUOTES:

Rool: 'Who are you calling a lizard? Your mother was a lizard!'

Madmartigan: 'Help! There's a peck here with an acorn pointed at me!'

MUSICAL NOTES: James Horner had previously provided scores for the second and third *Star Trek* theatrical features, as well as *Star Wars* pastiche *Battle Beyond the Stars* (Jimmy T Murakami, 1980). His career would reach its peak a decade later with his Oscar win for the score to James Cameron's bloated boat picture *Titanic*. A skilful player-with-themes in the John Williams mode, Horner's score draws heavily on Robert Schumann (1810–1856), whose *Symphony No. 3* (The *Rhenish* Symphony) provides much of the movie's main theme. The *Rhenish* was written by Schumann as a reaction to the countryside of Dusseldorf, a county for which he was appointed Municipal Music Director in 1850. Horner's theme acquires the lively energy and optimism of Schumann's work, and is integral to giving the picture its heart. The picture's other main theme appears to have been heavily influenced by Prokofiev's *Alexander Nevsky*, although this is less obvious than the Schumann pastiche.

Fundamentally different, but also impressive, is Horner's 'Nelwyn music', used to score a party within the little people's village, and reprised over much of the closing credits. Rhythmic and infectious, and obviously influenced by the African/folk fusion of Paul Simon's then contemporary *Graceland* album, it is far more effective than the similar piece by John Williams used at the end of the theatrical cut of *Return of the Jedi*.

The score itself has always been reacted to positively by film music fans; partially because of its huge scope. It was called one of the 'most ambitious projects of the 80s' and 'a favourite score for many [collectors]' as recently as January 2002 by the influential *Film Score Monthly*.

RECURRING CONCERNS: A child with a great prophesied destiny is central to the Republic trilogy. One character's comment that 'magic is the bloodstream of the universe' recalls Obi-Wan Kenobi's initial explanation of the force in *Star Wars* and anticipates the 'mitochlorain' explanation of it in *The Phantom Menace*. A wizard's advice that 'all you need is your intuition' also seems to anticipate Liam Neeson's protestations of '*feel*, don't think' from the latter film. As with *Star Wars* there's again repeated emphasis on how one individual can make a huge difference. The romance between a self-confessed 'scoundrel' (Madmartigan) and a princess (Sorsha) is obviously reminiscent of *The Empire Strikes Back*. It should be noted as well that as in most other Lucas projects, teamwork is the solution to achieving what is perceived to be impossible (in this case besting the devil dogs) and a group of disparate characters is brought together – despite their differences – for the achievement of a common greater goal. The conflict between a parent and child is central to the Imperial trilogy. Queen Bavmorda is, like the Emperor Palpatine, a usurper defeated by a coalition of different races within her kingdom.

When the similarities between Madmartigan and characters like Indiana Jones or – more strikingly – Han Solo were put to Lucas, he responded that, 'I happen to like rogues with a heart of gold . . . I like this kind of character, I've used it before . . . it's close to my heart, and [a character] not unusual in filmmaking. John Ford did it. Howard Hawks did it. John Huston did it. Everybody! It's a character repeated in [many] movies . . . movies [audiences] have empathy with.'

VISUAL INTERESTS: *Willow* saw some of the earliest use of computer technology to augment special effects. It was in order to achieve the multiple transformations of Fin Raziel to and from various kinds of animal (and finally into a human) that ILM invented the computer-assisted technique later termed morphing. Building on what they had achieved on the Steven Spielberg-produced *Young Sherlock Holmes and the Pyramid of Fear* (Barry Levinson, 1985), ILM's Dennis Muren and Doug Smythe created a process they called MORF. This involved manipulating filmed footage inside a computer using a grid system to slowly switch between one image and another. The lengthy morphing sequence at the film's climax is estimated to have involved two billion calculations. It took Muran and Smythe between September and December 1987 to devise the technology, and until March the following year to complete the actual shots required by the movie. Each of the two men generously credits the other with doing the bulk of the work and coming up with the term.

Ron Howard was hugely impressed by the finished sequence, which staged the entire lengthy transformation in camera without cutting away once. Muran is absolutely confident that the sequence is the 'first time real-world objects had been manipulated in a computer and then put back on film'. Oddly Lucasfilm neglected to copyright the technology that made the process possible, and it passed into the public domain soon after. Home morphing kits are now available for reasonably advanced PCs at a cost of less than $100.

The castle of Nockmaar seen in the film's final act is visibly indebted to that seen in Akira Kurosawa's *Macbeth* adaptation *Throne of Blood* (1957).

It's ironic, given *Willow*'s obvious parallels to JRR Tolkien's *The Lord of the Rings* novels, that the New Zealand locations mean that the film frequently visually anticipates – at least during its first half hour – Peter Jackson's Oscar-winning film adaptation of *The Lord of the Rings: The Fellowship of the Ring* (2001).

EXTERNAL REFERENCES: The baby-in-the-bulrushes motif is obviously straight out of the Biblical book of Exodus. As Lucas commented, 'This is not the first baby to go down a river – and not the last. [It's] a motif. A river means life, the baby means birth, and these mythological motifs give you [something] that is correct, psychologically. They're classic symbolic images that have come down – and worked – for several thousand years . . . we use the symbols, consciously or unconsciously, to invoke . . . emotion.'

The basic quest structure, along with the fact that the hero is one of a frowned-upon race of small humans, has led to many comparisons with JRR Tolkien's Middle Earth books, particularly *The Hobbit* and *The Lord of the Rings* trilogy. Whilst there are undoubtedly parallels between Frodo/Willow and Aragorn/Madmartigan, and Cherlindrea and Tolkien's elves (and Lucas is undoubtedly familiar with Tolkien), it is disingenuous to suggest that such character archetypes began with Tolkien, or that they haven't been used by many other writers since.

Fin Raziel's transformation sequence seems to be a riff on some of Merlin's powers in TH White's Arthurian stories, and the sequence in which Willow and Meegosh are tied down by 'brownies' has obvious resonance with Gulliver's capture by Lilliputians in Jonathan Swift's *Gulliver's Travels*. The twist here, of course, is that the two Nelwyns consider themselves small, and to be attacked by someone for being large seems to them bizarrely ironic.

Queen Bavmorda's chief enforcer is called General Kael, an obvious reference to film critic Pauline. This is made more obvious by the presence in the film of a two-headed beast called an Ebersisk, an equally obvious nod to film-reviewing duo Gene Siskel and Roger Ebert. An extreme reading of these nods, and one adopted by biographer John Baxter amongst others, is to see them as textual indicators that the story of the picture is essentially autobiographical. Willow is Lucas – a man of short stature and good heart who has a desire to be a magician/filmmaker. Surrounded by nay-sayers and fair-weather friends, he carries his precious cargo on a long journey, ultimately emerging triumphant. In this reading Queen Bavmorda (who is a usurper sitting on someone else's throne) would be the massed forces of old Hollywood, and the Elora Danan a symbol of the desire to place creative people back in charge of filmmaking. The revered village elder who sets Willow out on his quest represents Kurosawa (and looks not unlike him) and Burglekutt – not a bad man but an untrustworthy and power-led one, albeit one who is a key ally early on – would be Coppola. To extrapolate from Baxter's reading, Madmartigan perhaps represents Steven Spielberg; taller, better-looking and initially more successful than Willow, he's a suspicious figure and perhaps a rival who eventually becomes the only person that the hero can really trust, a needed collaborator and valued friend. One can make a case for this 'reading', certainly, but that doesn't mean one is obliged to agree with any of it.

RELEASE: Released to a large number of theatres in the US on 20 May 1988, Willow took only $27 million when – thanks to marketing and other costs – it needed to make $90 million to go into profit. Seeking to explain the film's poor showing Lucas told newspapers that it was possibly down to it being a fantasy film, part of 'a genre that has seemed to be poison at the box office'. The film's non-performance in theatres killed the idea of any filmic Willow sequels (Lucas had hinted that these were a possibility during a pre-release press conference at the Cannes film festival), but Lucas's storylines for future adventures in the world of Willow eventually found expression in another medium (see **TRIVIA**).

In the UK the picture received a Royal Premiere in the presence of the Prince and Princess of Wales. Warwick Davis recalls that Princess Diana, talking to him about the film after the screening, mentioned the character of Sorsha and exclaimed, 'You give us princesses a rough ride [in this film]'.

CRITICISM: Reviews for *Willow* were not positive, reacting against what was seen as a commercially-minded children's film. *Variety* called it a 'medieval mish-mash', and spent much of the review pointing out from where they felt the picture's elements had all been derived. Nevertheless there was the concession that 'kids probably will love it' and the unshakeable belief that for MGM there was the inevitable 'box office recoupment (sic) of its large investment'. The only positive comments the paper made about the film concerned its technical excellence and the fact that the New Zealand scenery was 'stunning'. A few days later the *New York Times* had much the same to say. 'As vast as it is second-hand', commented the paper's Janet Maslin, although she approved of the film's 'easy-going sense of humour'. Maslin felt Ron Howard's directorial style, 'more matter-of-fact' than Lucas's own, was unsuited to the picture, and that he failed to bring 'any particular colour or personality' to the material, resulting in a film which 'lacked emotional centre'.

Films and Filming felt pretty much the same way, condemning the 'sentimentality and predictability' that they felt undermined the entire film. Director Howard was 'out of his depth' and the film relied on 'magnificent locations and special effects' to evoke any interest. There is also (interestingly) the revisionist suggestion that only the Lucas films made under Coppola's supervision have 'any real life'. Here too there was, as with some reviews of *The Ewok Adventure*, the suggestion that the reviewer felt the film was too innately commercial to deserve any real consideration, author Brian Baxter conceding he would 'probably have been more sympathetic' to the film had it not been pegged to be so huge – which of course ultimately it wasn't.

Willow is in the final analysis an above-average children's film, albeit one with a rather dark final half hour. It has less to offer an adult viewer than, say, Lucas's USC comrade Walter Murch's equally financially disastrous *Return to Oz* (1985). This is perhaps unsurprising considering that its director insisted during interviews that the primary question in his and Lucas's minds at all times was 'what would our children think of this?' It has a few good lines, some excellent set-pieces and even a few genuinely beautiful shots, and whilst it's difficult to pinpoint anything actually *wrong* with *Willow*, it doesn't cohere in the same way that Lucas's best work does.

Warwick Davis is excellent throughout and Val Kilmer's performance here is sufficiently charismatic and likeable to make you pine at the current state of his career. Whilst it is unfair, even disingenuous, to criticise a film made to please ten-year-olds for only pleasing ten-year-olds, Lucas's work so often transcends such limitations that the simple fact that *Willow* doesn't meant it was heavily criticised on its original release. Rather than being – as its innovative use of computers might suggest – the first of a new kind of summer film, it is in fact the last in a long line of big-budget 80s pictures aimed too squarely at children; the inheritor not of Indiana Jones's mantle of accessible, demographic-crossing thrills, but of pictures such as *Labyrinth* (Jim Henson, 1986), *The Dark Crystal* (Jim Henson, 1982), *The Goonies* (Richard Donner, 1985), and *Flight of the Navigator* (Randall Kleiser, 1986). *Willow* is – like those – the exact opposite of *Star Wars*, an *over*-budgeted film that everyone *knew* would be huge but which failed to become a genuine crossover hit; satisfactory only to its core audience when it needed to reach out to far more people.

Ironically *Willow*'s popularity is now greater than it ever has been, the children of the 1980s – now adults – finding nostalgia value in it even whilst further generations of ten-year-olds are discovering its innocent thrills. It is entirely possible that the indulging reviews that greeted the recent DVD release may lead to a shift in the picture's reputation.

Whatever happens in the future won't change the fact that *Willow* was neither a financial nor a critical success at the time of its release. 'Roll up! Roll up!' gabbled Ron Howard during the movie's electronic presspack. 'Get your *Willow* tickets here!' Unfortunately not enough people did.

AWARDS: At the 1989 Academy Awards *Willow* was Oscar-nominated for both Best Effects – Sound Effects Editing (Ben Burtt and Richard Hymns) and Best Effects – Visual Effects (Dennis Muren, Phil Tippett, Michael J McAlister and Christopher Evans) but lost out in both instances to Robert Zemeckis's *Who*

Framed Roger Rabbit? It won Best Costumes for costumier Barbara Lane at the 1989 Saturn Awards, and was nominated for the Hugo Best Dramatic Presentation but didn't win.

TRIVIA: Queen Bavmorda's devil dogs were played by two rottweilers in masks, except in close-up where the snarling beasts' heads were animatronic.

Despite the film being originally produced with money from MGM and the VHS being issued by Columbia, the (splendid) 2002 DVD edition was issued through Fox.

In August 1995 Bantam Books/Doubleday released *Shadow Moon*, a novel co-written by Lucas and comics writer Chris Claremont, which continued Willow Ufgood's adventures on the printed page. Despite suggestions from some quarters that Lucas had had no direct involvement in the book, there are passages in it with strong stylistic similarities to the *Star Wars* novelisation that Lucas co-wrote with Alan Dean Foster in the 1970s. A charming and involving (if scarcely innovative) sequel, *Shadow Dawn*, was published in January 2001 with a further instalment *Shadow Star* the following year.

These were penned solely by, and credited to, Claremont, although Lucas did receive an ostentatiously large cover credit for devising the characters and storyline. The latter books concentrate on the Elora Danan, rather than Willow himself. The baby of the film grows up into a vivacious, magically inclined (and frankly clichéd) adolescent whose personality and adventures fail to hold the attention.

EXPERT WITNESS: 'George is very clear about having the director be the leader, the decision maker. All he asks is to be a creative producer – and be rationally listened to when he has a point [to make].' Director Ron Howard

LUCAS ON WILLOW: 'I've always gotten about 50/50 reviews, at best . . . the initial *Willow* reviews were not . . . favourable. Most American reviews are . . . very glib, tell you what the movie's about, then some sort of very sticky little statement. That's about all they amount to. I don't really give them much concern.'

Indiana Jones and the Last Crusade (1989)

(122 minutes)

Paramount
A Lucasfilm Ltd Production
Screenplay by Jeffrey Boam
Story by George Lucas and Menno Meyjes
Director of Photography: Douglas Slocombe, BSC
Production Designer: Elliot Scott
Produced by Robert Watts
Executive Producers: George Lucas, Frank Marshall
Music: John Williams
Edited by Michael Kahn
Directed by Steven Spielberg

PRINCIPAL CAST: Harrison Ford (*Dr Henry 'Indiana' Jones Junior*), Sean Connery (*Professor Henry Jones Senior*), Denholm Elliott (*Dr Marcus Brody*), Alison Doody (*Dr Elsa Schneider*), John Rhys Davies (*Sallah*), Julian Glover (*Walter Donovan*), River Phoenix (*Young Indy*), Michael Byrne (*Colonel Vogel*), Kevork Malikyan (*Kazim*), Robert Eddison (*Grail Knight*), Richard Young (*Fedora*), Alexei Sayle (*Sultan*), Alex Hyde-White (*Young Henry*), Paul Maxwell (*Panama Hat*), Isla Blair (*Mrs Donovan*), Vernon Dobtcheff (*Butler*), J J Hardy (*Herman*), Bradley Gregg (*Roscoe*), Jeff O'Haco (*Half Breed*), Vince Deadrick (*Rough Rider*), Marc Miles (*Sheriff*), Ted Grossman (*Deputy Sheriff*), Tim Hiser (*Young Panama Hat*), Larry Sanders (*Scout Master Havelock*), Will Miles (*Scout #1*), David Murray (*Scout #2*), Frederick Jaeger (*World War One Ace*), Jerry Harte (*Professor Stanton*), Billy J Mitchell (*Dr Mulbray*), Pat Roach (*Gestapo*), Suzanne Rocquette (*Film Director*), Michael Sheard (*Adolf Hitler*)

TAGLINE: The man with the hat is back and this time he's bringing his dad!

SUMMARY: Utah, 1912 – thirteen-year-old Indiana Jones, on a scout trip, tries to stop grave robbers from taking the cross of Coronado but is frustrated when local authorities hand it back to his adversaries. 26 years later Indy finally retrieves the cross and takes it back to his university. Shortly afterwards antiques collector Walter Donovan contacts him; Donovan asks Indy to take over a research project whose leader has disappeared. The project is the quest for the Holy Grail. On hearing this Indy tells Donovan that he's got the wrong Jones; the man he needs is his father, Henry Jones Senior. Donovan tells Indy that his father is the project leader who has disappeared. Indy reluctantly accepts the assignment – not because he's interested in finding the grail, but out of concern for his father, from whom he is already estranged. Indy travels with museum curator Marcus Brody to Venice to meet the project's assistant director Dr Elsa Schneider and pick up where his father left off.

Elsa and Indy follow the clues in Henry's 'grail diary' and find the tomb of a crusader in catacombs under the city. The crusader's shield has an inscription on it which tells of the resting place of the grail. Indy is attacked by the Brotherhood of the Cruciform Sword, a fanatical Christian group devoted to protecting the grail, but Indy explains that he only wants to find his father. The cult's leader tells Indy that Henry is being held in a castle on the German border, and Indy and Elsa go there to break him out, while Marcus meets up with Indy's friend Sallah.

Indy retrieves his father, but they are both captured by a German army contingent under the brutal SS Colonel Vogel. Elsa is a Nazi spy. It transpires that Donovan has been working with the Nazis all along. Donovan and the Nazis head off to retrieve the grail, leaving Indy and Henry to die. Indy and Henry escape and give chase, pausing only to visit Berlin to recover Henry's grail diary, which contains information on how to pass the many tests that lie in wait for someone who penetrates the grail temple.

At the grail temple Indy passes the tests, and meets the grail's guardian, a 1,000-year-old knight kept alive by the power of the grail, the brother of the crusader in whose tomb they'd found the clues. Donovan dies drinking from a false grail, but the real one is lost forever when the temple collapses, and only Indy, Henry, Marcus and Sallah escape with their lives. Father and son are reconciled and all four ride off into the sunset.

SCREENPLAY: The writing of *Last Crusade* was a lengthy, complex and tortuous process, the long gap between it and *Temple of Doom* in part the result of the difficulties faced by

Lucas and Spielberg in coming up with an appropriate storyline for a third *Indiana Jones* picture. Lucas wanted to do a 'haunted house' story, with Indy leading a group of explorers who penetrate a sealed mansion and have to face a variety of tricks and tests. Lucas commissioned a script from Diane Thomas (who had written the *Raiders*-lite *Romancing the Stone* [Robert Zemeckis, 1985]) but this was rejected. Spielberg had never been keen on the idea anyway, having felt that he had covered the 'haunted house' genre with *Poltergeist* (Tobe Hooper, 1982), which he wrote and produced.

Discussions began to centre on the quest for the Holy Grail, but this was another idea with which Spielberg was dissatisfied. As he came from a specifically Judaic rather than a Judaeo-Christian heritage the story had little or no resonance for him personally, and whenever it was mentioned he immediately thought of Monty Python and their *Monty Python and the Holy Grail* film (1974).

Chris Columbus[1] was asked to write a screenplay set in Africa and concentrating on the Chinese myth of the Monkey King. Columbus wrote a draft but again it wasn't judged suitable, so Lucas again returned to the idea of the grail, a topic into which he had done more research whilst other ideas were being discussed. Dutch-born writer Menno Meyjes, who had scripted Spielberg's Alice Walker adaptation *The Color Purple* (1985), became the third writer to script a version of *Indy III*, this time concentrating on Lucas's grail quest narrative. Another idea he was given to play with was the notion of including Indy's father, an elderly professor obsessed with the grail. It was with the introduction of this plot strand that Spielberg became enthusiastic about the grail storyline. 'The grail is symbolic [of] finding the truth in one's life', he later opined. 'They actually go after the Holy Grail but their quest is . . . symbolic of their search for each other'. In this context hunting for the grail appealed to him, and he later commented that Indy and Henry's difficulties were based on his uncomfortable relationship with his own father: '[They] follow a similar curve to me and my dad', he admitted. He was also charmed by the idea that whereas in *Raiders* and *Temple* Indy retrieves an ancient treasure, in this story Indy would lose what he

---

[1] Chris Columbus, writer *Gremlins* (Joe Dante, 1984), *The Goonies* (Barry Levinson, 1984), *Young Sherlock Holmes* (Barry Levinson, 1985); director *Home Alone* (1991), *Home Alone 2: Lost in New York* (1992), *Harry Potter and the Philosopher's/Sorcerer's Stone* (2001), *Harry Potter and the Chamber of Secrets* (2002).

was ostensibly looking for but instead rescue his relationship with his father.

Meyjes's script introduced the version of the 'tests' faced by Indy that was actually used at the film's climax, but virtually everything else he came up with was rejected. Jeffrey Boam, the writer of the Spielberg-produced *Innerspace* (Joe Dante, 1985) took a pass at the script, and one of his innovations was to bring the character of Henry in much earlier than Meyjes had. Boam paired father and son off throughout the film's second hour and established them as a comic double act. Another of Boam's tasks was to write some of the screenplay around various storyboards that Spielberg had produced based upon earlier drafts (for example an epic tank chase used in the finished film had begun life in Columbus's rejected script, but Spielberg was sufficiently enthusiastic about shooting it that Boam was asked to work it back in to his).

Meyjes was given a joint 'Story' credit with Lucas for the work he'd done, with the screenplay credited solely to Boam despite the final rewrite performed on it by British playwright Tom Stoppard. Stoppard was then performing uncredited 'script doctor' duties on several American pictures and would later win an Oscar for his screenplay for *Shakespeare in Love* (John Madden, 1999). Madden had, incidentally, directed two radio adaptations of the *Star Wars* films for Lucas at the beginning of the 80s, and another in 1996.

CASTING: When creating the character of Professor Henry Jones Senior, Lucas initially visualised an elderly British character actor or an actor in the mould of John Houseman (Houseman was an American producer born in 1902; he worked in such a capacity with Orson Welles before turning to acting in his sixties to considerable acclaim, winning an Oscar for *Paper Chase* [James Bridges, 1974]. He died in 1988). Sean Connery – a screen icon, and former James Bond – was in the process of rescuing a career which had been in decline for over a decade. He was doing this by choosing to play wittier, lower-key character roles which gave him the opportunity to demonstrate his considerable abilities as an actor rather than picking films which forced him to hang foolishly on to matinee idol status. He won an Oscar for his role in *The Untouchables* (Brian De Palma, 1987). For Spielberg Connery was 'the only person on the face of the planet Earth I could imagine . . . who could intimidate Harrison Ford', and the fact that Connery was only twelve years Ford's senior was judged immaterial. Ford would be playing down his age anyway (he was 46 during filming, while Indy is 38 in *Last Crusade*), and a grey beard and tweedy wardrobe would add years to Connery's appearance without difficulty. Once the actor was suggested to him Lucas made no bones about the fact that he thought Connery would be 'perfect'. That the James Bond films in sense begat the *Indiana Jones* series also made the casting of cinema's first – and for many greatest – Bond as Indy's father add a nice, if obvious, metatextual frisson.

The character of Henry as originally conceived was a more bookish, traditional professor archetype incapable of coping with the stresses of Indiana's adventures, but Connery's casting changed all that. Connery saw the character as being in the mould of the explorer Sir Richard Burton – an ageing intellectual with retained physical vigour. Emotionally speaking he should be 'someone who would have been indifferent to his son growing up and would have gone off and not been heard of for six months and think nothing of it and not feel guilty at all'.

Eighteen-year-old River Phoenix was Spielberg's first and only choice for the role of the thirteen-year-old Indy. An experienced juvenile lead, he would – shortly after production on *Last Crusade* finished – be Oscar-nominated for his previous role in *Running on Empty* (Sidney Lumet, 1988). Phoenix had previously worked with Harrison Ford in *The Mosquito Coast* (Peter Weir, 1986), playing his son; although Ford was obviously not required to be on set during Phoenix's scenes in *Last Crusade* he nevertheless visited the studio in order to reacquaint himself with a young actor everyone agreed had a bright future. Despite a publicly declared anti-drugs stance Phoenix died of an overdose of heroin and cocaine outside the Viper Room nightclub, LA in 1993.

Alison Doody, cast as Nazi babe Elsa Schneider, both the most obvious traitor in screen history and an ideal source of friction between father and son, was a minor Bond girl, having played Jenny Flex in *A View to a Kill* (John Glen, 1985); she had also impressed in *A Prayer for the Dying* (Mike Hodges, 1987). Elsa is sufficiently different from either *Raiders'* Marion or *Temple of Doom's* Willie for the series to avoid repeating itself, dabbling in another love-interest archetype (the Hitchcockian ice maiden with a secret) instead. Doody's performance is a subtle blend of cold sensuality and excellent comic timing.

Rounding out the cast were Denholm Elliott and John Rhys Davies (both returning from *Raiders*, a clue to potential cinemagoers that this would be in the style of the more popular of the other two *Indiana Jones* adventures) and British stage actor Julian Glover. Glover, a member of the Royal Shakespeare Company who has mixed acclaimed interpretations of great stage roles – such as Shakespeare's *Henry IV* – with film and television work (he'd had a minor role in *The Empire Strikes Back* and a larger one in the James Bond film *For Your Eyes Only* [John Glen, 1981], as well as appearing more than once in *Doctor Who*). For the role of grail seeker Walter Donovan Glover adopts an American accent which seems odd to fans of his stage career, but which seems to have convinced American critics *en masse*.

PRODUCTION: On 16 May 1988 Spielberg's crew – largely that which had produced the two earlier *Jones* adventures – started shooting in Almeira, Spain before moving to Elstree Studios, England for a ten-week residency. After this they headed to Jordan and the tourist attraction of the ancient city of Petra, which was used to represent the Grail Temple in the Canyon of the Crescent Moon. Shooting was, by all accounts, a smooth process with no major upsets and a contented cast and crew, although Julian Glover later expressed regret that the precise requirements of the script didn't involve him travelling to Jordan even though his character did (Donovan only appears in interiors in Jordan; all of his scenes in the country were accomplished either in Spain or at Elstree).

ALTERNATIVE VERSIONS: TV prints have Indy and Henry's exchange in which Indy swears ('Jesus Christ, Dad') and Henry slaps Indy around the face deleted. This is unfortunate given that the scene is not merely revealing in character terms (Henry is driven by his faith in a way that Indiana never has been), but also insofar as Henry's reaction explicitly condemns Indy's blasphemy as strongly as the people who cut it would. Essentially, the scene sides with those who would delete it.

CUT SCENES: Boam's screenplay opened not with Young Indy but with a lengthy western pastiche set in a Mexico bar. Lucas ejected it from the screenplay, instead crafting the myth-making teen Indy sequence to take its place. Thematically the latter works better, giving the audience a hint of the nature of the relationship between Henry and Indy. As shot it was much longer, and featured Alex Hyde-White (who is still credited on the finished film, despite only appearing as a pair of hands accompanied by a Connery voice-over) as the younger Henry.

Further cuts hinted at by the cast list include a scene with a disgruntled World War One ace played by Frederick Jaeger. This was to have taken place on the zeppelin and Jaeger can be briefly glimpsed – dressed in full Luftwaffe uniform – as Henry and Indy book their places on the Airship.

Also removed from the film were a number of shots showing the presence of a documentary camera team at the Nuremberg rally which Indy and Henry accidentally attend. The team is led by a female director (played by Suzanne Rocquette). This was a reference to Leni Riefenstahl, the director of *Triumph of the Will* (1936) and other Nazi propaganda pieces. A filmmaker whose talent is impossible to ignore no matter how strongly one rejects the use to which she put it, Riefenstahl was still alive in 1989, and this, as well as concerns over the length of the film, may account for the deletion of these scenes.

QUOTES:
Marcus: 'The search for the cup of Christ is the search for the divine in all of us.'

Elsa: 'You have your father's eyes.'
Indy: 'And my mother's ears, but the rest belongs to you.'
Elsa: 'Looks like the best parts have already been spoken for.'

Indy: 'You know Marcus, he got lost once in his own museum.'

Donovan: 'Germany has declared war on the Jones boys.'

Indy: 'Archaeology is the search for fact, not truth. If it's truth you're interested in then Dr Tyree's philosophy class is just down the hall.'

Indy: 'Remember the last time we had a quiet drink? I had milkshake.'

MUSICAL NOTES: The score for *Last Crusade* is virtually an exercise in avoiding the 'Raiders March'. This means that the theme is all the more effective when it does appear, and Williams comes up with numerous excellent new themes to fill out the action, including a pastoral grail theme and a chirpy passage to represent the younger Indiana.

Williams's imaginative, lyrical score covers over 110 minutes of a 127-minute film and almost all of it is new material. We get bursts of the 'Raiders March' on very few occasions: when young Indy runs away from the train, as Indy machine-guns down Nazi troopers whilst arguing with his dad, as he throws Vogel out of the airship and as he's on the verge of being crushed into a rockface by a German tank.

RECURRING CONCERNS: There's an obvious, but successful, attempt to place Indy in the heritage of the heroic archetypes that populate western fiction. Indy already has elements of the gumshoe and the cowboy, but *Last Crusade* makes him literally a boy-scout hero (and the TV series will, retroactively, make Indy a soldier – see **Young Indiana Jones**). This process is complete when Indy meets the knight who guards the grail: 'you're strangely dressed for a knight', the crusader says, looking at Indy's clothes. He assumes that Dr Jones is the twentieth century's equivalent of a knight (and even tries to present Indy with his sword) – which, archetypally speaking, he is. When Indy rides a motorbike towards another one ridden by a Nazi soldier and then attacks it with a long pole in imitation of a joust, the point is really rammed home.

Obviously *Last Crusade* is partially about the conflict between parent and child; this occurs in much of Lucas's work, and the assumption often made is that the fractious, difficult parent/child battles of *Star Wars* or *Willow* reflect Lucas's own relationship with his father. It seems that the Lucases' famous argument about George Jr's intention to go to film school has caused the autobiographical nature of such an element to be overstated by biographers – the Lucases were reconciled shortly afterwards, and George Jr's parents seem to have been thoroughly supportive of him once he was at USC. Lucas seems to have focused on parent/child conflict because of its obvious dramatic usefulness and mythic resonance rather than because it reflects aspects of his own life. Steven Spielberg, on the other hand, has repeatedly talked about how the conflict between Indy and Henry (which, although acerbic and marked by a lack of communication, is altogether different to that between Luke and Vader) is in a sense based on his relationship with *his* father. It *is* Lucas, however, not Spielberg, who is named after his father and who, like so many American children, suffered the indignity of being known as 'Junior' through much of his early life.

Indy's declaration that you 'can't take mythology at face value' could well be Lucas's mantra, judging by his work.

BACKWARDS/FORWARDS: Henry is surprised that Indy can fly a plane; he learned during his World War One service (see **Young Indiana Jones** – 'Attack of the Hawkmen'). The TV series also has rather a lot to say about the conflict between Henry Jones Senior and Junior. When Indy mentions the Ark of the Covenant John Williams's 'Ark Theme' from *Raiders* makes a brief, unobtrusive appearance.

RELEASE: Released on 24 May 1989 to 2,327 screens *Last Crusade* earned $46.9 million in its opening weekend.

CRITICISM: Reviews of *Last Crusade* split into two categories, those who saw that it was a cut above the kind of action-adventure genre to which it ostensibly belonged, and those who couldn't really see the point of that kind of movie at all. In the former camp was *Time*'s Richard Corliss, who called it 'the same . . . and better', delighted with the way it infused 'vitality into a movie staple [otherwise] nearly exhausted'. The latter camp was best summed up by *Sight and Sound*'s reviewer, who felt that Spielberg was wasting his time 'running on the spot in Boy's Own territory'. Pauline Kael, once one of the champions of the Lucas/Spielberg way of doing things, noted in the *New Yorker* that the film was 'familiar . . . repetitive . . . a rehash. The movie isn't bad; most of it *is* enjoyable'.

Last Crusade's greatest strength and yet also its greatest weakness is that it is such a rerun of *Raiders* – albeit one even lighter in tone and in which the rough edges of Indy's character as seen in *Raiders* but minimalised in *Temple of Doom* are further smoothed out. There is also (unlike in *Temple*) no real attempt to find a different filmic landscape for the character to function in.

The opening acts of *Raiders* and *Last Crusade* are almost identical. Both, after an action sequence, begin with Indy lecturing in Princeton; the lesson ends slightly prematurely and as his students leave he mentions his university office duties. Marcus enters the classroom and Indy gives him something for the museum – something captured during the aforementioned action sequence. Indy is then contacted by someone who wants him to find something for them, and he tells them they instead want a revered figure from his personal history – a father, or substitute father. The middle third of the film sees the grail diary/the ark change hands and Indy trapped with someone with whom he has issues to resolve; this is followed by escape and a journey to catch up with the Nazis.

Other clear points of comparison include seeing Indy in tweeds, a comic action sequence in a marketplace, Nazi villains, Indy's rival destroyed by the wrath of God at the end, the appearance of Sallah and Marcus, Indy disguising himself as a Wehrmacht officer, an English actor doing an accent as one of the villains, and Indy's reconciliation with a figure from his past.

What makes *Last Crusade* effective and distinctive, and prevents it from being simply '*Raiders* again', is the comic sparring between Connery and Ford. Even leaving them aside it's resolutely one of the most straightforwardly pleasurable movies ever committed to celluloid: fast and funny, beautifully made and beautifully played. Like all of Lucas's best work it's both warm-hearted and sincere, packed with great jokes and peerless action sequences and has a simple but effective point to make.

AWARDS: The 1990 Oscars saw Ben Burtt and Richard Hymns pick up an Academy Award for Best Effects, Sound Effects Editing but they were denied the double when their other nomination for Best Sound failed to win. Also nominated was John Williams for the score. Sean Connery won a Golden Globe for his performance, and the film won the Hugo for Best Dramatic Presentation. At the BAFTAs the film was nominated for Best Sound, Best Special Effects, and Sean Connery received a nomination for Best Actor in a Supporting Role.

TRIVIA: ILM built a three-quarter-scale model tank and physically threw it off a cliff in order to create a representation of such an event as authentically as possible.

Young Indiana Jones
(1992–1996)

Paramount
Lucasfilm Ltd
Amblin Entertainment
Created by George Lucas
Director of Photography: David Tattersall (except 15, 16,
20, 21)
Production Designer: Gavin Bocquet (except 21)
Produced by Rick McCallum
Executive Producer: George Lucas
Theme by Laurence Rosenthal

STARRING: Sean Patrick Flannery (*Henry 'Indiana' Jones Junior except 3, 15, 19, 20, 21, 25*), Corey Carrier (*Henry 'Indiana' Jones Junior 1, 3, 15, 19, 20, 21, 25, 32*), George Hall (*Dr Henry 'Indiana' Jones Junior except 11, 17, 23, 24, 26, 27, 28, 29, 30, 31, 32*), Lloyd Owen (*Professor Henry Jones Senior 1, 3, 15, 19, 20, 21, 25, 32*), Ronny Coutteure (*Remy 1, 2, 4, 5, 6, 8, 17, 18, 22, 30*)

TITLE TATTLE: As originally produced for broadcast the series carries the on-screen title *The Young Indiana Jones Chronicles* and the individual episodes (with some exceptions) carry a title which consists of a date and the location in which the episode occurs. The later re-edited TV Movie versions (see **ALTERNATIVE VERSIONS**) don't have an overall series title, and are instead given longer, more dramatic titles of their own. In this form the series is usually referred to as *The Adventures of Young Indiana Jones*, as per the covers of the VHS releases, but is sometimes given its previous title (for example by the BBC's Ceefax service during the 2002 repeat run).

SUMMARY: The life, adventures and military career of Henry Jones Junior, from his pre-teen tours of the world accompanying his parents through his service during World War One and on into the 1920s.

CASTING: As the principal hero of his series Lucas cast Sean Patrick Flannery, a virtual unknown. Flannery did six screen tests for the part and met the producer several times before finally being cast. Flannery spent virtually five years working on the series, and as part of the show's 'educational' remit was given pages of research to read concerning the historical background to each episode.

To play the younger 'Young Indy' Lucas cast Corey Carrier, known as a child stand-up comedian who had opened for Jay Leno and appeared in various TV variety series. He had also made an impression on US television by playing a child with AIDS in an episode of *The Equalizer*.

PRODUCTION: *Young Indiana Jones* is one of the great unknown quantities of 90s television. The history of the series is one of lavish filming, changes of network, changes of format and changes of cast. Additionally, as with the Imperial trilogy, George Lucas has proved incapable of leaving the series alone, producing multiple versions of episodes, incorporating new titles, new effects and even new shooting in attempts to iron out problems both perceived and real, and in order to make the series more to his – and audiences' – liking.

The series grew out of the action sequence at the beginning of the third *Indiana Jones* movie, which featured River Phoenix as a thirteen-year-old Indy (see **Indiana Jones and the Last Crusade**). The idea of showing Indy's formative years was initially simply a way of inventing an intriguing action sequence that would be suitably distinct from those of the other Indiana Jones films, but it came to dominate Lucas's creative thinking for a while; would it be desirable – even possible – to explore in greater detail what Indiana Jones had been like as a pre-teen, a teenager, a young man? Here was someone as old as the twentieth century, who could be put in almost any pre-World War Two situation. 'A bunch of ideas popped out', Lucas later explained, describing his enthusiasm for the basic notion: 'I turned them into screenplays [and] I came up with seventeen hours. It was like a fountain!'

When he was asked about why he was pursuing *Young Indiana Jones* as the first live-action serial television project of his career, Lucas replied, 'It's not the kind of idea that works in features because it's so big and sprawling'. Of the initial seventeen hours of television that comprised the first production block, every episode was storylined and partially written by Lucas himself.

Before the series began its creator stressed that, although it would be an adventure series, there was also a strong educational angle to many episodes, part of the point of the show being to expose American children to history in an involving way.

As was usual at this point in Lucas's career he is simply credited for 'Story' on these episodes. As a prolific ideas man who dislikes the process of writing screenplays he chose – as he had done on *Willow* and *The Empire Strikes Back* – to turn over notes and a detailed outline to another writer to turn into a finished script, whilst contributing to and keeping an eye on the process in his capacity as executive producer.

The series' first production block, with shooting taking place on five continents, consisted of fifteen one-hour episodes and one two-hour episode designed as the series premiere. Five of these starred Corey Carrier as a pre-pubescent Indiana, travelling the world with his father, and ten revolved around actor Sean Patrick Flannery playing a late-teens Indy who enlists in the Belgian army before US entry into World War One. The opening special 'Young Indiana Jones and the Curse of the Jackal' featured them both.

RELEASE: The series premiered on ABC on 4 March 1992 with 'Young Indiana Jones and the Curse of the Jackal'. Lucas himself penned an article in *TV Guide* to launch the series, encouraging young people to look into the lives of the historical figures presented in the show and talking of his hopes for a show which combined education and adventure in equal measure.

The series ratings, bolstered by the reputations of both Lucas and Indy, were initially very high but dropped off quickly, and the network dumped the series after running it for only six consecutive weeks. The problems of this 'first season' are real, but the network should be condemned for canning it so swiftly. 'Young Indiana Jones and the Curse of the Jackal' is a smartly witty, epic adventure on a scale unprecedented for television, 'Verdun, September 1916' is an effective illustration of the horrors of trench warfare which skilfully avoids becoming gung-ho, jingoistic or crass and the 'German East Africa, December 1916/Congo, January 1917' two-parter grapples bravely with issues of colonialism and ideas of friendship. None of the World

War One episodes ever descends simply into claiming the First World War as 'a just war'. The London-based romantic episode and the 'British East Africa, September 1909' instalments are less satisfactory, but they are watchable and handsomely mounted pieces of television all the same.

The series' initial network failure can be put down to a number of factors, not least amongst them ABC's needless speed in suspending the show. One of the series' faults was its anti-chronological attitude, with Carrier and Flannery episodes jumbled together seemingly at random – a source of confusion for more casual viewers. Another was the uninvolving introductions common to all the episodes. These featured eye-patched 80-something actor George Hall as Indy, and slowed the pace of the opening moments of any episode to a crawl. The need to cut back to Hall at the end of the hour often meant that a final scene of some wit or catharsis was ruined by the sudden intrusion of the framing sequence. Also problematic was the opening episode's use of the pre-teen Corey Carrier Indy. Adults, and even more so teenagers, can rarely be engaged by a series which has a lead under ten, while children tend to look up to adult heroes rather than identifying with adventurous contemporaries.

The series' biggest asset, right from the beginning, was Flannery – charming, funny and well up to both the action and character scenes that were asked of him. What's more, like River Phoenix before him, he really looked as if he could believably grow up to be Harrison Ford.

Despite these problems, the power of Lucasfilm, combined with the fact that seventeen hours of exceptionally expensive television had been already shot and paid for, meant the show would inevitably return. This it eventually did in the fall of 1992, bolstered by its receipt of no less than four well-deserved technical Emmys in that year's awards ceremony.

In transmission terms this second season consisted of a mix of unaired first-season episodes and instalments from a second recording block (of twelve episodes) that had begun over the summer. The newly produced episodes differed in some ways from those already made. Only one new episode featured the younger 'Young Indy', with Flannery headlining the rest, and the sequences with Hall's aged Indiana became briefer before being dropped entirely.

The series was beautifully produced, partially – although not entirely – because it was so expensive to make. A glance at the cast lists and guest directors of many episodes (see below) demonstrates the amount of money being made available to the show, and the quality of creative collaborator Lucas was able to tempt into television as a result. Equally his eye for talent is easily demonstrated by the number of young writers and directors who have gone on to greater acclaim and success since working for him on *Young Indiana Jones*.

In one 'season two' episode the budget of the feature-length 'Mystery of the Blues' even ran to an appearance by Harrison Ford, whose portrayal of a bearded, 50-something Indiana perhaps gave some indication of how he intends to approach the role of an older Dr Jones in any future film appearance (see **Indiana Jones IV**).

This 'second season', which included long breaks without any new episodes, concluded in Summer 1993 with several produced episodes unshown. By unlucky chance these included some of the best of the second block, such as the witty Kafka pastiche, 'Prague, August 1917'.

At this point even the most ardent admirers of the series could not have expected a third season, and yet this is precisely what happened. The 'USA Family Channel' made four TV movies in 1996. Noticeably cheaper than many of the previous episodes, the second of the four, 'Young Indiana Jones and The Treasure of the Peacock's Eye', is perhaps the closest the series ever got to emulating the tone of the films.

In 2000 Lucasfilm released twelve *Young Indy* videos on sell-through in the US. These were three of the 'Family Channel'-backed TV movies, plus a couple of the series' ABC-made feature-length episodes and a number of newly retitled features sewn together out of two disparate one-hour episodes (see **ALTERNATIVE VERSIONS**). Ten of the tapes were also released in the UK.

The series was not a popular success on video either, and the remaining ten/twelve have not yet been released in either market despite the available VHSs having volume numbers on the spines.

1. Young Indiana Jones and the Curse of the Jackal

Music by Laurence Rosenthal
Written by Jonathan Hales
Story by George Lucas
Egypt Segment Directed by Jim O'Brien
Directed by Carl Schultz
First US Transmission: 4 March 1992

GUEST CAST: Margaret Tyzack (*Helen Seymour*), Mike Moroff (*Pancho Villa*), Francesco Quinn (*Francois*), Ruth De Sosa (*Anna Jones*)

SUMMARY: Indy leaves his home town of Princeton in 1908, accompanying his father on a worldwide series of lectures. One of the countries they visit is Egypt, where Indy meets TE ('Ned') Lawrence, who becomes a life-long friend. A priceless artefact with a top shaped like a jackal's head is stolen during their visit and eight years later the sixteen-year-old Indy finds himself in a position to retrieve it, having run away to Mexico and inadvertently joined up with revolutionary Pancho Villa.

CAST & CREW: Margaret Tyzack, making here the first of many appearances as Indy's childhood tutor Helen Seymour, was well known for roles on British television, including in *I, Claudius* and *The Forsyte Saga*, and had made odd film appearances such as *A Clockwork Orange* (Stanley Kubrick, 1971).

TRIVIA: Mike Moroff, playing Pancho Villa, has relatives who actually rode in the historical Villa's gang.

2. London, May 1916

Music by Joel McNeely
Written by Rosemary Anne Sisson
Story by George Lucas
Directed by Carl Schultz
First US Transmission: 11 March 1992

GUEST CAST: Margaret Tyzack (*Helen Seymour*), Elizabeth Hurley (*Vicky Prentiss*), Vanessa Redgrave (*Mrs Prentiss*), Jane Wyatt (*Older Vicky*), Kika Markham (*Sylvia Pankhurst*)

SUMMARY: Indy arrives in London with Remy – previously one of Villa's gang – and romances a beautiful suffragette, before deciding to enlist for service in the Belgian army and fight in the Great War.

CAST & CREW: Elizabeth Hurley, former model turned actress, plays Indy's girlfriend Vicky. Later well known for comic roles such as that in *Austin Powers – International Man of Mystery* (Mike Myers, 1997) and as a successful producer, her role here is not so much that of a guest star as a 'before they were famous' sighting.

Vanessa Redgrave, of the immense acting clan, plays Vicky's mother. In constant work since the 1950s both on stage and in films, her career includes two Oscar nominations for *Mary Queen of Scots* (Charles Jarrot, 1971) and *Gods and Monsters* (Bill Condon, 1999).

Rosemary Anne Sisson has worked extensively in British television. Her screenplays for the BBC include the first episode of *The Six Wives of Henry VIII* (1970) and the second episode of *Elizabeth R* (1971), and she wrote no fewer than eleven episodes of ITV's *Upstairs, Downstairs* for creator/star Jean Marsh.

3. British East Africa, September 1909

Music by Laurence Rosenthal
Written by Matthew Jacobs
Story by George Lucas
Directed by Carl Schultz
First US Transmission: 18 March 1992

GUEST CAST: Margaret Tyzack (*Helen Seymour*), Ruth De Sosa (*Anna Jones*), Isaac Senteu Supeyo (*Meto*), James Gammon (*Teddy Roosevelt*), Paul Freeman (*Frederick Selous*)

SUMMARY: Indy and his parents travel to Africa, where they join then recently retired President Theodore Roosevelt on safari.

CAST & CREW: Paul Freeman played Belloq in *Raiders of the Lost Ark*.

TRIVIA: Disclaimer at beginning and end of episode: *No animals were harmed or killed for the purposes of the production.*

4. Verdun, September 1916

Music by Joel McNeely
Written by Jonathan Hensleigh
Story by George Lucas
Directed by Rene Manzor
First US Transmission: 25 March 1992

GUEST CAST: Bernard Fresson (*Joffre*), Jean Rougerie (*Henri-Philippe Petain*), Igor De Savitch (*Robert Nivelle*), Cris Campion (*Lieutenant Gaston*)

SUMMARY: Indy is a runner for the Belgian army during one of the most horrific engagements of the trench conflict.

CAST & CREW: Jonathan Hensleigh's first script for the series is impressive, but gives little indication of his subsequent career as one of Hollywood's busiest screenwriters of action cinema, responsible for *Die Hard: With a Vengeance* (John McTiernan, 1995), *Armageddon* (Michael Bay, 1998) and *Jumanji* (Joe Johnston, 1995); his screenplay for *The Saint* (Philip Noyce, 1996) was rewritten by other hands but still credited to him alone.

5. German East Africa, December 1916

Music by Joel McNeely
Written by Frank Darabont
Story by George Lucas
Directed by Simon Wincer
First US Transmission: 1 April 1992

GUEST CAST: Bryan Pringle (*Sloat*), Michel Duchaussoy (*Maor Boucher*), Isaach De Bankole (*Sgt Barthelmy*), Friedrich Von Thunas (*Albert Schweitzer*)

SUMMARY: In North Africa Indy is second in command of a unit sent on a secret mission to move some weapons up the Congo. He quarrels with his harsh immediate superior, and through conversations with his own subordinates comes to a broader understanding of colonialism.

CAST & CREW: A veteran of numerous unremarkable television series, Simon Wincer was hired because of his work on the genuinely extraordinary *Lonesome Dove* mini-series in 1989. Since *Young Indiana Jones* he has moved into theatrical features including *Free Willy* (1993) and *The Phantom* (1996) starring Billy Zane.

This is the first episode by Frank Darabont, the screenwriter of *A Nightmare on Elm Street Part Three: Dream Warriors* (Chuck Russell, 1987) and *The Fly II* (Chris Walas, 1989). He went on to become the Oscar-nominated writer/director of *The Shawshank Redemption* (1994), *The Green Mile* (1999) and *The Majestic* (2001).

6. Congo, January 1917

Music by Joel McNeely
Written by Frank Darabont
Story by George Lucas
Directed by Simon Wincer
First US Transmission: 8 April 1992

GUEST CAST: Bryan Pringle (*Sloat*), Emile Abossolo M'Bo (*Joseph*), Isolde Barth (*Helene Schweitzer*), Yann Colette (*Colonel Pernod*), Friedrich Von Thunas (*Albert Schweitzer*)

SUMMARY: Half-dead through illness, Indy and his men encounter humanitarian Albert Schweitzer.

7. Austria, March 1917

Music by Laurence Rosenthal
Written by Frank Darabont
Story by George Lucas
Directed by Vic Armstrong
First US Transmission: 21 September 1992

GUEST CAST: Benedict Taylor (*Prince Sixtus*), Matthew Wait (*Prince Xavier*), Christopher Lee (*Count Ottokar Graf Czernin*), Patrick Ryecart (*Emperor Karl*), Jennifer Ehle (*Empress Zita*), Joss Ackland (*The Prussian*)

SUMMARY: Indy is sent, in the company of two young princes, to petition the Emperor of Austria to conclude a separate peace with France and Britain, thus leaving the Kaiser of Germany politically isolated in Europe.

CAST & CREW: Directed with a flair for action by former stuntman and regular James Bond second-unit director Vic Armstrong, this episode has one of the series' most impressive guest casts and was a good choice to relaunch the series after its transmission break.

Jennifer Ehle, American-born but thoroughly British, was in the process of shooting to fame – and becoming a sex symbol – through an impressive performance in Channel 4's adaptation of Mary Wesley's *The Camomile Lawn*. She later played Elizabeth Bennett in a well-received BBC adaptation of Jane Austen's *Pride and Prejudice* (1995) and her film roles include playing John Lennon's first wife, Cynthia, in *Backbeat* (Iain Softley, 1993), Oscar Wilde's wife Constance in *Wilde* (Brian Gilbert, 1997) and roles in *This Year's Love* (David Kane, 1999) and *Possession* (Neil LaBute, 2002).

TV legend Joss Ackland, here worldless as a sinister spy master, had a career then going back forty years. Best known to Americans at the time for his role in *Bill and Ted's Bogus Journey* (Peter Hewitt, 1991), his extensive résumé includes roles in plays by Shakespeare and Chekhov for the BBC and guest-villain roles in a dozen second-rate TV shows, like *The Persuaders*. He was perhaps most impressive in *Tinker, Tailer, Soldier, Spy*, also for the BBC, and as CS Lewis in the 1985 TV version of *Shadowlands*.

Christopher Lee remains one of cinema's great icons and needs little introduction. A great Bond villain, the definitive screen Dracula and a fine Sherlock Holmes, he has made more than 100 films in a career spanning half a century.

Patrick Ryecart remains one of those actors who concentrate on the stage, but his TV work includes playing Romeo for the BBC and guest appearances in *Poirot*, *Lovejoy* and *Rumpole of the*

Bailey as well as a particularly fine turn as a guest villain in a 1986 *Doctor Who* serial.

8. Somme, Early August 1916

Music by Frederic Talgorn
Written by Jonathan Hensleigh
Story by George Lucas
Directed by Simon Wincer
First US Transmission: 28 September 1992

GUEST CAST: Jason Flemyng (*Emile*), Richard Ridings (*Andre*), Simon Hepworth (*Tutu*), Jonathan Phillips (*Jacques*)

SUMMARY: The horrors of trench warfare as seen through the eyes of Indy who, as a young American, initially has no real idea of what to expect.

NOTE: Set before Episode 4 'Verdun, September 1916'.

9. Germany, Mid-August 1916

Music by Frederic Talgorn
Written by Jonathan Hensleigh
Story by George Lucas
Directed by Simon Wincer
First US Transmission: 5 October 1992

GUEST CAST: Jason Flemyng (*Emile*), Yves Beneyton (*Benet*), Herve Pauchon (*Charles De Gaulle*)

SUMMARY: Captured by German forces, Indy settles into a prisoner-of-war camp and befriends an energetic, remarkable young French officer, Charles De Gaulle, and together they plan to escape.

TRIVIA: This episode and the previous one were transmitted in Australia as a TV movie entitled *Young Indiana Jones and the Great Escape.*

10. Barcelona, May 1917

Music by Laurence Rosenthal
Written by Gavin Scott
Story by George Lucas
Directed by Terry Jones
First US Transmission: 12 October 1992

GUEST CAST: Amanda Ooms (*Nadia*), Timothy Spall (*Cunningham*), Harry Enfield (*Chauffeur*), Terry Jones (*Marcello*), William Hootkins (*Diaghilev*), Liz Smith (*Delfina*)

SUMMARY: Indy falls in with chaotically disorganised British agents in Spain in one of the series' most simply comic (and most effective) episodes.

CAST & CREW: Director/Guest Star Terry Jones was one-sixth of *Monty Python's Flying Circus*, the director or co-director of their four theatrical features and the writer of many of their most memorable sketches. As well as being the co-creator of television series *Ripping Yarns*, Jones is also a respected medieval historian and critic of Middle English literature.

The versatile, funny and deep Timothy Spall was one of the regulars in *Auf Wiedersehen, Pet*, the Dick Clement and Ian La Frenais-scripted series about British builders abroad which ran from 1983 to 1986 to great acclaim. It was revived in 2002 to even greater critical plaudits. RADA-trained (where he won the Special Prize), he has a long working relationship with Mike Leigh, appearing in *Secrets & Lies* (1992) and *All or Nothing* (2002). His role in *Vanilla Sky* (Cameron Crowe, 2002) saw him finally break into mainstream Hollywood pictures.

William Hootkins had featured in *Star Wars* and *Batman* (Tim Burton, 1989). As an American living in the UK he is often called upon by American-set productions based in Britain.

Harry Enfield remains best known as a comedian in Britain, the brains behind half a dozen sketch shows and sitcoms and the originator of too many catchphrases to count.

Liz Smith, despite a long career, will doubtlessly be remembered in the UK for her role as the permanently confused Nana in BBC sitcom *The Royle Family*, which began in 1998.

11. Young Indiana Jones and the Mystery of the Blues

Music Composed and Adapted by Joel McNeely
Written by Jule Selbo
Story by George Lucas
Directed by Carl Schultz
First US Transmission: 13 March 1993

GUEST CAST: Harrison Ford (*Doctor Henry 'Indiana' Jones Junior*), Jeffrey Wright (*Sidney Bechet*), Jay Underwood (*Ernest Hemingway*), Ray Serra (*Jim Colosimo*), Keith David (*King Oliver*), Frank Vincent (*John Torrio*), Frederick Weller (*Eliot Ness*), Maria Howell (*Goldie*), Nicholas Turturro (*Al Capone*), Saginaw Grant (*Great Cloud*), Jane Krakowski (*Mrs Colosimo*), David Arnott (*Clifford*), Victor Slezak (*O'Bannion*)

SUMMARY: Waiting tables in Chicago at night and attending university during the day, Indy clashes with Al Capone.

NOTES: This episode has a framing sequence set in Wyoming in 1950, in which Harrison Ford plays Indiana Jones. Although he appears for only a few minutes his undoubted celebrity entitled him to be second-billed after Flannery for the episode. Ford plays the older Indy with a full, greying beard, and whilst he manages to get an impressive action sequence into his brief screen time (a car chase on ice) it's a grizzled, contemplative Indy on show.

CAST & CREW: Jane Krakowski, here in the minor role of Colosimo's wife, later played Elaine in *Ally McBeal*.

CRITICISM: '. . . as good as series television gets' noted the *Hollywood Reporter* of this special-event episode, calling it a 'jazz-filled delight' of 'quality and imagination' and an example of a series which regularly demonstrated 'nothing but class and quality'. Harrison Ford's return to one of his most famous cinematic roles was also praised for its 'fun and flamboyance' and the way he played the role as 'more jester than adventurer' this time around. One of the series' most accomplished instalments, Ford's appearance gives it curiosity value and the setting is beautifully realised.

FORWARDS/BACKWARDS: Indy is shown attending the University of Chicago, mentioned as his alma mater in *Raiders of the Lost Ark*.

12. Princeton, February 1916

Music by Laurence Rosenthal
Written by Matthew Jacobs
Production Designers: Ricky Eyres, Barbara Kretschmer,
Jeffrey Ginn
Directed by Joe Johnston
First US Transmission: 20 March 1993

GUEST CAST: Lloyd Owen (*Professor Henry Jones Senior*), Robyn Lively (*Nancy Stratemeyer*), Mark L Taylor (*Professor Thompson*), Clark Gregg (*Dickinson*)

SUMMARY: While at school Indy and his girlfriend Nancy investigate the theft of an electrical device invented by Thomas Edison.

BACKWARDS/FORWARDS: A large leap back in the series' own chronology, with this episode set before the Flannery sections of the series premiere 'Young Indiana Jones and the Curse of the Jackal'. Flannery, although game, looks uncomfortable pretending to be at school.

EXTERNAL REFERENCES: Indy's high-school sweetheart, Nancy Stratemeyer, is the daughter of the creator of the Nancy Drew series of girls' mystery adventure novellas. The character in the episode is clearly based on the character from the books, implying that in 'truth' it was the other way around.

13. Petrograd, July 1917

Music by Laurence Rosenthal
Written by Gavin Scott
Story by George Lucas
Directed by Simon Wincer
First US Transmission: 27 March 1993

GUEST CAST: Julia Stemberger (*Rosa*), Jean-Pierre Cassel (*Ambassador*), Beata Pozniak (*Irena*), Ravil Isyanov (*Sergei*), Gary Olsen (*Boris*), Roger Sloman (*Lenin*)

SUMMARY: Sent to infiltrate a group of Communists in Russia, Indy finds his sympathy for their predicament quickly conflicts with his orders.

CAST & CREW: Roger Sloman had previously played Lenin in *Reds* (Warren Beatty, 1981).

CRITICISM: Astoundingly beautifully shot on location in St Petersburg, this intelligent episode asks young Americans to think of the social origins of European communism and consider the human dimension of revolution. It also points out that there was more than one Russian revolution in 1917, in a non-patronising but informative way. This is one of the episodes that really live up to the series' potential to educate *and* entertain. The final massacre is horrifying.

14. Young Indiana Jones and the Scandal of 1920

Music Composed and Adapted by Joel McNeely
Written by Jonathan Hales
Production Designer: Jeff Ginn
Directed by Syd MaCartney
First US Transmission: 3 April 1993

GUEST CAST: Alexandra Powers (*Gloria*), Anne Heche (*Kate*), Jennifer Stevens (*Peggy*), Christopher John Fields (*George White*), Tom Beckett (*George Gershwin*), Michelle Nicastro (*Ann Penington*), Bill McKinney (*Mack*), Robert Trebor (*Schwarz*), Peter Appel (*Ross*), Annabelle Gurwitch (*Dottie*), Mark Holton (*Woolcott*), Terumi Matthews (*Edna Ferber*), Dylan Price (*Franklin Adams*), Joshua Rifkind (*Robert Sherwood*), Peter Spears (*Robert Benchley*), Brenda Strong (*Beatrice Kaufman*), Guri Weinberg (*George Kaufman*)

SUMMARY: Indy works with George Gershwin while romancing three women at once, with hilarious consequences.

CAST & CREW: The lovely Anne Heche was in Gus Van Sant's under-appreciated remake of *Psycho* (1998). In theatre from childhood, she was sensational as teen twins in TV soap *Another World*; her films include *Donnie Brasco* (Mike Newell, 1997) and writer/director Donald Cammell's criminally misunderstood *Wild Side* (1995).

15. Vienna, November 1908

Music by Laurence Rosenthal
Written by Matthew Jacobs
Story by George Lucas
Director of Photography: Jörgen Persson
Directed by Bille August
First US Transmission: 10 April 1993

GUEST CAST: Margaret Tyzack (*Helen Seymour*), Ruth De Sosa (*Anna Jones*), Lennart Hjulstrom (*Franz Ferdinand*), Ernst Hugo Jardegard (*Carl Jung*), Bjorn Granat (*Adler*), Amalie Alstrup (*Princess Sophie*), Max von Sydow (*Sigmund Freud*)

SUMMARY: Indy and his family visit the Hapsburg court, where pre-adolescent infatuation strikes Henry Junior like a thunderbolt at the first sight of the young Princess Sophie. He's advised by the three founding fathers of modern psychoanalysis as a result.

CAST & CREW: Director Bille August won the *Palme D'Or* at Cannes for the remarkable *Pelle the Conqueror* (1987) which he wrote and directed, a feat he repeated with *The Best Intentions* in 1992. *Pelle* also won the Best Foreign Film Academy Award. His movies since have included *Smilla's Feeling for Snow* (1997) and an uninspiring adaptation of Victor Hugo's *Les Miserables* (1998), both of which suffered from his lack of screenplay input. For this episode August brought his regular cinematographer Jörgen Persson to the series, and the two achieve some beautiful visuals with the Viennese locations.

Max von Sydow has appeared in some of the best and some of the worst movies ever made. Forever associated with his role in *The Seventh Seal* (Ingmar Bergman, 1956), he also made impressive appearances in that director's *Wild Strawberries* (1957) amongst others. Other fine performances include his

Oscar-nominated role in *Pelle the Conqueror* and his part in Woody Allen's *Hannah and Her Sisters*. Less wise choices include the bland *Judge Dredd* (Danny Cannon, 1995) and the awe-inspiringly dreadful *What Dreams May Come* (Vincent Ward, 1998) starring Robin Williams.

16. Northern Italy, June 1918

Music by Laurence Rosenthal
Director of Photography: Jörgen Persson
Written by Jonathan Hales
Directed by Bille August
First US Transmission: 17 April 1993

GUEST CAST: Jay Underwood (*Ernest Hemingway*), Veronika Logan (*Giulietta*), Pernilla August (*Mamma*)

SUMMARY: Indy asks the advice of his friend Ernie Hemingway on how to woo women.

17. Phantom Train of Doom

Music Composed by Joel McNeely
Written by Frank Darabont
Directed by Peter Macdonald
First US Transmission: 5 May 1993

GUEST CAST: Lynsey Baxter (*Margaret Trappe*), Tom Bell (*General Paul von Lettow-Vorbeck*), Paul Freeman (*Frederick Selous*), Ronald Fraser (*Donald*), Freddie Jones (*Birdy*), Norman Rodway (*General Smuts*)

SUMMARY: In Africa, Indy and Remy team up with some unlikely commandos to destroy what some insist is actually a ghost train.

CRITICISM: Action-packed and involving, this is a far simpler effort than the immediately preceding episodes, but also less in-joke-laden and more accessible to younger and/or less literate viewers.

LUCAS ON PHANTOM TRAIN OF DOOM: Lucas claimed he wanted 'to make a real old Indiana Jones adventure', and when his researches in World War One led him to an Africa-based regiment known colloquially as 'The Old and the Bold' he knew he had the material: 'This group of very old hunters and trackers formed a regiment together' and by putting Indy in with them the spectacle of 'old men on an adventure with this young teenager' was created. He later dubbed it '. . . one of my favourite episodes' and was sufficiently enthused about it years later to make it the *Young Indiana Jones* VHS given away with the UK edition of the three-film *Indiana Jones* VHS box set; a 'gift' partially intended to raise awareness of the series and encourage purchase of further episodes by fans of the films.

18. Ireland, April 1916

Music by Laurence Rosenthal
Written by Jonathan Hales
Directed by Gillies Mackinnon
First US Transmission: 12 June 1993

GUEST CAST: John Lynch (*Sean O'Casey*), Shane Connaughton (*WB Yeats*), Darrah Kelly (*Sean Lemass*), Susannah Doyle (*Maggie*), Nell Murphy (*Nuala*)

SUMMARY: In Dublin on his way to England (see 'London, May 1916') Indy gets a job at a pub, where he meets playwright Sean O'Casey and poet Yeats and discusses issues arising from Ireland's history and future.

19. Paris, September 1908

Music by Joel McNeely
Theme by Laurence Rosenthal
Written by Reg Gadney
Story by George Lucas
Directed by Rene Manzor
First US Transmission: 19 June 1993

GUEST CAST: Margaret Tyzack (*Helen Seymour*), Ruth De Sosa (*Anna Jones*), Danny Webb (*Pablo Picasso*), Jean Pierre Aumont (*Edgar Degas*), Lukas Haas (*Norman Rockwell*)

SUMMARY: Indy meets Norman Rockwell in Paris, and the two encounter Degas and Picasso, who quarrel about the nature of art.

TRIVIA: George Lucas is a noted collector of Norman Rockwell paintings.

20. Peking, March 1910

Music by Laurence Rosenthal
Written by Rosemary Anne Sisson
Story by George Lucas
Director of Photography: Oliver Stapleton
Directed by Gavin Millar
First US Transmission: 26 June 1993

GUEST CAST: Margaret Tyzack (*Helen Seymour*), Ruth De Sosa (*Anna Jones*), Ping Wu (*Li*), Nigel Fan (*Ah Pin*)

SUMMARY: Indy becomes ill on a visit to China.

21. Benares, January 1910

Music by Laurence Rosenthal
Written by Jonathan Hensleigh
Director of Photography: Giles Nuttgens
Production Designer: Lucy Richardson
Story by George Lucas
Directed by Deepa Mehta
First US Transmission: 3 July 1993

GUEST CAST: Margaret Tyzack (*Helen Seymour*), Ruth De Sosa (*Anna Jones*), John Wood (*Charles Leadbeater*), Dorothy Tutin (*Annie Besant*), Hemanth Raoas (*Jiddu Krishnamurti*)

SUMMARY: Indy's eyes are opened to comparative religion in India.

CAST & CREW: Indian director Deepa Mehta's films include *Martha, Ruth & Eddie* (1988) and *Sam & Me* (1991).

22. Paris, October 1916

Music by Joel McNeely
Theme by Laurence Rosenthal
Written by Carrie Fisher
Story by George Lucas
Directed by Nicholas Roeg
First US Transmission: 10 July 1993

GUEST CAST: Domiziana Giordano (*Mata Hari*), Kenneth Haigh (*War Minister*), Ian McDiarmid (*Professor Levi*), Jacqueline Pearce (*Annabelle*)

SUMMARY: Indy has an affair with Mata Hari.

CAST & CREW: Ian McDiarmid played Senator/Chancellor/ Emperor Palpatine in *Return of the Jedi*, *The Phantom Menace* and *Attack of the Clones*.

Former Hammer Horror actress Jacqueline Pearce is best known as Servalan from camp, cult space-fascism TV drama *Blake's 7* (1978–1981).

Writer Carrie Fisher of course played Princess Leia in the first three *Star Wars* films. Some highlights of her surprisingly extensive CV of other film roles include a startlingly funny cameo as a therapist in *Austin Powers – International Man of Mystery* (Jay Roach, 1997), her debut as young seductress Lorna in *Shampoo* (Hal Ashby, 1975), a part in the Oscar-winning *Hannah and Her Sisters* (Woody Allen, 1986), and roles in the flawed *The Burbs* (Joe Dante, 1989), the insipid *Drop Dead Fred* (Ate de Jong, 1991) and the wonderful *When Harry Met Sally* (Rob Reiner, 1987). As *de facto* Hollywood royalty from birth, she's had quite a tough time of it, as detailed in her fascinating memoir *Postcards from the Edge* which she adapted into an excellent film script for director Mike Nicholls in 1990. Other work as a writer includes the celebrated TV movie *These Old Broads* (Matthew Diamond, 2001), featuring her mother Debbie Reynolds, Joan Collins and Elizabeth Taylor, and the novels *Surrender the Pink* and *Delusions of Grandma*.

Director Nic Roeg, a former cinematographer, was the co-director of *Performance* (with Donald Cammell, 1969) and directed *Walkabout* (1972), *Don't Look Now* (1973) and *The Man Who Fell To Earth* (1976).

23. Istanbul, September 1918

Music by Laurence Rosenthal
Written by Rosemary Ann Sisson
Directed by Mike Newell
First US Transmission: 17 July 1993

GUEST CAST: Katherine Butler (*Molly*), Peter Firth (*Stefan*), Ahmet Levendoglu (*Mustafa Kemal*)

SUMMARY: On a spying mission, Indy keeps his identity a secret from a woman he is planning to marry.

CAST & CREW: Director Mike Newell worked in British television before becoming famous for directing *Four Weddings and a Funeral* (1994), the hugely popular all-star comedy of British upper-middle-class life which virtually kick-started a new genre. He followed it with the quintessentially American story of *Donnie Brasco* (1997), starring Al Pacino and Johnny Depp.

24. Paris, May 1919

Music by Joel McNeely
Written by Jonathan Hales
Directed by David Hare
First US Transmission: 24 July 1993

GUEST CAST: Cyril Cusack (*George Clemenceau*), Anna Massey (*Gertrude Bell*), Michael Maloney (*Arnold Toynbee*), Douglas Henshall (*TE Lawrence*), Alec Mapa (*Nguyen*), Michael Kitchen (*David Lloyd George*), Josef Sommer (*Woodrow Wilson*), Jeroen Krabbé (*Brockdorff*)

SUMMARY: Indy attends the Paris peace conferences to which he has been sent because of his expertise with numerous languages.

CAST & CREW: Michael Kitchen plays MI6's chief of staff in Eon Productions' more recent James Bond films. A busy and versatile actor, his most memorable role is as the future King Charles III (i.e. the present Prince of Wales) locked in a constitutional confrontation with a virtually totalitarian British government in TV's *To Play the King*.

Dutch actor Jeroen Krabbé also has Bond experience; he played KGB General Koskov in *The Living Daylights* (John Glen, 1987). His other American films include *Kafka* (Steven Soderbergh, 1991), *The Fugitive* (Andrew Davies, 1993) with Harrison Ford, exposé *Scandal* (Michael Caton-Jones, 1989) and Beethoven biopic *Immortal Beloved* (Bernard Rose, 1994).

Cyril Cusack, who made his professional acting debut in 1917, is another actor whose primary arena has been the stage. His movies include *Harold and Maude* (Hal Ashby, 1971), *Fahrenheit 451* (François Truffaut, 1966) and *My Left Foot* (Jim Sheridan, 1989).

Douglas Henshall plays Indy's friend Ned Lawrence (i.e. Lawrence of Arabia) in several episodes of this series. Henshall's other work includes TV series *Lipstick on Your Collar* (1993, with Ewan McGregor), *Common as Muck* (1994, with Edward Woodward) and the films *Angels & Insects* (Philip Haas, 1995) and *This Year's Love* (David Kane, 1999). He also starred in the heavily underrated Anglo-Spanish magical realist romantic comedy *If Only . . .* (aka *The Man With Rain in His Shoes*) (Maria Ripoll, 1998).

25. Florence, May 1908

Music Adapted by Laurence Rosenthal
Written by Jule Selbo
Directed by Mike Newell

GUEST CAST: Margaret Tyzack (*Helen Seymour*), Ruth De Sosa (*Anna Jones*), George Corraface (*Puccini*)

SUMMARY: While touring Florence, Italy, Indy meets opera composer Giacomo Puccini, who has romantic designs on Indy's mother.

NOTE: Made as part of the series' second production block but never shown in the US in its original form.

26. Prague, August 1917

Music by Laurence Rosenthal
Written by Gavin Scott
Directed by Robert Young

GUEST CAST: Tim McInnerny (*Franz Kafka*)

SUMMARY: Indy and his friend Franz face bureaucratic incompetence as they attempt to get a telephone installed in a Prague apartment.

CAST & CREW: The versatile and underrated Tim McInnerny (sometimes miscredited as McInnery) played two different Lords Percy Percy, both Dukes of Northumberland, in *The Black Adder* (1983) and *Blackadder II* (1986) respectively, Captain Darling in *Blackadder Goes Forth* (1989) and numerous members of the Darling family in *Blackadder Back and Forth* (1999). His other television work includes *Edge of Darkness* and his films include *Notting Hill* (Roger Michell, 1999) and *Richard III* (Richard Loncraine, 1995).

CRITICISM: A witty Kafka pastiche with notable lightness of touch, this is virtually a two-hander between Flannery and McInnerny; one of the series' most enjoyable but least accessible episodes.

NOTE: Made as part of the series' second production block but never shown in the US in its original form.

27. Palestine, October 1917

Music by Laurence Rosenthal
Written by Frank Darabont
Directed by Simon Wincer

GUEST CAST: Catherine Zeta Jones (*Maya*), Julian Firth (*Meinertzhagan*), Cameron Daddo (*Jack Anders*), Douglas Henshall (*TE Lawrence*)

CAST & CREW: Catherine Zeta Jones came to prominence in Britain via ITV's *The Darling Buds of May* (1991), but her subsequent transition to mainstream Hollywood movies surprised many. Memorable roles include playing Antonio Banderas's love interest in *The Mask of Zorro* (Martin Campbell, 1995) and a pregnant woman who discovers her upper-class husband is involved in drug-dealing in *Traffic* (Steven Soderbergh, 2000). Her marriage to Michael Douglas has seen her effectively become Hollywood royalty.

NOTE: Made as part of the series' second production block but never shown in the US in its original form (see 'Daredevils of the Desert').

28. Transylvania, January 1918

Music by Curt Sobel
Written by Jonathan Hensleigh
Directed by Dick Maas

GUEST CAST: Bob Peck (*General Targo*), Keith Szarabajka (*Colonel Waters*), Simone Bendix (*Maria*), Paul Kynman (*Nicholas Hunyadi*), Alan Polonski (*Agent McCall*), Michael Mellinger (*Paretti*), William Roberts (*Stanfill*), William Armstrong (*The Major*), Steven Hartley (*Agent Picard*), Ann Tirard (*Tarot Reader*), Petr Svarovsky (*Venetian Policeman*), David Gilliam (*Agent Thompson*)

SUMMARY: Indy goes behind enemy lines to investigate the sudden disappearance of all the prisoners at an Austrian POW camp.

CAST & CREW: Principally a stage actor, the late Bob Peck's best role remains the crusading policeman in the BBC's *Edge of Darkness* (1985), although he was also memorable in a small role in *Jurassic Park* (Steven Spielberg, 1993).

NOTE: Made as part of the series' second production block but never shown in the US in its original form.

29. Young Indiana Jones and the Hollywood Follies

Music Composed by Laurence Rosenthal
Written by Jonathan Hales and Matthew Jacobs
Directed by Michael Schultz
First US Transmission: 15 October 1994

GUEST CAST: Allison Smith (*Claire Lieberman*), Bill Cusack (*Irving Thalberg*), Julia Campbell (*Kitty*), Stephen Caffery (*John Ford*), Dana Gladstone (*Erich von Stroheim*), David Margulies (*Carl Lämmle*), Peter Dennis (*Pete*), Luigi Amodeo (*Massimo*), JD Hinton (*Harry Carey*), Leo Gordon (*Wyatt Earp*)

SUMMARY: Indy takes a job at a Hollywood studio, where he's told to get director Erich von Stroheim to bring his new picture in on time.

30. Treasure of the Peacock's Eye

Music Composed by Steven Bramson
Written by Jule Selbo
Directed by Carl Schultz
First US Transmission: 12 January 1995

GUEST CAST: Adrian Edmondson (*Zyke*), Jayne Ashbourne (*Lily*), Tom Courtenay (*Bronislaw Malinowski*)

SUMMARY: Indy and Remy spend months hunting for a diamond that once belonged to Alexander the Great, hoping that it will make their fortunes.

CASTING & CREW: The co-writer/star of *Bottom*, Vyvyan in *The Young Ones* and a frequent guest actor in *Blackadder* (all for the BBC), Adrian Edmondson's turn as an eye-patched, eye-rolling villain is one of the series' highlights.

Sir Tom Courtenay began his career as angry young man or victim of circumstance and matured into character roles and complex middle-aged men with great skill. Films include the title roles in *Billy Liar* (John Schlesinger, 1963) *Private Potter* (Caspar Wrede, 1962) and *Whatever Happened to Harold Smith?* (Peter

Hewitt, 1999). He was also in the wonderful *Last Orders* (Fred Schepisi, 2001) and *Let Him Have It* (Peter Medak, 1991) which concerned the case of Derek Bentley, who was hanged in 1953 for a crime he didn't commit. Courtenay has twice been Oscar nominated: for Pasha in *Doctor Zhivago* (David Lean, 1965) and for the role of Norman in *The Dresser* (Peter Yates, 1983). He was knighted in the Queen's 2001 New Year's Honours List.

31. Attack of the Hawkmen

Music Composed by Joel McNeely
Written by Matthew Jacobs, Rosemary Anne Sisson and Ben Burtt
Directed by Ben Burtt
First US Transmission: 8 October 1995

GUEST CAST: Patrick Toomey (*Charles Nungesser*), Marc Warren (*Baron von Richthofen*), Craig Kelly (*Anthony Fokker*), Daniel Kash (*Raoul Lufbery*), Ewan Bailey (*Hobie*), Lawrence Elman (*Len*), Nick Colicos (*Green*), Matt Bardock (*Carl*), Victor Spinetti (*Bragas*), John Warnaby (*British Officer*), Richard Ashcroft (*LeBlanc*), John Conroy (*Cartier*), Damien Dibben (*Corporal G*), Leon Silver (*Eugene*), Kenneth Collard (*Pierre*), Anthony Daniels (*Francois*), Gertran Klauber (*Maurice*), Bill Thomas (*Max*), Karl Dobry (*Goering*), Manuel Harlan (*Lothar*), Peter Clay (*Forssman*), Jon Pertwee (*General Von Kramer*)

SUMMARY: As part of the Lafayette Escadrille flying squadron, Indy encounters the notorious Baron von Richthofen and tries to persuade aircraft designer Anthony Fokker to defect from Germany.

CAST & CREW: Jon Pertwee was TV's Worzel Gummidge (1979–1986) and the third Doctor Who (1970–1975); he died in 1996. Anthony Daniels plays C-3PO in all of the *Star Wars* films. Craig Kelly went on to some fame and acclaim as Vince in Russell T Davies's *Queer As Folk* for Channel 4.

Ben Burtt won an Oscar for his sound designs on *Star Wars* and worked as a writer on Lucas's *Droids* cartoon series. He is the film editor of the *Star Wars* prequels.

32. Travels With Father

Music Composed by Laurence Rosenthal
Written by Frank Darabont, Matthew Jacobs, and Jonathan Hales
Greece Segment Directed by Deepa Mehta
Directed by Michael Schultz
First US Transmission: 16 June 1996

GUEST CAST: Ruth De Sosa (*Anna Jones*), Margaret Tyzack (*Helen Seymour*), Michael Gough (*Tolstoy*), George Jackos (*Nikos Kazantzakis*), George Yiasoumi (*Aristotle*)

SUMMARY: The Joneses tour Russia and Athens together.

ALTERNATIVE VERSIONS: At some point in 1996 Lucas appears to have made the decision to comprehensively re-edit the entire series into 23 episodes of around an hour-and-a-half in length, and arrange them in chronological sequence. The 'Old Indy' framing sequences were to be removed, the title sequences made uniform and, where necessary, new footage shot to make the material run smoothly in its new format. The new linear approach to the series chronology presented particular problems with 'Young Indiana Jones and the Curse of the Jackal' which, by jumping, mid-plot, from 1909 to 1916 as it did, required major surgery. In the end a large amount of new footage was shot and the story split into *two* movie-length instalments, which were tagged to be (1) and (6) in the series' new numbering system. In a frankly astonishing bit of technical legerdemain new scenes shot with actor Corey Carrier as the pre-teen Indy were matched with film from five years before by digitally shrinking the actor to make him appear the right size in relation to other performers. Once the re-edits were complete, repeats of the series in its new form began running on the USA cable channel and (eventually) BBC1. In this – regarded by Lucasfilm as the series' definitive form – the episode numbers and titles are as follows (the episodes from which these new versions were derived are noted in brackets):
1. My First Adventure (Young Indiana Jones and the Curse of the Jackal [First Half], Tangiers 1908 [new])
2. Passion for Life (British East Africa 1909, Paris 1908)

3. The Perils of Cupid (Vienna 1908, Florence 1908)
4. Travels With Father (Travels With Father)
5. Journey of Radiance (Benares 1910, China 1910)
6. Spring Break Adventure (Princeton 1916, Young Indiana Jones and the Curse of the Jackal [Second Half])
7. Love's Sweet Song (Ireland 1916, London 1916)
8. Trenches of Hell (Somme 1916, Germany 1916)
9. Demons of Deception (Verdun 1916, Paris 1916)
10. Phantom Train of Doom (Phantom Train Of Doom)
11. Ogang, the Giver and Taker of Life (German East Africa 1916, Congo 1917)
12. Attack of the Hawkmen (Attack of the Hawkmen)
13. Adventures in the Secret Service (Austria 1917, Petrograd 1917)
14. Espionage Escapades (Barcelona 1917, Prague 1917)
15. Daredevils of the Desert (Palestine 1917, plus new filming)
16. Tales of Innocence (Northern Italy 1918, Morocco 1917 [new])
17. Masks of Evil (Transylvania 1918, Istanbul 1918)
18. Treasure of the Peacock's Eye (Treasure of the Peacock's Eye)
19. Winds of Change (Paris 1919, Princeton 1919 [new])
20. Young Indiana Jones and the Mystery of the Blues (Young Indiana Jones and the Mystery of the Blues)
21. Scandal of 1920 (Scandal of 1920)
22. Young Indiana Jones and the Hollywood Follies (Young Indiana Jones and the Hollywood Follies)

CRITICISM: *Young Indiana Jones* is a unique and remarkable television series which genuinely deserves far more respect and credit that it currently receives. While Indy's habit of bumping into famous and influential people wherever he goes can be irritating, and at times seems to strain credulity, it's a necessary offshoot of Lucas's desire to use an adventure series to inform as well as entertain. One of the series' strengths is that it never patronises its audience, and another is that for the most part it can be purely enjoyed as a series of extraordinarily lavish historical vignettes. Flannery is excellent in the title role, and the quality of guest actor he often gets to play against should at the very least make the series an interesting curio for the film-literate. The only other television series to have episodes directed by *Palme D'Or* winning filmmakers is *Twin Peaks*. There's no doubt that some of the episodes, even in their video special-edition form, are fundamentally lacking – but it's equally certain that others, such as the epic and action-packed 'Daredevils of the Desert', the hugely atmospheric 'Mystery of the Blues' or the literate and humane 'Trenches of Hell', have an enormous amount to offer both fans of the movies and a general audience bemused by the series' shapeless history and inconclusive legacy.

The undervaluing of the series is itself interesting in that it goes to prove that no matter what people say Lucas is incapable of forcing his whims and fancies onto the public if they are fundamentally uninterested in what he has to offer. In this instance more than any other it is the general public's loss.

Radioland Murders (1994)

(100 minutes)

Universal
A Lucasfilm Limited Production
Screenplay by Willard Huyck & Gloria Katz and Jeff Reno &
Ron Osborn
Story by George Lucas
Director of Photography: David Tattersall, BSC
Production Designer: Gavin Bocquet
Producer: Rick McCallum
Producer: Fred Roos
Executive Producer: George Lucas
Music by Joel McNeely
Edited by Paul Trejo
Directed by Mel Smith

PRINCIPAL CAST: Brian Benben (*Roger Henderson*), Mary Stuart Masterson (*Penny Henderson*), Ned Beatty (*General Walt Whalen*), George Burns (*Milt Lackey*), Scott Michael Campbell (*Billy*), Brion James (*Bernie King*), Michael Lerner (*Lieutenant Cross*), Michael McKean (*Rick Rochester*), Jeffrey Tambor (*Walt Whalen Junior*), Stephen Tobolowsky (*Max Applewhite*), Christopher Lloyd (*Zoltan*), Larry Miller (*Herman Katzenback*), Anita Morris (*Claudette Katzenback*), Corbin Bernsen (*Dexter Morris*), Rosemary Clooney (*Anna*), Bobcat Goldthwait (*Wild Writer*), Robert Walden (*Tommy*), Dylan Baker (*Jasper*), Billy

Barty (*Himself*), Tracy Byrd (*Himself*), Candy Clark (*Billy's Mom*), Anne De Salvo (*Female Writer*), Jennifer Dundas (*Deirdre*), Bo Hopkins (*Billy's Father*), Robert Klein (*Father Writer*), Harvey Korman (*Jules Cogley*), Joey Lawrence (*Frankie Marshall*), Peter MacNicol (*Son Writer*), Frank J Aard (*Rollerskating Penguin*)

TAGLINE: At station WBN, the hits just keep on coming!

SUMMARY: At a gala all-night broadcast at radio station WBN, which is both the first night the station has been transmitted nationally *and* an evening during which the station's headquarters are filled with potential sponsors, someone starts killing members of the station's crew. Each murder is prefixed by a riddle read out over the station's airwaves by a cackling maniac. Employees Roger and Penny Henderson try to solve the murders whilst patching their marriage back together – something that becomes more difficult when circumstantial evidence convinces the investigating police officer that Roger himself is responsible. The real murderer, a WBN sound engineer, is tricked into admitting his guilt live on air. His motivation? He invented television and then had his invention suppressed by the radio moguls he's been killing off.

PRODUCTION: *Radioland Murders* was one of the batch of ideas George Lucas had been carrying around studios in the early 1970s. It was part of the presentation that also included *American Graffiti* and an embryonic *Star Wars* and it boasted a draft script by Willard Huyck & Gloria Katz (see **American Graffiti**). As with *Star Wars* Universal Pictures acquired first option on producing it as part of their deal funding *American Graffiti*. After *Graffiti*, *Star Wars* and then its spin-offs and sequels began to dominate Lucas's professional life and *Radioland* was forgotten.

In the early 1990s Lucasfilm was developing Sabre, a real-time CGI imaging system (and a development of Quantel's 'Domino' system) for use in movies and television series. It had already proved its worth on several episodes of *Young Indiana Jones* but a suitable feature vehicle was needed to see if the system could really work at the high resolution necessary for cinematic projection. Lucas dusted off the long-delayed screenplay and took it to Universal. They agreed to finance it (offering a paltry $10 million) provided the film featured recognisable TV stars, who would provide the vital elements of being both recognisable names and affordable within the budget.

To rework the now twenty-year-old script Lucas hired Jeff Reno & Ron Osborn, two of the driving talents behind the genre-shattering Bruce Willis/Cybill Shepherd series *Moonlighting* (1985), who would later go on to work on Aaron Sorkin's TV masterwork *The West Wing* (1999). For a director he went to Mel Smith. A British comedic writer/performer who had come to prominence in satirical sketch show *Not the Nine O'Clock News* (1979–1981), Smith had moved into film directing with the Emma Thompson/Jeff Goldblum-starring *The Tall Guy* (1989), a caustic look at the life of an American actor in London. Since *Radioland* he has directed *Bean* (1997), starring his *Not the Nine O' Clock News* cohort Rowan Atkinson, which was for a while the most successful British movie ever made. Smith's crew consisted of the then standard Lucasfilm repertory, people who were working on *Young Indiana Jones* for the executive producer. This included the editor, the producer, the composer and the director of photography.

The picture was shot in 40 days – which included a lot of blue-screen work – and the crew were encouraged by Lucas to think of *Radioland* as a film which could be 'fixed' in a technical sense in post-production (see **AFTERLIFE**).

CASTING: Brian Benben had starred in *Dream On*, a popular television series about a man so obsessed with film and television culture he's almost incapable of communicating without film references, and sees everything in relation to old movies. Conceptually speaking this makes him the most perfect lead imaginable for a Lucas film, of course.

Mary Stuart Masterson was a minor film, rather than major TV, actress. A former child star, she had then recently appeared in *Fried Green Tomatoes at the Whistlestop Café* (John Avnet, 1991) and *Benny and Joon* (Jeremiah Chechik, 1993). Other members of the almost 100-strong speaking cast included *Back to the Future* and *Taxi* (1978–1981) star Christopher Lloyd, Corbin Bernsen (then one of the leads of *LA Law*) and Peter MacNicol, a popular guest actor then a few years away from his career-defining role as John 'The Biscuit' Cage in *Ally McBeal* (1997–2002). Amongst the acts appearing as part of the radio station's fictitious broadcast were unfeasibly old comedian George Burns, legendary small actor Billy Barty (who had appeared in *Willow*) and singer Rosemary Clooney.

TV and film actress Anita Morris, playing amoral sex bomb Claudette Katzenback, had had a career in similar parts. Between the shooting and release of the picture she lost her long battle against cancer – the finished film is dedicated to her memory.

QUOTES:
Passer-by: 'Catch your head in a threshing machine, *that's* horrible.'

Penny: 'I'm trying to stay on top of things.'
Roger: 'I always liked you on top.'

Bernie King: 'A philosophy professor who murders people by convincing them they don't exist?'
Penny: 'It's satire!'
Bernie King: 'It's crapola!'

MUSICAL NOTES: The background music in *Radioland* mostly consists of period tunes: Irving Berlin's 'What'll I Do' performed by Joey Lawrence, or Lew Brown and Sammy Fain's 'That Old Feeling' sung here by Rosemary Clooney. These in-character renditions, alongside Billy Barty's performance of 'That Old Black Magic' (Harold Arlen/Johnny Mercer), give a suitable period ambience. Other distinctly noticeable tunes utilised include 'In the Mood' as popularized by Glenn Miller and 'Let's Face the Music and Dance', along with a snatch of Nicolai Rimsky-Korsakoff's 'Flight of the Bumblebee'.

RECURRING CONCERNS: Like *American Graffiti* all the action of *Radioland* takes place across one night, and like *Graffiti* it's essentially a Lucas nostalgia piece looking back on an earlier period in his life.

VISUAL INTERESTS: The opening CG matte shot is a brilliant piece of work – the camera pans down from the Universal logo past a radio mast extending into the sky and down to a live-action plate of people milling around outside the radio station.

FORWARDS/BACKWARDS: According to Lucas, Penny and Roger Henderson go on to be the parents of Curt, Andrew and

GEORGE LUCAS Radioland Murders

Laurie (**American Graffiti, More American Graffiti**), making this a prequel of sorts.

EXTERNAL REFERENCES: There are clips from classic radio shows *The Lone Ranger* and *I Love a Mystery* played during the opening shot.

Penny's dress is based on that worn by Katharine Hepburn in the Oscar-winning *Woman of the Year* (George Stevens, 1942).

As well as genuine stars of the period (George Burns, Rosemary Clooney and Billy Barty) there are background characters who seem to be meant to represent contemporary talent such as Gene Autry, Cab Calloway, the Andrews Sisters, Spike Jones (whose estate is thanked on the closing credits), Frank Sinatra and Fred Astaire and Ginger Rogers.

RELEASE: Lucas's name alone was not enough to sell *Radioland*; put out on 21 October 1994 to generally dismal reviews, to date it has taken only $1,299,060, substantially under its budget.

CRITICISM: Whilst conceding that the production was 'bright and flashy' and that the actors' performances were full of energy, the *Chicago Sun-Times*'s respected Roger Ebert felt that the film 'doesn't work. It's all action and no character, all situation and no comedy'. To his mind the pace was partly to blame: 'we don't have an opportunity to . . . care about the characters in a way that would make their actions funny'. For the *San Francisco Chronicle*'s Mick LaSalle, however, the pace was one of the movie's saving graces; it moved at 'a velocity . . . and like it or not it takes you with it'. This wasn't enough, however, to make it 'a particularly good movie', but it wasn't 'a bad one either', albeit with a 'slightly canned, airless feel about it'. *Variety* felt that the film was 'annoyingly shrill' and an 'exercise virtually devoid of romance, suspense or wit', and was convinced that the movie's setting would mean it had 'scant appeal to the MTV generation', even as the pace made it unpalatable to those who could remember the era it was attempting to portray.

Radioland Murders is not a bad film – it's opulent, well played and quite funny, and it more than achieves its technical goals – but it's far from essential viewing for even the keenest moviegoer.

AFTERLIFE: Lucas openly admitted that the film was, in the words of one commentator, a 'testing ground for the grand

experiment of digital filmaking' (see **PRODUCTION**). The huge
lobby, seen in only two sequences, was constructed almost
entirely inside a computer and then dropped into the completed
scenes. Equally experimental was the shooting of some of the
movie on Hi 8 digital videotape, and yet more of it on
three-quarter inch digital video. Computers were used to add
lighting effects, correct continuity errors (such as making sure
there were always blinds across Christopher Lloyd's windows or
putting missing microphones into long shots of the studio
interiors) and adding depth and height to sets. All of these
techniques were intended to be used in Lucas's then planned new
Star Wars trilogy; *Radioland* was a way of getting another
company to underwrite the research costs for Sabre, whilst
actually doing something with a long-gestated idea. Putting the
technology in the service of one of his own stories and then letting
the movie be judged was a far more effective way for Lucas to see
whether or not the technology was up to the tasks ahead of it than
simply shooting endless test footage. That the special effects were
the only aspect of the movie singled out for praise suggests that
whilst *Radioland* achieved its primary objective, it fell some way
short of providing a popular product in the process.

LUCAS ON RADIOLAND MURDERS: 'Soon *Radioland*'s fix-it
shots and digital set extensions and enhancements will be so
commonplace we will not regard them as special effects', declared
Lucas to *American Cinematographer*. Less than a decade later,
when even TV sitcoms and 'realistic' dramas have a small CGI
budget to deal with problems in post-production, he's been
proved absolutely right.

Star Wars: Episode I – The Phantom Menace (1999)

(127 minutes theatrical cut/131 minutes DVD version)

Twentieth Century Fox
Lucasfilm Ltd
Director of Photography: David Tattersall, BSC
Production Designer: Gavin Bouquet

Produced by Rick McCallum
Executive Producer: George Lucas
Music by John Williams
Edited by Ben Burtt, Paul Martin Smith
Written and Directed by George Lucas

PRINCIPAL CAST: Liam Neeson (*Qui-Gon Ginn*), Ewan McGregor (*Obi-Wan Kenobi*), Natalie Portman (*Queen Amidala*), Jake Lloyd (*Anakin Skywalker*), Pernilla August (*Shmi Skywalker*), Ian McDiarmid (*Senator Palpatine*), Oliver Ford Davies (*Sio Bibble*), Hugh Quarshie (*Captain Panaka*), Ahmed Best (*Jar Jar Binks*), Anthony Daniels (*C-3PO*), Kenny Baker (*R2-D2*), Frank Oz (*Yoda*), Terence Stamp (*Chancellor Valorum*), Samuel L. Jackson (*Mace Windu*), Brian Blessed (*Boss Nass*), Andrew Secombe (*Watto*), Ray Park (*Darth Maul*), Peter Serafinowicz (*Darth Maul [voice]*), Lewis Macleod (*Sebulba*), Steven Spiers (*Captain Tarpals*), Silas Carson (*Nute Gunray/Ki-Adi-Mundi/Lott Dodd/Radiant VII pilot*), Ralph Brown (*I/Ric Olié*), Dhruv Chanchani (*Kitster*), John Fensom (*TC-14*), Lindsay Duncan (*TC-14 [voice]*), Keira Knightley (*Handmaiden Sabé*), Sofia Coppola (*Handmaiden Saché*), Toby Longworth (*Senator Lott Dodd*)

TAGLINE: Every generation has a legend. Every journey has a first step. Every story has a beginning.

SUMMARY: A long time ago, in a galaxy far, far away, there existed a vast democratic Republic which covered nearly the entire galaxy. The Republic's ruling body, the senate, has passed a law taxing trade routes to far-off star systems, and in protest the Trade Federation, a sovereign collective of alien traders, has blockaded the distant planet of Naboo. Supreme Chancellor Valorum, the elected head of the senate, has despatched Jedi Knight Qui-Gon Ginn and his apprentice Obi-Wan Kenobi to meet the heads of the Trade Federation aboard one of the Federation's orbiting blockade ships and bring about a settlement.

Unbeknownst to the senate or the Jedi the Trade Federation is in league with a mysterious figure they address as Lord Sidious – who appears to have orchestrated the blockade for reasons of his own. On his orders the Trade Federation invade and occupy the planet Naboo and attempt to kill the two Jedi. The Jedi escape to the surface of the planet, where they encounter an orange, frog-headed alien named Jar Jar Binks who introduces them to his people, the aquatic Gungans. The Gungans assist the two Jedi in getting to the now heavily guarded capital city, where the two Jedi and Jar Jar rescue Queen Amidala of Naboo and – accompanied by much of her palace retinue – escape the planet in a royal spaceship.

The ship is damaged running the blockade, and forced to set down on the planet Tatooine for repairs. Amidala accompanies Qui-Gon, Jar Jar and R2 into the nearby city disguised as one of her own handmaidens (and calling herself Padmé) because she is interested in seeing the culture of this far-off planet. In the city they meet nine-year-old slave boy Anakin Skywalker and his mother, as well as the slaves' owner, the sly but ultimately fair Watto. Unable to use the currency of the Republic to buy parts and labour on such a backward world Qui-Gon indulges in a series of cumulative bets which also result in him winning ownership of the boy whom he then frees. He's motivated to this because he believes that the boy has special powers and should be trained as a Jedi. Anakin sets out to quit the planet with Qui-Gon's party, after bidding a tearful farewell to his mother, who is still a slave.

Before leaving Qui-Gon and Anakin are attacked by Darth Maul, apprentice to Lord Sidious, who has been sent to apprehend them and force the queen to sign a treaty that will legitimise the Trade Federation's occupation of Naboo. Qui-Gon fights Maul off, and his party heads to Coruscant, the capital world of the Republic and seat of the senate. While Amidala makes a plea to the senate for their help in freeing her planet and people, Qui-Gon tells the Jedi Council that he believes the warrior who attacked him was 'well trained in the Jedi arts', possibly 'a Sith Lord', although this is judged by the council to be unlikely as 'the Sith have been extinct for millennia'. Qui-Gon also introduces Anakin to the council and reveals that he believes the boy to be 'the chosen one', the child prophesied as the one who will 'bring balance to the force'. The force is an energy field created by life which can be communicated with by listening to midichlorians, microscopic lifeforms living in symbiosis with humans and other sentient beings which communicate the will of the force. Qui-Gon's belief in Anakin is inspired by his discovery that Anakin's blood contains an unusually high level of midichlorians.

The council turns down Qui-Gon's request that Anakin be trained, despite Jedi Masters Mace Windu and Yoda clearly believing Qui-Gon's claims about Anakin's potential. Rebelliously Qui-Gon declares he will make Anakin his apprentice; but Yoda points out that Qui-Gon already has an apprentice and the code of their order forbids any master having two.

Palpatine, the senator for Naboo, suggests to his queen that given the senate's inability to deal with their world's problems perhaps she should suggest a vote of no confidence in the chancellor; he would probably lose and then a new chancellor would be elected. She does this, and Palpatine himself is nominated to become chancellor; Palpatine subsequently wins this election.

Amidala returns to the still-occupied Naboo with Qui-Gon and Obi-Wan as her protectors and Anakin, R2-D2 and Jar Jar in tow. She goes to the Gungans and asks for help in freeing their world. The Gungans attack the Trade Federation's vast droid army as a diversion whilst a group consisting of the two Jedi, Amidala, Anakin and several palace guards sneak into the city in an attempt to capture the Trade Federation's viceroy. They will then force the Trade Federation to leave their world. Several of the palace guards manage to take fighter ships from the hangar bays and attack the Trade Federation's orbiting battleships.

Qui-Gon and Obi-Wan are attacked by Darth Maul, who kills Qui-Gon before being himself despatched by Obi-Wan Kenobi. With his dying breath Qui-Gon begs Obi-Wan to take Anakin as his own apprentice once he's made a full Jedi himself, and Obi-Wan agrees as Qui-Gon dies in his arms. Amidala's party capture the viceroy, and the fighter flown by the child Anakin Skywalker eventually destroys the ship which controls the Federation's droid armies. The Gungans win their battle by default. Naboo is restored to its own people, and a party consisting of several important Jedi and the newly elected Supreme Chancellor Palpatine arrives on Naboo shortly afterwards. Qui-Gon is cremated and Master Yoda confers on Obi-Wan the rank of Jedi Knight; Yoda reveals that the council have acquiesced to the request that Anakin be trained as a Jedi, but explains that he himself disagreed with the decision.

Mace Windu and Yoda discuss recent events and concur that Maul must have been a Sith Lord. 'Always two there are, a master and an apprentice', Yoda states, leaving Mace Windu to ponder which it was that Obi-Wan killed. Lord Sidious, a presence never revealed to any of the film's heroic characters, goes undetected and unpunished for his role in events.

TRAILER: The first trailer for *Episode I* was released in December 1998, tagged to the front of the second week of existential romantic comedy *Meet Joe Black* (Martin Brest). The three-minute 'teaser' featured numerous shots from *The Phantom Menace*, backed by music from the earlier films. It is emblematic of the near-hysteria surrounding the project that some US cinemas made clear on their exterior billboards which screenings carried the trailer. There were reports on international news television stations such as BBC News 24 and CNN that people paid for entry to *Meet Joe Black* and then left the theatre after the *Star Wars* trailer had finished. While this may sound like hyperbole a large increase in takings between the first and second weeks of *Joe Black*'s business strongly suggests that, at the very least, people were paying to see the film because of the presence of the trailer.

In the UK the trailer was transmitted – well before its UK theatrical premiere – in its entirety, and as a news item, on BBC News 24 – an instance then unique in television history, albeit one since replicated with the trailer for *Harry Potter and the Chamber of Secrets* (Chris Columbus, 2002).

The second trailer, put out early in 1999 on both sides of the Atlantic, saw a *slightly* more muted version of the same extreme reaction.

SCREENPLAY: On 1 November 1994 a divorced father of three took his children to school and then returned home to work in his office. Sitting at his desk George Lucas began what he'd long put off, writing the first draft screenplay for the first of his three projected *Star Wars* prequels. He began by transcribing his various 'backstory' notes, some of them prepared as long ago as 1975, and with a video cassette of *Keystone Cops* movies playing in the background, a man who'd often professed to hating the process of writing scripts threw himself into creating the screenplay for arguably the most eagerly anticipated movie of all time. Pausing occasionally to consult a copy of Julius Caesar's *The Civil Wars* – in his eyes vital research material – he worked in pencil and in longhand on pads of lined paper which were, in a self-consciously myth-making exercise, placed into the same ring binder in which he'd written the screenplays to *American Graffiti* and the original *Star Wars*.

He later explained to a documentary crew that, while had he worked out 'the broad strokes' of the plot of the prequel trilogy decades before (it had been necessary, he claimed, in order to write the script for 1977's *Star Wars*) large amounts of the detail and 'a lot of the subtleties' had not yet been finalised. The success f the *Star Wars* universe had given him the freedom to explore this background material, 'to go back and tell . . . the story of how everybody got there'. He had fifteen pages of notes covering the 30 or so years before the beginning of *Star Wars: Episode IV – A New Hope*, and the next two months saw him involved in the long process of expanding the first five of these pages into a screenplay.

Earlier in 1994 he'd talked to Carrie Fisher – once Princess Leia, and now an award-winning writer – about her contributing script material to the new trilogy ('we have spoken about the possibility of me writing one', she told reporters in May – 'wouldn't that be neat?'). Although she'd written one of best-received episodes of *Young Indiana Jones* it was an opportunity the producer/director/creator chose not to pursue. Lawrence Kasdan, co-writer of *Empire* and *Jedi* as well as the author of *Raiders of the Lost Ark*, had become a writer/director in his own right and no longer wrote screenplays for others to direct; he wouldn't have been interested in returning to Lucas's galaxy far, far away even if he'd been asked. Although proud of his Lucasfilm work, he'd regarded doing the final screenplay for *Jedi* as 'a favour' to Lucas more than ten years previously. So it was that despite his dislike of writing Lucas had decided that the script would be all – or at least primarily – his own work, just as the original *Star Wars* had been.

Lucas completed a first draft by his self-imposed deadline of 13 January 1995. It was given the generic title of *The Beginning* and copies – sometimes of the whole script, sometimes of single scenes – were passed to relevant production people to allow casting, costing and design work to begin in earnest.

CASTING: Five previous *Star Wars* principals were immediately asked back to take part in the first prequel. Anthony Daniels signed on to portray the then freshly built C-3PO across *Episodes I, II* and *III* and Kenny Baker agreed to return to the inside of R2-D2. Ian McDiarmid, cast as the Emperor in *Return of the Jedi*, was asked to return to play the same character as a younger man. Only in his thirties when he played the aged, monstrous Emperor under heavy make-up, the long gap between *Star Wars* movies means that by the time *Episode I* was being shot McDiarmid would be the same age as his character in the new film. McDiarmid was also called upon to play Lord Sidious, Palpatine's dark alter-ego (see **FORWARDS/BACKWARDS**). When interviewed McDiarmid said he saw his character as 'conventional on the outside, demonic inside', and compared him to Shakespeare's Iago in terms of sheer malevolence. In deference to Palpatine's role as the architect of the fall of the Galactic Republic and head of the fascistic Empire already seen in the Imperial trilogy, he described the politician as 'on the edge, he's trying to go beyond what's possible'. The years since *Jedi* had been good to McDiarmid, at the time of casting the toast of the London theatre scene thanks to his assured, innovative stewardship of the Almeida Theatre in London's Angel district.

Frank Oz was again called upon to perform Yoda. Oz had also seen his career move forwards considerably since the last time he had worked for Lucas. Although he'd begun directing films before *Jedi* the late 80s had seen him move from 'creature features' such as *The Dark Crystal* (1982) and into comedy, with films such as *What About Bob?* (1991), *Dirty Rotten Scoundrels* (1988) and *Little Shop of Horrors* (1986) on his CV.

Last of the returning actors was Warwick Davis, who although not returning to the part of Wicket the Ewok plays three roles in the finished movie. He's Anakin's lizard friend on Tatooine, a wild-haired spectator at the pod race and one of the attendants at the final victory parade on Naboo. Davis also stood in for Yoda during scenes in which Frank Oz's puppet was absent or when a computer-generated/assisted Yoda was intended to be added in post-production.

As the prequel's principal new character, Jedi Master Qui-Gon Ginn, Lucas cast Northern Irish actor Liam Neeson, best known for his Academy Award-nominated role in Steven Spielberg's *Schindler's List* (1993). Production and costume design art for Qui-Gon which uses Neeson's features exists dating back as far as 1994, indicating that Lucas was interested in the actor from the very beginning of pre-production. Neeson explained to reporters that he saw his role as being like that of 'Alan Ladd in *Shane*', a previous example of a peculiarly Zen action hero.

Ewan McGregor, cast as Jedi apprentice Obi-Wan Kenobi, was known for committed performances in small-scale British independent films. A hard-working actor who made more than a dozen films in the second half of the 1990s alone, his three collaborations with director and fellow Scot Danny Boyle, *Shallow Grave* (1994), *Trainspotting* (1995) and *A Life Less Ordinary* (1996), saw him cement his reputation as one of Britain's most interesting and versatile young actors; a reputation built from fine work in TV dramas such as Dennis Potter's exceptional *Lipstick on Your Collar* (1993) and a BBC adaptation of Stendhal's *Scarlet and Black* (1992).

Despite having previously declared in interviews that he would rather shoot himself than be in a Hollywood blockbuster like *Independence Day* (Roland Emmerich, 1994), McGregor found himself unable to resist Lucasfilm's overtures and signed up for three films as the younger version of the character previously portrayed by Alec Guinness. As far as McGregor was concerned he hadn't contravened his previous statement'; '*Star Wars* isn't a part of that [Hollywood blockbusters]; it's a fairy tale', he insisted in more than one interview. 'You have the prince, the princess, the jester and the wizard. You have characters that we understand there. The fight of good against evil'. McGregor's uncle, Denis Lawson, who played rebel fighter pilot Wedge in all three of the previous *Star Wars* films, advised the young actor not to accept the role, fearing that his nephew might become typecast and throw away a massively promising career in the process. Nevertheless when offered the part McGregor found it impossible to resist, admitting 'I wanted to be in it because of what it meant to me . . . I saw the first one when I was six – at six I absolutely got it'.

The actor's relationship with the film series that he signed to become an integral part of remains complicated. He has frequently stated that the *Star Wars* series is 'more than just movies' and is on record as saying that being part of *Star Wars* is like 'being part of the Bible', but has also later expressed dissatisfaction with *Episode I* as released. He has been quoted in interviews as saying that making the film was often 'boring' due to the large amount of blue-screen effects work, but has also been known to enthuse wildly about the thrill of wielding a lightsaber and has boasted more than once that 'there's nothing cooler than being a Jedi Knight'. In 2002 he told a Channel 4 interviewer of the excitement he felt looking at himself in the mirror in costume for the first time and exclaiming, 'I'm in fucking *Star Wars*'.

Aside from the strange schoolboy thrill of participating in cinema's biggest ongoing series McGregor had higher motives, which were related to his craft as an actor. He saw portraying a younger Obi-Wan Kenobi as a unique acting challenge. The opportunity to try and emulate an acknowledged great actor performing one of his most famous roles interested him greatly. With both the younger Guinness and Obi-Wan being so well known it was never going to be easy; 'becoming him . . . that was one of the most interesting things about [it]', McGregor told reporters. He saw the process as being to 'try and track back from a guy we know as an older man . . . without doing an impersonation . . . I watched a lot of his old films, but I never met him'.

One critic singled out McGregor's work in the film for particular praise, commenting on the way the actor's 'sometimes uncanny attempt to emulate Alec Guinness transcends simple impersonation. Believably portraying the same man and ever aware of the role's previous incumbent, he nevertheless makes the part his own'.

Israeli-born actress Natalie Portman (a stage name) had come to the public's attention in Luc Besson's controversial *Leon* (1995) in which, aged fourteen, she played a young girl involved in an ambiguous teacher/pupil relationship with Jean Reno's eponymous assassin. Further impressive screen roles followed in Woody Allen's *Everyone Says I Love You* (1996) and Tim Burton's witty and chaotic *Mars Attacks!* (1997). Despite never having seen any of the previous *Star Wars* films, she too signed a three-film contract.

Screen tests for the role of Anakin Skywalker were shot on 8 March 1997, with a skeleton crew of Lucas, McCallum and Tattersall behind the camera. Of the initial three thousand applicants Lucas and McCallum arrived at a short list of three. These hopefuls – all aged between seven and ten – read scenes from the draft screenplay opposite Natalie Portman. Jake Lloyd, whose primary screen experience was as Arnold Schwarzenegger's son in comedy *Jingle All the Way* (Brian Levant, 1996), won the role.

Pernilla August, taking the role of Shmi, Anakin's mother, had previously worked for Lucas on *Young Indiana Jones* (she was formerly the wife of one of that series' directors, Bille August).

On 18 June a selection of the cast consisting of Pernilla August, Ahmed Best, Dhruv Chanchani, Jake Lloyd, Ian McDiarmid, Ewan McGregor, Liam Neeson, Frank Oz, Natalie Portman and Hugh Quarshie attended a first read-through of the entire script along with Lucas and producer Rick McCallum at Skywalker Ranch.

Not present was Samuel L Jackson. Although not at the time attached to *Episode I* Jackson plays Mace Windu in the film, and was cast after appearing on British television offering to play anything from 'Lando Calrissian's grandfather to Luke Skywalker's slave'. Jackson, despite a long career that embraced much stage work and impressive supporting roles in films, had only really come to prominence with Spike Lee's *Jungle Fever* (1991). He had since featured in *Jurassic Park* (Steven Spielberg, 1993), *Die Hard: With a Vengeance* (John McTiernan, 1995), and *Menace II Society* (Allen Hughes, Albert Hughes, 1993), and been nominated for an Oscar for playing Jules, the quipping hit man in Quentin Tarantino's *Pulp Fiction* (1994), a role which gained him cult status. The actor – a huge fan of the *Star Wars* series – was thrilled on receiving his script to discover he had the line 'May the force be with you', and playing a revered Jedi Master. Jackson's enthusiasm caused Lucas to promise him that Windu could have an expanded role in the second film of the prequel trilogy if he wanted.

PRODUCTION: One of the first people to see Lucas's draft was Taiwanese-born director of concept design Doug Chiang, whose job it would be – alongside British production designer Gavin Bouquet – to design what Lucas was creating. Chiang was responsible for the creature and starship designs for the film and chose – in conjunction with Lucas – to blend an Asiatic aesthetic with elements of art deco. The look was decided upon by a simple logical process; Chiang's art style had always featured smooth lines and curves suggestive of Japanese *anime* and the original *Star Wars* often looks, despite attempts to create timeless visuals, distinctly 70s in style. It was intuitive then that something set thirty or so years before the original film should have elements of western pre-war design to it, albeit filtered through Chiang's own primary influences.

When interviewed Chiang explained that he saw the main difference between the worlds of the Imperial trilogy he'd seen as a child and the Republic trilogy it would partially be his job to create as one of 'manufacturing process'. The Empire was industrial, while the Republic would be hand-crafted. Lucas met his design teams every Friday from early 1995 onwards, giving advice and feedback to Chiang and his team and making sure that the world of the first prequel would be exactly as he wanted it. Lucas, as well as writing and directing the film, would be funding its budget – all $100-plus million dollars of it – out of his own personal fortune without any recourse to bank or studio loans. It was to be *his* picture in every last detail; as success or failure it would be his responsibility.

Many of the production crew for Lucas's new episode were inherited from his television project *Young Indiana Jones*. Producer Rick McCallum, production designer Gavin Bouquet and director of photography David Tattersall had all worked on some or all of that epic TV undertaking.

Studio shooting for *The Phantom Menace* began on 16 July 1997 at Leavesden Studios near London, a converted Rolls-Royce factory which had previously been used by Lucas and McCallum on *Young Indiana Jones* and by Eon Productions for the seventeenth James Bond adventure *GoldenEye*. The first scene shot was of Qui-Gon's party being greeted by the Supreme Chancellor of the Republic (Terence Stamp) and Senator Palpatine. Neeson has since claimed that the process was strangely calming, saying that there was '. . . a wonderful ease in doing *Star Wars*', generated by the simple fact that the director was paying for the production: 'nobody [was] breathing down your neck, there was no studio, no producer checking his watch . . .'

By late July much of the first unit had moved to Tunisia in order to film sequences set on the planet Tatooine. On 29 July many of the exterior sets constructed for the film, including the lavishly expensive free-standing podracers (small vehicles with enormous engines attached to them by thin horizontal poles) were torn to pieces in a sandstorm which lasted all night. 'Making of' footage shot that day saw producer McCallum call the disaster 'heartbreaking', but Lucas was seen to be surprisingly upbeat. He recalled a similar incident which occurred at almost exactly the same point during the shooting of *Episode IV* in 1976 (see **Star Wars**) and dubbed the storm 'good luck'.

By September principal photography on *Episode I* had been completed, having included location work in Whippendal Woods, Hertfordshire, and Italy (both standing in for Naboo). Studios used also included Pinewood and Ealing, the latter of which was where pick-ups and reshoots were already scheduled to take place in early 1998. The main task was now to begin the extensive special-effects sequence that would be as integral a part of the film as *Star Wars*' own innovative FX were over 20 years before. The main difference between the techniques used on *Episode IV* (described by Mark Hamill as 'Scotch tape and popsicle sticks') and those used on *Episode I* is the advent of CGI. Computer Generated Imagery had been pioneered by ILM for Lucas's own *Willow* but had been further developed by them for James Cameron's *Terminator 2: Judgment Day* in 1991, and Steven Spielberg's Oscar-winning *Jurassic Park* in 1993. ILM had used CGI when refitting the original trilogy for the Special Edition releases, and intended to make extensive use of it on *Episode I* (see **VISUAL INTERESTS**).

ALTERNATIVE VERSIONS: The version of *The Phantom Menace* released on DVD on 19 November 2001 differs from the cinematic release in a number of small ways. There have been a number of alterations to the CGI special effects; these are too numerous to list in full, but include new shots inserted into the battle for control of the Naboo palace at the end of the film and some new effects added to the space battle above the planet that occurs simultaneously. More noticeable are the additions to the pod race sequence, including an extension to the second lap, featuring much more local colour and whimsy and a much lengthier 'starting line-up' which features an introduction to every single driver participating. There is also an additional short scene on Coruscant of Amidala, Jar Jar and Anakin riding to Senator Palpatine's apartments in an air car.

CUT SCENES: The 2001 DVD of *Episode I* features several cut scenes: a brief character moment on the morning before the pod race where Amidala wakes Anakin up; a lengthy sequence which features Qui-Gon, Obi-Wan and Jar Jar Binks escaping from their Bongo (submarine) before it crashes over a waterfall; Anakin Skywalker fighting with an alien child after winning the pod race; and a short scene of Anakin saying goodbye to market trader Jira before leaving Tatooine for good, which is closely followed by Qui-Gon becoming suspicious about the floating probe droid which is following him and the boy.

Of these the most interesting, and indeed the one that should most obviously have been cut, is that featuring Anakin and the alien child (the race are referred to as 'Rodians' in much *Star Wars* ancillary material, but this is never stated on screen). The child is the same kind of alien as the bounty hunter, Greedo, who is shot dead by Han Solo in the Mos Eisley cantina in *Star Wars*, and this scene confirms that this is the same person: 'You're going to have to watch that temper of yours, Greedo, or you're going to come to a bad end', says another character slyly. Self-indulgent and unfunny, this is a rare, ill-judged off-shoot of Lucas's clear desire to bind the series together with a web of interconnecting references (see **FORWARDS/BACKWARDS**) and its removal is to be applauded.

Three other scenes were added to the DVD edition of the film itself (see **ALTERNATIVE VERSIONS**), increasing its running time by around three minutes.

QUOTES:

Palpatine: 'We are indebted to you, Obi-Wan Kenobi, for your bravery. And to you, young Skywalker – we will follow your career with great interest.'

Qui-Gon: 'Feel, don't think. Your focus determines your reality.'

Qui-Gon: 'There's always a bigger fish.'

Yoda (to Anakin): 'Fear leads to anger, anger leads to hate, hate leads to suffering. I sense much fear in you.'

MUSICAL NOTES: John Williams was not so much the obvious as the only choice to score *Episode I*, and was contacted by Lucas about doing so early in the production process. Williams later described himself as being 'uniquely fortunate' among filmic composers in being able to work on such a wide-ranging, epic project that encompassed so many years of narrative, themes and characters. Although unable to draw on many of the themes he'd created for previous *Star Wars* pictures (such as 'Han Solo and the Princess' or 'Luke and Leia') because the characters represented by them were not present in the new film, he was still able to utilise the themes for the Emperor, the force and (thanks to some cunning re-instrumentation) Darth Vader.

Williams's 'Anakin's Theme', a light, airy piece for woodwind and strings meant to represent Anakin's innocence, is given an undercurrent of sadness by its use of a refrain from 'Imperial March/Darth Vader's Theme'. This means the piece (which finishes in a minor key) serves as a constant reminder of Anakin's destiny and represents Williams's assumption of Lucas's mode of backwards/forwards storytelling (see **FORWARDS/ BACKWARDS**). For an audience beginning at *Episode I*, 'Anakin's Theme' is a lush yet never sentimental piece which they can witness evolving into the bombastic refrain heard in *Episode V* and *Episode VI*. For an audience coming to the beginning after seeing the end, it adds an air of melancholy that would not otherwise be so strongly present.

Among the new music composed by Williams for the film is 'The Duel of the Fates', a huge piece for a full orchestra which features a choir singing in Sanskrit. Used to underscore virtually all of the final battle scene in the movie, the piece was played on several music television channels in the run-up to the film's release, backed by a 'pop video'-style compilation of clips from the movie and behind-the-scenes footage.

Williams's score began recording on 10 February 1999 at EMI Abbey Road Studios, London and was completed within a month.

VISUAL INTERESTS: *The Phantom Menace*'s production design is so eye-popping that at times it borders on the distracting. It doesn't matter how many times a viewer watches it, there are always details in its backgrounds and settings that one has simply not seen before: the flock of unreal birds that lift into an unreal sky as a spaceship lands between unreal trees, or the moment when one of the CG animals 'breathes' onto a camera lens *which isn't actually there* and mists it up. 'If this picture works', commented Lucas at an early production meeting for *Episode I*, 'then everybody else will want [its technical innovations] for *their* picture'. He couldn't have been more right. As mentioned many times in the press during the film's original release, much of *The Phantom Menace* was shot against blue drapes rather than sets; those sets that were constructed were minimal, with only those elements that were strictly necessary for actor comfort and orientation (such as doors) built, and no set was taller than the production's tallest actor (Liam Neeson). Almost everything else was added into the film later using a computer.

Episode I placed actors in real-seeming CG environments for the first time in cinema history. It also placed three-dimensional

CG creatures into real environments with real actors more successfully than even *Jurassic Park* did. Raptors may run, but Watto can hold a conversation with Liam Neeson whilst looking like nothing that's ever existed on Earth. The film makes more extensive use, both obtrusively and unobtrusively, of CGI than any live-action picture made before it, and its techniques have been much imitated since. Critic Roger Ebert commented at the time on the way the picture 'seamlessly integrates real characters and digital ones, real landscapes and imaginary places', and concluded that audiences were standing on the threshold of 'a new age of epic cinema . . . in which digital techniques mean that . . . filmmakers will be able to show us just about anything they can imagine.'

On a scale unprecedented at the time, this technique has already become commonplace. When the *New York Times* predicted in the week of its release that *The Phantom Menace* would beget 'a new generation of computer-generated sci-fi' it was actually understating its point. Compare *The Mummy* (Stephen Sommers, 1999), made roughly contemporaneously to *The Phantom Menace*, with *The Mummy Returns* (Stephen Sommers, 2001), made shortly afterwards. Despite the two *Mummy* films being made by almost exactly the same crew, the former looks like *Raiders of the Lost Ark* and the latter looks like *The Phantom Menace*. Films such as those in the *Harry Potter* series and *The Lord of the Rings* trilogy are noticeably indebted to *The Phantom Menace*, developing its techniques and in some instances, its actual software and hardware for their own purposes (*The Lord of the Rings'* Gollum simply wouldn't be possible without the technology developed to realize Jar Jar Binks). Use of these techniques is moreover not only on the kind of films which audiences expect to be effects-intensive, but also on pictures such as *Shakespeare in Love* (John Madden, 1999), *Gladiator* (Ridley Scott, 2001), *Moulin Rouge* (Baz Luhrmann, 2001), *O Brother, Where Art Thou?* (Ethan Coen, 2001), *Pearl Harbor* (Michael Bay, 2001) and *28 Days Later* (Danny Boyle, 2002). *The Phantom Menace* already borders on being as technically influential a piece of filmmaking as the original *Star Wars*. It's virtually a manifesto for a new way of making movies, and vast swathes of the film business have adopted it wholesale – whether they know it or not.

FORWARDS/BACKWARDS: While it is manifestly untrue that a detailed knowledge of *Star Wars* (1977) and its sequels is needed to appreciate *Episode I*, a detailed understanding of the Imperial trilogy does create a totally different, diametrically opposed reading of the events of the film to that understood by viewers who have not seen the earlier-made/later-set films. Seen in isolation *The Phantom Menace* is a straightforward, albeit lavish, action-adventure movie about a likeable group of characters attempting to repel a planetary invasion. The real villain – identified only as Lord Sidious – escapes and his involvement in events is never revealed to any of the film's heroic characters. While it is strongly implied that Sidious and Palpatine, an ambitious yet genial politician allied to the film's heroes, are one and the same, it nevertheless appears to some audiences that the heroes have won; an impression the sun-drenched, jovially scored, smiling finale goes a long way to support. Ian McDiarmid plays both Sidious and Palpatine, the former uncredited, and as Sidious we never see his whole face (he's permanently wearing a hood); additionally when Sidious gives orders to Maul he is clearly on the balcony of Palpatine's apartments on Coruscant. This scene is set at night, and shot from an angle from which the audience never sees the balcony during the day; although there are a few lingering shots of the balcony from other angles to help less attentive viewers. There are a few other clues, mostly within the subtleties of McDiarmid's performances – such as the sudden coldness in Palpatine's voice and eyes when he says 'they will elect a new chancellor, a strong chancellor'.

However, a greater awareness of the content of Episodes IV – VI alters this perspective drastically. Palpatine and Sidious are indeed the same person. Ian McDiarmid played Palpatine – by then styled 'the Emperor' – in *Episode VI*, dressed as Sidious is in *Episode I*, and the musical underscore (vital in all of the *Star Wars* films to perceptions of characters) used for Palpatine/the Emperor in *Episode VI* is used for Sidious in *Episode I*, clueing in a more informed viewer immediately. This does more, however, than simply confirm that the two characters are one and the same. If Palpatine and Sidious are the same character then Palpatine has contrived the entire invasion of Naboo merely to ensure his elevation to the chancellorship – a stepping-stone to acquiring for himself the as yet unknown title of Emperor. Thus when Amidala and the Jedi repel the Trade Federation's occupation of Naboo they are unknowingly assisting Sidious/Palpatine, who will be less likely to be suspected of having contrived his election to the chancellorship if his tracks are covered by the defeat of the Trade Federation. No wonder Palpatine seems so upbeat as he returns to Naboo at the end of the film. The riotous joy of the celebration at the film's end now seems blackly ironic; the semiotic gap between what the characters think has happened (or how the drama treats what has happened) and what the audience knows has actually happened is vast. *The Phantom Menace*'s plot has two completely different, incompatible, diametrically opposed meanings simultaneously depending on the viewer's familiarity with the Imperial trilogy.

This backwards-and-forwards storytelling is one of *Episode I*'s greatest strengths, and some of the audience's foreknowledge of certain characters' fates allows Lucas to play along with, and occasionally work against, its expectations. A good example is the first meeting of Obi-Wan and Anakin: 'Anakin Skywalker, meet Obi-Wan Kenobi', says Qui-Gon, and the two shake hands smiling; even the least attentive viewer must be aware that the grinning boy will one day murder the Jedi in cold blood.

Equally nasty is Palpatine's assertion that he hopes to bring 'peace and prosperity to the Republic', when anyone who has seen the Imperial trilogy knows what 20 years of his brutal personal rule will do. His comment that he will watch Anakin Skywalker's career 'with great interest' is, when combined with the knowledge that Anakin becomes Darth Vader, and that it will be Palpatine who is responsible for his corruption, quite chilling.

More than this, *Episode I* also contains moments of narrative cleverness – spoken or visual moments that feed back into the pre-existing films and add extra layers to sequences from them. Sometimes it's simply the dramatisation of past events that are remembered by characters in the Imperial trilogy; on other occasions plot points, images or dialogue in *Episode I* seem designed to change the viewer's perceptions of scenes in *Star Wars*, *Empire* or *Jedi*.

A straightforward example of the former technique is the scene in *Jedi* where Obi-Wan tells Luke, 'When I first knew him your father was already a great pilot, but I was amazed how strongly the force was with him'. In *Episode I* we see the events that Kenobi is remembering. Anakin demonstrates that he is a great pilot when he wins the pod race, and again later when he takes part in the dogfight over Naboo, and there's another scene in which Obi-Wan tests Anakin's blood in order to see the midichlorian level of his blood – a scientific test of how strongly the force is with him. McGregor's performance of Kenobi's comment that 'The reading's off the chart!' shows that the character's meant to be amazed.

An example of the second technique concerns one of the most famous lines of dialogue from *The Phantom Menace*: Yoda's assertion to Anakin that 'Fear leads to anger, anger leads to hate, hate leads to suffering. I sense much fear in you'. This relates to the scene in *Empire* in which Yoda becomes angry when Luke claims he is 'not afraid': Yoda's reacting to his memories of Anakin in a film which hasn't been made yet. Another example comes later in *Empire*, as Vader and Luke fight and Vader attempts to convince Luke to turn to the dark side; he tells the young Jedi, 'You have controlled your fear. Now unleash your anger. Only your hatred can destroy me.' He's attempting to push Luke down his own prior path, and again the character is reacting to his own memories of a film which has not yet been scripted or shot.

Furthermore, if you watch the original *Star Wars* having seen *Episode I* it is possible to see that R2-D2 makes his way to the Lars homestead through the ruins of the pod-race ring, and that the ledge on which Luke fights a Tusken Raider is the rock shelf from which the sand people fire at the unsuspecting pod-race contestants in *Episode I*.

In normal drama this would be simple cause and effect – what makes Lucas's version of it clever is that it works *backwards*. Whether Lucas is working to some unfeasibly complicated pre-existing plan, or just skilfully working within the margins of what he has already created, is open to debate. Either he has constructed a generation-spanning epic of enormous complexity and then deliberately made it in the wrong order, seeding the earliest-made latest-set instalments with subtleties that only become noticeable once the earlier-set instalments have been made or, more believably, he's built an internally consistent set of 'prequels' out of the coincidences and ambiguities of his biggest successes. Either option is very clever indeed.

What is especially remarkable is that despite all this meta-narrative activity *The Phantom Menace* functions equally well when watched as either the fourth or first *Star Wars* film, a unique balancing act that Lucas pulls off with aplomb. *The Phantom Menace*'s narrative approach is perhaps unprecedented in mainstream American film.

RELEASE: Asked about the box office potential of *Episode I* before its release Lucas demurred, 'We're never going to beat *Titanic* [then the highest grossing film of all time], it's not possible', and even when assured that the popularity of the series would ensure a vast turnout he seemed unmoved, quoting the abysmal box office failure of *More American Graffiti* as proof that a hugely profitable and beloved film can have a sequel which utterly tanks; 'You can destroy these things,' he insisted during production. 'It is possible.' On 19 May 1999, *Star Wars: Episode I – The Phantom Menace* opened across America. Hardcore fans queued outside Mann's Chinese Theater in Hollywood in order to see *Episode I* at the cinema where *Star Wars* itself had premiered over twenty years earlier, but US time zones meant that the first screenings were actually on the East Coast. Across the country many cinemas opened for special one-minute-past-midnight showings, and some – such as the famous Ziegfeld on 54th St in New York – devoted themselves entirely to screening this one film on a 24-hour schedule. The massive Union Square Cinema (also in New York) devoted four of its ten screens to the picture, resulting in screenings which started at less than hourly intervals 24 hours a day seven days a week. As a consequence the film made $200 million faster than any other picture in history, a record which stood until the release of Sam Raimi's *Spider-Man* (to more than three times as many screens) on 3 May 2002.

CRITICISM: As has often been observed *The Phantom Menace* received some bad notices; what is less often reported is that it received some extremely good ones as well. Critical disdain for summer-released popcorn films, especially those perceived as being part of 'franchises', had swelled in the years that *Star Wars* had been away. However, the not-exactly pro-blockbuster Janet Maslin of the *New York Times* (a critic who had not particularly liked *The Empire Strikes Back* nineteen years before) was unashamedly impressed. She confessed to 'a happy surprise: it's up to snuff. It sustains the gee-whiz spirit of the series and offers a swashbuckling extragalactic getaway'. She continued by expressing further shock that, whilst there are 'film series that grow palpably desperate for inspiration as they age', Lucas's was not one of them. Roger Ebert, writing in the *Chicago Sun-Times*, was sufficiently confident in his appreciation to quietly attack less positive reviewers – he claimed that if *The Phantom Menace* had been the first *Star Wars* film it would 'be hailed as a visionary breakthrough', and went on to chide his fellow professionals for being 'blasé' to the wonders of Lucasfilm. He himself hailed *The Phantom Menace* as 'an astonishing achievement in imaginative filmmaking' and, while acknowledging that the 'flat and awkward dialogue' could have been better, he was also firm in his assertions that 'Lucas tells a good story' and that his new picture 'raised the curtain on new freedom for filmmakers'. Other overwhelmingly positive reviews included those in British movie magazines *Empire* and *Film Review*, whereas that in *Sight and Sound*, bizarrely, spent most of its word count arguing that the Jedi were a sect of Wagnerian Parsifals and that any film involving them was therefore morally dubious by default (that the Jedi are obviously samurai rather than Teutonic templars is something that appeared to have passed the reviewer by).

Other negative reviews such as those in *Newsweek*, the *Los Angeles Times* and *Variety* tended to concentrate on an abstract sense of disappointment, without explaining what it was they had expected to see. Anthony Lane's attack on the film (or more accurately Lucas generally) in the *New Yorker* seemed particularly harsh, especially when he called it 'childishly unknowing and rotten with cynicism'; quite how something could be *both* defies explanation, and the whole point of *Star Wars* is, and always has been, the utter sincerity of its story.

Regardless, the harshest critics of *Episode I* were not professional film reviewers, for the most part – they were *Star Wars* fans. Every year George Lucas left between the release of *Jedi* in 1983 and any follow-up could only increase anticipation. As time moved on, the critical reputation of the first three *Star Wars* films increased, and they began to be seen as one unit, rather than three films. A generation for whom the struggle between Rebel Alliance and Empire was the most important fiction of their childhoods grew up into taxpayers and film critics.

When *Episode I* arrived many were disappointed; some were vitriolic in their anger at how savage the disappointment was. It didn't live up to what they believed *Star Wars* was – but then *nothing* could have lived up to what they believed *Star Wars* was. Faced with this disappointment Lucas's fans lashed out, comparing *Episode I* unfavourably with the three previous films in the series and showering the movie with criticisms that, for the most part, could be equally applied to their beloved original trilogy.

Comparing the achievements and flaws of one film with those of three is critically invalid, but in practice it's very hard not to do – especially when the flaws of those three films have been dulled by repeated viewings and smoothed over by the first (not even the best) of them repeatedly winning polls acclaiming it to be 'The Greatest Movie Ever Made'.

It has been claimed that *The Phantom Menace* is purely a 'children's movie'. It isn't. It *is,* like the original *Star Wars*, a film that children can enjoy, and much like its predecessors, it does contain elements that are targeted at a child audience.

Episode I has Jar Jar, but *Star Wars* itself has a comically prissy android, *Empire* has a constantly giggling Muppet played by the actor who plays Miss Piggy and *Jedi* has an army of Teddy bears. All four films are, to a roughly equal degree, made for children to enjoy. That's why the tie-in merchandise has always included *toys*. And yet, like the other *Star Wars* films, *The Phantom Menace* has intelligence and concerns which set it far apart from actual 'children's movies' such as *The Little Vampire* (Uli Edel, 2000) or virtually any live-action Disney film. It also lacks the outright sentimentality and lazy plotting that often characterise films made solely for children (such as, for example, Lucas's own two Ewok TV movies of the 1980s), and its technical brilliance sets it far apart from other popcorn films.

Another allegation made against *Episode I* is that it leaves what it starts unfinished; a nonsensical criticism of what is unashamedly the first episode of a three-part story, a story that is itself half of a larger sequence of six parts. It is true that See-Threepio is built in *The Phantom Menace* and then has no role in the plot. It is equally true that aspects of the 'mitichlorian' plotline remain unclear at the film's end; but these aspects are clearly left dangling to be dealt with in the remaining instalments of the trilogy.

An analogous example from the original trilogy is that large chunks of *Episode IV* place enormous emphasis on Luke's lightsaber. He is presented with it by Kenobi, and later scenes show him practicing with it, moving towards the day when he will finally carry it into battle; and then in the film's grand finale . . . it lies useless at his side whilst he blows up a space station with a different weapon entirely. Ultimately he gets to use the lightsaber, and in rather spectacular fashion, in *The Empire Strikes Back*.

One of *Episode I*'s greatest strengths – yet also one of the reasons for the vitriolic fan reaction against it – is the film it *isn't*. It isn't the *Star Wars* prequel that the series fans were expecting. It isn't the story of a wise Jedi called Obi-Wan Kenobi who finds an angry young boy called Anakin and trains him to be a Jedi. It's something else. And this is because what they expected is a film that doesn't need to be made, a story that doesn't need telling (in fact much of it happens *off screen* between *Episode I* and *II*, so little does the audience need to see it). *Episode I* throws multiple curveballs at even the most informed audience; Anakin is a pleasant, fairly innocent child; Obi-Wan is himself a young, brash apprentice and a marginal figure. He's not, in *Episode I*, already a Jedi at the height of his powers. It's the small, grunting R2-D2 who works for the royal family, and prissy protocol-obsessed See-Threepio who is handmade on a farm by a slave. The fascistic Empire of the pre-existing films doesn't displace the prelapsarian Republic spoken of by Obi-Wan in *Star Wars*, it *is* the Republic under different leadership. The Republic isn't taken over from the outside, it rots from the *inside* – destroyed by its own corruption, ripped apart by Palpatine, one of its own ruling class.

The Phantom Menace works because of a combination of two seemingly contradictory things: firstly it's as much like the other *Star Wars* films as they are like each other and so, like *The Godfather Part III* (Francis Ford Coppola, 1991), it's for some audiences such a welcome return to a unique cinematic aesthetic that it's simply pleasing to see it. Secondly it is constantly subverting the assumptions of those films. In between the space-borne dogfights, clashes of primitive weapons against superior technology and huge chase sequences, Lucas somehow both aggrandises *and* demystifies his own universe. He strips the force of its pseudo-religious status whilst making Darth Vader overtly messianic. He shows the Republic of which the older characters mourned the passing, and makes it a far from perfect world (Tatooine seems to be in a worse position under the Republic than the Empire). He subtly raises the idea that Ben and Yoda are manipulating Luke in the Imperial trilogy, and even seems to flat-out contradict the later pictures on a couple of occasions. Seems to, that is, until the viewer looks at them, particularly *Star Wars*, afresh and realises that they dovetail with fearful precision. It's only the audience's mistaken assumptions that *The Phantom Menace* disregards, never the other films' own few certainties.

For all its flaws, and despite the level of scrutiny to which it has been subjected, *Episode I* remains a hugely enjoyable film. It's beautifully made and has an exceptionally fine score. It's daring and complex in both its approach to its narrative and its attitude to the hysterically appreciated series of which it is a part, *and* it once again demonstrate Lucas's unparalleled ability to push forward the technical side of film production.

Even in the best of all possible worlds *The Phantom Menace* was never going to be perceived as equalling what the previous instalments had been built up to be; at most it could be a film to equal what the previous three *actually were*, blockbusters with hidden depth and honest intentions, produced with the care and attention to detail of an obsessive master craftsman. In the author's opinion it was. *The Phantom Menace* is one of the most unfairly maligned, quietly sophisticated and important American movies ever made.

TRIVIA: *The Phantom Menace* is, to date, the only film in the *Star Wars* sequence in which nobody gets part of an arm sliced off with a lightsaber.

TITLE TATTLE: Objections were raised by many *Star Wars* fans to the film's subtitle *The Phantom Menace*, with complaints including suggestions that it was 'tacky' or that it made no sense. It *is* tacky, conjuring images of the chapter plays which Lucas took as initial inspiration in exactly the way that *The Empire Strikes Back* does, but it certainly makes sense.

The 'phantom menace' is a number of things. It's Lord Sidious, mostly seen throughout the film in phantom-like holographic form. Less prosaically it refers to the way the heroic characters never know what's actually going on at any point in the film. The 'phantom menace' is the invasion of Naboo, a diversion that one of the film's major characters dies trying to end. It's also arguable that the 'phantom menace' is Vader, a shade of the future, whose shadow hangs over the film's action and whose instantly familiar rasping breathing is heard over the closing credits.

EXPERT WITNESS: 'George knows cameras inside out . . . his knowledge of storytelling is profound . . . the camera is like an

Racism

One of the most persistent charges thrown at *The Phantom Menace* by several commentators during 1999 was of racism. These accusations generally, although not exclusively, concerned the character of Jar Jar Binks, Qui-Gon Ginn's comedy Gungan sidekick, as played by African-American actor Ahmed Best.

Lucas was upset by such accusations, and seemed bewildered, 'How in the world could you take an orange amphibian and say that he's a Jamaican? It's completely absurd!' he countered when asked by the BBC's Kirsty Wark on 13 July 1999. It is certainly true that there's no attempt within the plot of *Episode I* to suggest that the Gungans on Naboo are somehow analogous to black people within American society, and it is *not* true to say that some mythical intrinsically 'black characteristics' are being applied exclusively to this alien race (indeed the other Gungans in the film are played by British actors with received pronunciation accents). The suggestion that Binks – who speaks, like Yoda, in broken English – was in some sense speaking Jamaican patois was also rigorously denied by Lucas: '... those criticisms are made by people who've obviously never met a Jamaican', he commented scathingly.

Some commentators chose to extend the accusation further: they suggested that CGI slaver Watto was an anti-Semitic stereotype and that the Trade Federation Nemodians were caricatures (although reviewers were themselves confused on this issue, some suggesting they were stereotypically Chinese, others that they were an offensive evocation of the perceived Japanese economic 'red menace').

The answer to these suggestions must be that the *Star Wars* universe has always been one populated by archetypes. That's why, for example, the diner visited by Obi Wan in *Attack of the Clones* resembles a slice of 50s Americana or why the principal characters in the original *Star Wars* are essentially a cowboy, a wizard, a virgin and a prince. Archetypal characteristics, both positive and negative, heroic and villainous, which have been the key to storytelling for centuries – but which have on occasions been used to 'define' or demean a particular ethnicity or culture – are scattered across characters of multiple ethnic backgrounds, both human and non-human. The result is that *The Phantom Menace* doesn't unthinkingly regard 'European White' as some sort of ethnic and cultural neutral, but does mean that some of the character traits exhibited by the non-human characters are open to deliberate misinterpretation.

Other characters that could be termed 'racist', if they were to have been played by a black actor, include Anakin (a slave boy rescued by explorers from another, ostensibly more advanced, civilisation) and Obi Wan Kenobi (a younger man bonded to an older, doing his every bidding and constantly addressing him as Master), among others but – unlike with Jar Jar – there's no accidental casting link between Lucas's utilisation of said archetype and previous ones (*The Phantom Menace* also has two noticeable black heroes in Panaka and Mace Windu).

It's inarguable that the heroic Jedi are far more influenced by Japanese culture, both visually and ethically, than the villainous Nemodians are

(Lucasfilm has since identified the accent the principal Nemodian speaks in as Transylvanian, incidentally) and worth noting that much of the animé aesthetic exhibited by the film is the result of the art style of Korean-born designer Doug Chiang. Palpatine, the overarching villain of the entire *Star Wars* series, and the root of all evil, is also a middle-aged, white Englishman. Similar complaints about 'racism' were raised against *Clones* for casting its only 'Latino' actor as a villain – until it was pointed out that actor Temeura Morrison is a Maori from New Zealand.

While it is hard to deny that there are resemblances between Watto and Charles Dickens' Fagin, for example, it is equally true that the character archetype existed before, and independently of, its anti-Semitic application. If the application of it in *Star Wars* to an alien implies to a viewer the connotations of some previous, ideologically motivated, applications then this is hardly Lucas's fault and, in the writer/director's mind, reflected more on 'the people who are making the comments than it does the movie'.

extra appendage. He can just "paint" with it.' Actor Liam Neeson (Qui-Gon Jinn)

'There were a couple of kids [in the cinema] in front of me and watching their emotion reminded me very much of being six when I watched the first one. And it's great. It's a lovely feeling because children are brilliant.' Actor Ewan McGregor (Obi-Wan Kenobi)

LUCAS ON THE PHANTOM MENACE: 'I made this film because I like to make movies [and] I wanted to finish this. I like the whole movie. I've taken some chances in storytelling and the way I put it together and by and large I think I've been successful.'

Star Wars: Episode II – Attack of the Clones (2002)

(142 minutes)

Twentieth Century Fox
A Lucasfilm Production
Screenplay by George Lucas & Jonathan Hales
Story by George Lucas
Director of Photography: David Tattersall, BSC
Production Designer: Gavin Bouquet
Produced by Rick McCallum

Executive Producer: George Lucas
Music by John Williams
Edited by Ben Burtt
Directed by George Lucas

PRINCIPAL CAST: Ewan McGregor (*Obi-Wan Kenobi*), Natalie Portman (*Padmé Amidala*), Hayden Christiansen (*Anakin Skywalker*), Samuel L Jackson (*Mace Windu*), Christopher Lee (*Count Dooku*), Frank Oz (*Yoda*), Ian McDiarmid (*Supreme Chancellor Palpatine*), Anthony Daniels (*C-3PO*), Pernilla August (*Shmi Skywalker*), Temeura Morrison (*Jango Fett*), Jimmy Smits (*Senator Bail Organa*), Jack Thompson (*Cliegg Lars*), Leanna Walsman (*Zam Wesell*), Ahmed Best (*Jar Jar Binks*), Rose Byrne (*Dormé*), Oliver Ford Davies (*Sio Bibble*), Ronald Falk (*Dexter Jettster*), Jay Laga'aia (*Captain Typho*), Andy Secombe (*Watto*), Silas Carson (*Ki-Adi-Mundi/Nute Gunray*), Ayesha Dharker (*Queen Jamillia*), Daniel Logan (*Boba Fett*), Joel Edgerton (*Owen Lars*), Bonnie Marie Piesse (*Beru*), Anthony Phelan (*Lama Su*), Rena Owen (*Taun We*), Kenny Baker (*R2-D2*)

TAGLINE: A Jedi shall not know anger. Nor hatred. Nor love.

SUMMARY: A long time ago, in a galaxy far, far away, the senate is debating the Military Creation Act, a bill that will create for the Republic a standing army of soldiers in addition to the Jedi. Principal among the opposition to the bill is Padmé Amidala, ten years previously the queen of Naboo and now the senator representing her planet. After an assassination attempt on her fails, Supreme Chancellor Palpatine assigns Obi-Wan Kenobi and his apprentice Anakin Skywalker to protect her. Padmé believes that retired Jedi Knight Count Dooku, now an influential politician, is behind the attacks on her. Dooku has become the figurehead and spokesman for a group of several thousand planets which wish to secede from the Republic.

Another attempt is made on the senator's life, and following clues given to him by the dying would-be assassin, Obi-Wan Kenobi makes his way to the planet of Kamino, while Anakin accompanies the senator back to Naboo. Obi-Wan discovers that on Kamino the population are creating a cloned army for the Republic and have been doing so for nearly ten years, despite the senate never authorising such a thing. The basis for their clone

245

army is a bounty hunter called Jango Fett, who is staying on
Kamino with a clone of himself that he is raising as his son –
Boba.

On Naboo, Anakin and Padmé begin to fall in love; but they
agree that they cannot act upon their emotions. Troubled by
dreams of his mother suffering, Anakin flies to Tatooine to see
her, only to be told by her husband and stepson that she has been
kidnapped by Tusken Raiders. He sets out to rescue her, but only
manages to find her moments before she dies. Enraged, he
massacres everyone in the Tusken encampment to which she has
been taken, including the women and children.

Jango attempts to leave Kamino, having worked out that
Obi-Wan is investigating the clone army rather than checking up
on the order for it. Kenobi follows him to the planet Genosys.
Here Obi-Wan discovers Count Dooku raising an army of droids,
and building an alliance to make war; if Palpatine will not let
them leave then they will secede by force. The reason that the
alliance wants Padmé dead is that among their number are
representatives of the Trade Federation (see *The Phantom
Menace*) who want revenge on her.

Obi-Wan sends a message to Coruscant asking for assistance,
which thanks to equipment failure he has to reroute via Anakin's
ship on Tatooine. Obi-Wan is then captured by battle droids sent
by Dooku.

Ignoring the Jedi Council's instructions to remain where they
are, Anakin and Padmé attempt to rescue Obi-Wan but are
themselves captured. As the three of them try to fight their way
out they are rescued by a party of Jedi led by Mace Windu; during
the rescue Jango Fett is killed. Just as the Jedi are on the verge of
being outfought by the sheer number of battle droids Dooku has
at his disposal, Yoda arrives with the clone army in tow. Count
Dooku escapes with the plans for the ultimate weapon – a Death
Star – but war breaks out between the secessionists and the
Republic. It is revealed to the audience, but not the characters,
that Dooku was working for Sidious all along, provoking war for
the chancellor's own purposes – the shoring up of his personal
power.

As the vast clone armies leave Coruscant to fight the war, and
Yoda, Windu and Kenobi ponder on recent events, Anakin and
Amidala marry in secret on Naboo.

TRAILERS: The film's first trailer was released on 9 November 2001 in the US, tagged to the front of Pixar's animated children's comedy *Monsters, Inc.* As with *Episode I* there were contemporary reports of fans paying to see the film solely to watch the trailer. This teaser itself is less than a minute of rain-soaked, dialogue-free clips backed by a discordant drumbeat and Darth Vader's ragged breathing. Three more trailers, subtitled 'Mystery', 'Forbidden Love' and 'Clone War' by Lucasfilm, followed. 'Mystery' was available exclusively via Lucasfilm's *Star Wars* website.

SCREENPLAY: Lucas began writing the screenplay for *Episode II* while *Episode I* was about to be released. Possibly stung by press criticisms of the dialogue of his solo-scripted screenplay for *Episode I*, Lucas chose to collaborate on the script for *Episode II* with British writer Jonathan Hales – author of many of the best episodes of *Young Indiana Jones*, and now carving for himself a career as a mainstream Hollywood screenwriter (indeed in the year of *Clones*' release, Hales would contribute to another of that summer's big movies, *The Scorpion King* [Chuck Russell, 2002]).

CASTING: The most vital piece of casting for *Episode II* was that of Anakin Skywalker (Jake Lloyd being obviously too young to reprise the character in a story set ten years after the events of *The Phantom Menace*). Lucasfilm was reported in the press as having spoken to Ryan Philippe (*Cruel Intentions*, 1999) and *Titanic* (James Cameron, 1997) star Leonardo DiCaprio, but Lucas ultimately chose Hayden Christiansen for the role. A nineteen-year-old Canadian actor with a career in television and commercials going back twelve years, Christiansen signed to appear in both *Episode II* and *Episode III*.

The other three major roles went to much more experienced performers. The septuagenarian Christopher Lee, cast as Count Dooku, remains one of cinema's great icons. The star of pictures as diverse as *Jinnah* (Jamil Dehlavi, 1998), in which he played the title role of Muhammad Ali Jinnah, the founder of Pakistan, and *The Wicker Man* (Robin Hardy, 1973), Lee's career experienced its Nth renaissance at the very end of the twentieth century with roles such as that of wizard Saruman the White in Peter Jackson's *Lord of the Rings* adaptation. Lee is bearded as Dooku, to fulfil Lucas's desire for the count to physically resemble Obi-Wan Kenobi as an older man (i.e. as played by Alec Guinness in *Star Wars*).

Anthony Daniels was very happy working with the series' new principals, calling Lee 'a wonderful storyteller and the most astounding figure of a man . . . physically, vocally, philosophically' and describing Hayden Christiansen as 'such a hero, and (a) terrific, clever actor'.

New Zealand-born Temeura Morrison, cast as Jango Fett, had had an impressive career in his country's own cinema – including an outstanding role in *Once Were Warriors* (Lee Tamahori, 1994) – but remains best known to many audiences for his role in TV soap opera *Shortland Street*.

Two small parts, albeit significant ones in the overall *Star Wars* series, are Owen Lars and Beru Whitesun, Luke's Uncle Owen and Aunt Beru from the original *Star Wars*, as played there by Phil Brown and Shelagh Fraser. To play the parts in *Episode II* young Australian actors Joel Edgerton and Bonnie Marie Piesse were hired.

PRODUCTION: *Clones* was not filmed; it was shot on digital videotape using a new 24-frame High Definition Progressive Scan camera, developed by Sony and fitted with Panavision Lens. Lucas reported happily during production that the new cameras worked flawlessly even in temperatures of 125 degrees Fahrenheit. The system also allows immediate playback (unlike film, where rushes need to be developed) and enables an editor to resize and crop images without losing picture quality.

Principal shooting began 26 June 2000 at Fox Studios, Sydney, Australia where Lucas had decided to shoot because the strong pound had pushed up the cost of making films in Britain. *Clones* used the same stages on which Ewan McGregor had worked while filming *Moulin Rouge* (Baz Luhrmann, 2001). As on *Episode I* most of the sets were only partially constructed, the intention being to add detail with special effects later. Hayden Christiansen estimated on British television that only one set on the whole film featured no blue-screen drapes at all, although he had little time for the suggestion that acting without detailed settings and reacting to objects and characters who weren't there during shooting was unnatural or awkward: 'it's like doing theatre,' he shrugged. Samuel L Jackson, back as Mace Windu, concurred, describing his technique as 'get out there and act like everything's natural'. One setting not constructed full-size at all was the ocean world of Kamino; all the interiors were built as ten scale models and then footage of McGregor acting on a blue-screen stage was added into the models using a computer. McGregor reported himself delighted with his expanded role in *Episode II*, particularly his character's pseudo-Bond detective mission and the opportunity to fly 'my own ship . . . to take off in it on [my] own little adventure'.

Both Christiansen and McGregor later quoted the worst part of the studio shoot as being the day they spent sitting in a prop airspeeder being buffeted from side to side by crew, as Lucas shot their reactions for the lengthy air-car chase early in the film; McGregor in particular found the process made him feel slightly sick.

Much of the cast and crew then moved to Tunisia to begin recording on location for scenes set on Tatooine. For these sequences the interior 'pit' of the Lars home used in *Star Wars* – the Sidi Driss hotel in Matmata – was rehired, and the domed, igloo-like exterior rebuilt. For Anthony Daniels the Tunisia shoot was his first return to the country in which he made See-Threepio his own since 1976. Behind-the-scenes footage of the first day of shooting captures Daniels standing outside the Lars homestead, in exactly the same place where he shot his first scenes as Threepio; the actor looks around and then motions to the director – 'George, I'm getting spine tingles'. Also accomplished during the shoot were some scenes for *Episode III*, although when asked Lucas refuses to be drawn on what they were, merely saying that they were being done with *Episode II* so that he didn't have to return to Tunisia during the shooting of *Episode III*.

After Tunisia, Lucas and his team moved to the Place de Espana in Seville, and the shores of Lake Coma, Spain, where the scenes taking place on Naboo were shot. It was here that Portman's Amidala and Christiansen's Anakin began in earnest what the actress called their 'big *Gone With The Wind* romance', which will eventually produce the Imperial trilogy's hero and heroine, Luke and Leia. Shooting wrapped mid-afternoon on 13 September 2000, a few hours ahead of schedule, and Portman and Christiansen used their unexpected free time to sign autographs for children who had gathered to watch the day's shooting.

The cast and crew reassembled months later at Ealing studios, London, to undertake extra shooting; as with *Episode I* Lucas had built a specified amount of extra time into his schedule both to allow reshoots of material he was unhappy with and to incorporate ideas which had arisen since the original recording concluded. Speaking about the Ealing material on the internet he described it as 'a chase, a fight, another chase, another fight, and three lines of dialogue'.

ALTERNATIVE VERSIONS: The version of *Clones* released in the UK was cut by one second to ensure a PG rating (a '12' was available but judged unacceptable by Lucasfilm). The missing footage is a headbutt during the fight between Obi-Wan and Jango Fett on Kamino. Headbutts are very much the *bête noire* of the contemporary BBFC (much as the board spent the 1980s obsessing over nunchakas) and have been needlessly removed from, among other things, the James Bond thriller *Goldeneye* (Martin Campbell, 1995).

In one of the trailers for the film, Yoda says 'Begun, this clone war has', but in the film as released he says, 'Begun, the clone war has'.

The version of *Clones* released on DVD differs in some small ways from the theatrical version. In the theatrical release the scene in the Lars homestead where Anakin confesses his slaughter of the Tuskens ends after Anakin breaks down and slumps to the floor (1 hr 24 minutes in). On the DVD the scene continues with Padmé stating, 'To be angry is to be human', and a tearful Anakin responding, 'I'm a Jedi. I know I'm better than this'. Additionally after Padmé falls from the gunship she replies to the clone trooper's question 'Are you all right?' with a pained groan and a nod, instead of the comically brisk 'Yes' of the cinema version.

There are, of course, two cinema versions of *Clones*: the purely digital one distributed to digital cinemas, and the one copied onto 35mm film prints shown in less advanced theatres. While the two versions are, technically speaking, totally different, there are a small number of editing differences too. One of the most noticeable is that in the digital edition, the film's final scene on Naboo features a close-up of Padmé taking Anakin's cybernetic hand in hers before she kisses him. The version shown from film prints features a slow pan up from Anakin's hand, which Padmé does not place in her own before kissing him.

Clones became the first *Star Wars* film to be reformatted and then rereleased for IMAX screens; released on 1 November 2002 this version is eight storeys high, and has over 12,000 watts of uncompressed sound. More than anything this version vindicates

Lucas's belief in the urgency and primacy of almost purely visual cinema.

CUT SCENES: A scene where Anakin and Padmé pay a visit to her family home was one of several sequences shot but not included in the released edit. The sequences featured Padmé's mother (Trisha Noble), father (Graeme Blundell) and sister (Claudia Karvan). This scene is included on the DVD edition, though not in the main part of the film.

Anthony Daniels has revealed that he did shoot scenes using the See-Threepio wire-frame puppet used in *Episode I*, but that these were cut. One of these appears to have been an additional scene with Shmi Skywalker (occurring before her capture by sand people) and another with Padmé and Threepio; the latter takes place while Anakin is looking for his mother in the Jundland wastes. In this Padmé removes the droid's battered metal coverings and cleans his endoskeleton, a mindless task she performs to take her mind off worrying about young Skywalker. These scenes have never been released.

QUOTES:
Obi-Wan (to Anakin): 'Why do I get the feeling you're going to be the death of me?'

Padmé: 'You're not all-powerful.'
Anakin: 'I should be. Someday I will be the most powerful Jedi ever.'

Anakin: 'We went into aggressive negotiations . . .'
Padmé: 'Aggressive negotiations? What's that?'
Anakin: 'Well, negotiations . . . with a lightsaber.'

Yoda: 'Lost a planet Master Obi-Wan has. How embarrassing. How embarrassing.'

Palpatine: 'I love democracy. I love the Republic. The power you give me I will lay down once this crisis has abated.'

Dooku: 'As you see my Jedi powers are far beyond yours; now back down.'
Obi-Wan: 'I don't think so.'

MUSICAL NOTES: Chronologically the first point in the series in which we hear the fully-fledged 'Imperial March/Darth Vader's

Theme' is at 1 hr 24 minutes into this film, as Anakin confesses to Padmé that in his rage he murdered all of the Tusken raiders he could find. The theme is later used to score the scene in which the army of clone troopers leaves Coruscant to go and fight the war; the music was also used to represent this same army when seen in *The Empire Strikes Back*.

One of Williams's new themes, 'Across The Stars', which is used to underscore the romance between Anakin and Amidala, is musically related to 'Han Solo and The Princess', the love theme from *The Empire Strikes Back*. Featuring similar musical leaps between notes and similar instrumentation, it is clearly meant to remind those who have already seen *Empire* of Williams's previous romantic theme. A major difference between the two themes, however, is that 'Across the Stars' is always in a minor key, creating an underlying air of melancholy to the romance which is, as any viewer of the Imperial trilogy must know, a doomed love.

Williams wrote fewer new themes for *Clones* than for any of the other *Star Wars* films, but in all fairness he already has many relevant ones to play with. One of the new tunes is an unsettling underscore meant to emphasise unease; most noticeably used when the audience first sees the ocean on Kamino, it also features under many of Yoda and Mace Windu's more worried conversations and – sped up – provides the Bernard Hermann-style sting as Anakin looks up from his mother's corpse before massacring the sand people.

RECURRING CONCERNS: Lucas always maintained that the Emperor Palpatine was in a sense based on disgraced US President Richard Milhouse Nixon (20 January 1969–9 August 1974), the first holder of the office to be forced to resign. Bearing this in mind the Clone War can be said to be the Republic's Vietnam. This is certainly how critic Tom Paulin saw it, calling the film 'a treatise on the death of the American republic' and 'a masterpiece' on British television's *Newsnight Review*. In this context it is tempting to see the battle of Genosys as Lucas's attempt to get more of his vision for *Apocalypse Now* on screen (see **More American Graffiti**).

One of the film's most impressive, and most misunderstood, aspects is the relationship between Padmé and Anakin. Those who attack it as a stereotypical romance seem unaware that this is what it is meant to be. Deliberately shot like scenes from a film by

Golden Age Hollywood romance maestro Douglas Sirk, the traditional representation of 'romance' is there to underscore and parody the simple fact that the two characters aren't falling in love at all. Padmé loves Anakin, but while he clearly desires her in a way he doesn't understand (she's a substitute mother, lover, friend, all the things the Jedi order won't let him have) he doesn't *love* her. The whole point of the much-criticised scene by the fire is not that he is falling in love with her, but rather that he's failing to articulate the simple fact that he wants to have sex with her. When she asks him if he could 'live a lie' he denies it, but the way Christiansen plays the reply can leave no doubt that he easily could, and that he's telling her what he knows she wants to hear.

One of the most important scenes in the film is when Padmé tells Anakin that she loves him on Genosys. His reply? 'You love me?' Compare this with the reciprocated, twice-repeated 'I love you' – 'I know' of the Imperial trilogy's Han and Leia. Anakin even then goes on to mock Padmé for her declaration of love, demanding to know how she has changed her mind so quickly and asking contemptuously, 'I thought we had decided not to fall in love?' He never tells her he loves her, but just lets her insist she loves him over and over again.

Just as *The Phantom Menace* goes about its story in an unexpected way, *Clones* confounds expectations by not really being a love story at all. Just as importantly its characterisation of Anakin is another very deliberate subversion. Suddenly the prequel trilogy is not, as *Return of the Jedi* strongly implies, the story of a good man going bad – it's the story of how an angry, troubled adolescent finally lost his self-control.

VISUAL INTERESTS: When Anakin awakens from his nightmare on Naboo and meditates on the balcony at dawn, a ying and yang symbol-shaped cloud is visible in the sunrise.

When Amidala's ship arrives on Coruscant at the film's opening, the city is under both a literal cloud as well as the metaphorical one caused by the political turmoil.

Due to the hairstyle given to Hayden Christiansen, his height and the style of his Jedi robes (plus some occasional CG trickery), Anakin often casts Darth Vader's shadow. A good example is when Anakin talks to Padmé just before he goes to search for his mother.

The final shot of Padmé and Anakin looking out on the lake in Naboo with R2-D2 and C-3PO to their right is evocative of (although in no sense an duplicate of) the final shot of *The Empire Strikes Back*. Equally, the shot of Padmé and some clone troopers firing at Dooku's fleeing speeder is clearly designed to remind the audience of Leia firing at *Slave-1* as it escapes Bespin, also in *Empire*.

The chancellor's blue-robed guards (as seen in *The Phantom Menace*) have here been replaced by red-robed, face-masked guards exactly like those protecting the Emperor in *Return of the Jedi*, a subtle indication of how Palpatine is building up his personal power. In a similar vein, the chancellor's chair in his office is the same shape and design as the Emperor's throne in *Jedi*.

When Obi-Wan and Anakin enter the bar on Coruscant several actors who elsewhere play characters achieved with make-up, masks and/or CGI can be seen in the crowd without make-up, including Anthony Daniels (C-3PO) and Ahmed Best (Jar Jar Binks); also present is Lucas's younger daughter Katie, playing a blue-skinned alien woman.

The scene of the clone army embarking on board the prototype Star Destroyers right at the end features more than a million men in a single shot, although none of them ever existed outside the special-effects computers at ILM.

Anakin has most of his right arm cut off by Count Dooku; and it is replaced by a mechanical prosthetic – it is this prosthetic hand that Luke Skywalker cuts off in *Jedi*, the action that causes Luke to halt his attack on his injured father.

When in the Jedi archive on Coruscant (33 minutes), Obi-Wan takes a moment to look sadly at a statue of the late Qui-Gon Ginn (see *The Phantom Menace*).

The lightsaber fight between Dooku and Anakin sees Lucas playing a little more with the kind of filmic abstraction he had delighted in pre-*THX-1138*, with the only light in the scene coming from the lightsabers wielded by the two men, causing blue and red patterns to pass over their faces as they duel. Actors Hayden Christiansen and Christopher Lee were recorded using neon tubes as weapons instead of the prop lightsabers normally utilised, casting the light onto their faces during shooting.

Jango Fett's ship *Slave-1*, previously seen in *Empire*, is hinted in *Clones* to be the product of Kaminoan civilisation; almost all of Kamino's technology, and indeed buildings shown during Obi-Wan's visit to the world, shares design features (such as multiple curved lines and low hanging protrusions) with the ship. Conceptual designer Doug Chiang extrapolated the Kamino technology from the twenty-year old design for *Slave-1* just to achieve this desired effect.

One thing that *Episode I* suggests and *Clones* confirms is the aesthetic shift between Republic and Empire: the Imperial trilogy's designs often rely on straight lines and muted colours and a large amount of black and white, while the Republic as represented in *The Phantom Menace* is a riot of strong, warm colours and ostentatious design. The world seen in *Clones* is a compromise between the two extremes, indicating a shift from one to the other that is indicative not only of the change in a society's aesthetics over time, but also the slow debasement of its culture. The Republic is presented as essentially prelapsarian in *The Phantom Menace*, and *Clones* sees it becoming more like the oppressive autocracy seen in the Imperial trilogy.

This is also seen in the way *Clones* takes us into murky and tacky areas of Coruscant (such as the lower area, full of bars and gamblers) which aren't even hinted at as being part of the beautiful city we are introduced to in *The Phantom Menace*.

It is also worth noting that the increased tonal, metaphorical darkness of *Clones* as compared to *Episode I* is matched by an increased aesthetic darkness. This film has more scenes at night, dirtier colours, more battered technology and is often illuminated with harsh neon lighting. The first film has the permanently sunny skies of midday, yet by *Episode II* even Naboo is covered in shadows (and appears to have become industrialised inside a decade) while Tatooine is blood-orange for much of the time.

Another aspect of this is that in *Clones*, unlike in *The Phantom Menace*, people bleed, and even adults cry when hurt or upset. The film echoes Anakin Skywalker's adolescence as much as *Episode I* consciously absorbs his childish innocence and works that into its atmosphere.

FORWARDS/BACKWARDS: It is notable that after more than twenty years of fan speculation that Luke's Uncle Owen as seen in *Star Wars* cannot possibly be Anakin Skywalker's brother, *Clones* reveals Owen to be simply Anakin's adoptive brother.

When Anakin and Padmé's ship lands on Naboo, ships of the same type as the *Millennium Falcon* can be seen on the landing platform.

Yoda is seen training pre-teen Jedi padewan learners, who are
using the same kind of masked helmets and floating target balls
Obi-Wan used to teach Luke in *Star Wars*. Yoda's role in training
the youngest Jedi answers what some *Star Wars* fans held to be a
continuity error. In *The Empire Strikes Back*, Obi-Wan says that
Yoda trained him. In *The Phantom Menace* Obi-Wan's master is
Qui-Gonn Jinn, but *Clones* makes it clear that Yoda has a role in
training all Jedi.

In one of the production's best and subtlest jokes Jango Fett
bumps his head on the underside of a closing door as he's
boarding *Slave-1*. In *Star Wars* a stormtrooper (all of whom are
revealed in this film to be clones of Fett) bumps his head on a door
in the Death Star in the same manner, one of the original film's
most noted 'bloopers'.

C-3PO's line (ad-libbed by Anthony Daniels) 'It seems that he is
carrying a message from an Obi-Wan Kenobi. Master Ani, does
that name mean anything to you?' is meant to resonate with the
robot's line 'He says he is the property of Obi-Wan Kenobi, and it is
a private message for him' from *Star Wars*. Daniels has also stated
in interviews that he saw Threepio's line about Anakin 'returning'
to be a deliberate foreshadowing of the end of *Return of the Jedi*.

The grave of Shmi Skywalker, buried outside the Lars home in
this film, is – astonishingly – visible in *Star Wars*.

The fate of young Boba Fett, last seen cradling his father's
discarded headgear after Jango's death at Mace Windu's hands, is
revealed in *Star Wars*, *Empire* and *Jedi*.

Anakin advises the clone troopers on where to aim their
weapons to cause maximum damage to the Trade Federation's
vehicles – he is able to do this because of his experiences inside the
droid control ship in *The Phantom Menace*.

Count Dooku demonstrates the same ability to expel painful
electrical energy from his fingers as the Emperor himself does in
Episode VI – an early hint to viewers that Dooku has fallen to the
dark side himself.

The emblem of the Imperial Starfleet used in *The Imperial
Trilogy* is seen on the Jedi starfighter flown by Obi-Wan Kenobi
in this film.

It has been suggested that Owen Lars's failure to recognize
See-Threepio in *Episode IV* despite him having owned the droid
previously is a continuity error. It is worth pointing out that all
five *Star Wars* films demonstrate that a large number of protocol

droids are built to exactly the same design as Threepio; the droid Owen buys in *Star Wars* is a different colour to the one he gives away in *Clones*, and at no point in *Star Wars* does Threepio tell Owen his name/number. Lucas has also publicly stated that Threepio has his memory wiped at some point before the events of *Episode IV*.

It is also interesting that while Palpatine/Sidious operates in the same way in *Episode II* as in *The Phantom Menace* (working within in the system and getting the film's heroes unwittingly to do his dirty work for him) his plan this time around ensures that whatever the outcome of the battle on Genosys, he still has an army at his disposal: a clone army if one side triumphs, an advanced droid army if the other succeeds.

It is also Palpatine who assigns Obi-Wan and Anakin to protect Amidala, presumably because he is aware that the emotional turmoil of being brought back into contact with Padmé is one of the triggers likely to assist in pushing Anakin towards the dark side of the force.

Just as there are many similarities between *Star Wars* and *The Phantom Menace*, there are equally numerous points of correlation between *Clones* and *Empire*. Both feature a romance strongly in their middle section (see **MUSICAL NOTES**), both feature a young Jedi losing his right hand in battle with a Sith Lord, both concern that Jedi confronting the dark side of the force after being traumatised by a revelation concerning a parent, both end with very similar shots (see **VISUAL INTERESTS**) and both have notably downbeat endings – especially when compared to their immediate predecessors. It is also tempting to see Count Dooku tempting Obi-Wan as a deliberate echo of Vader tempting Luke; all this is in line with Lucas's declared desire for drama which 'rhymes' and his uniquely symphonic approach to dramatic structure (see *The Phantom Menace*). It goes without saying that the line 'I have a bad feeling about this' occurs in this film too (Anakin says it as he's tied up in the arena on Genosys).

EXTERNAL REFERENCES: Anakin's speeder looks more than a little like Paul Le Mat's car from *American Graffiti*.

Padmé running over the hill in the lake country on Naboo is a straight lift of a shot from *The Sound of Music* (Robert Wise, 1965), and similarly during the arena sequence there are visual references to the famous fight with a giant crab from Ray Harryhausen's *The Seventh Voyage of Sinbad* (1958).

Jango Fett is named after the exceptionally violent spaghetti western *Django, Kill!* (Giulio Questi, 1967). Jango spins his pistol around his trigger finger, an action from several classic westerns which is also referenced in *RoboCop* (Paul Verhoeven, 1987).

Palpatine utters, on accepting special powers, words similar to those traditionally ascribed to Octavius Caesar when he accepted the title/name Augustus and became, in effect, the first emperor of Rome.

In the bar on Coruscant it looks very much like the LucasArts videogame *Star Wars: Episode 1 – Pod Racer* running on the left hand of the viewscreen.

There is a reference to Padmé being unable to serve more than two terms as elected queen of Naboo, an obvious gesture to the fifteenth amendment to the US constitution, which prevents a president from serving more than two terms of elected office. Lucas is also clearly thinking of the US as well as Galactic senate when Obi-Wan scathingly comments that senators tend to worry only about pleasing those who fund their campaigns: 'Not another lecture . . . on the economics of politics,' complains Anakin.

In one of the clearest examples of pop culture eating itself, Steven Spielberg's *Minority Report*, which was released a few months after *Clones* and worked on by some of the same special-effects people, has a conveyer belt-set action sequence which is partially a parody of the one in *Clones*. John Williams's music for *Minority Report* even very briefly reprises a phrase from his *Clones* score at one moment during it.

RELEASE: *Episode II* was released worldwide at midnight on 16 May 2002 in several countries including the USA and Britain. Midnight screenings were held in both countries and due to the vagaries of international time zones fans in Britain saw it before their American counterparts. Doors opened at the Leicester Square Odeon at 11.30 p.m. on 15 May, and anxious fans were entertained before the film by Anthony Daniels, who drolly mixed the roles of MC and stand-up comedian. He was supported in his endeavours by producer McCallum, who had remained in London following the previous day's charity gala premiere at the same theatre. 'Two words,' he told the crowd when asked to describe the atmosphere – 'fucking awesome.' In the US *Clones* took $30 million in the US on its opening day and $80 million across the following three-day weekend, giving it a four-day US total of

$110.2 million, the third biggest opening for a movie ever. Over its second weekend the movie took a further $47.8 million, and another $21 million across its third. In the US this made it the second biggest film of the summer, just behind *Spider-Man* (Sam Raimi, 2002). Thanks to its simultaneous worldwide release, however, *Attack of the Clones*' worldwide opening day gross of $97 million was easily the highest in cinema history.

CRITICISM: Reviews for *Attack of the Clones* were generally not very positive. The film was regarded by most commentators as an effective if slightly hamfisted blockbuster which many reviewers compared unfavourably with Peter Jackson's *The Fellowship of the Ring*, released the previous December. An admirable summary of the reviews was given in the *Sunday Telegraph* where a journalist interviewing Lucas told her readers that most critics agreed that 'The dialogue is dire [and] the acting half-hearted but the visuals are stunning'. In the same piece Lucas reiterated his utter lack of interest in reviews, insisting he made the films he wanted to make and that he didn't care if a film failed critically or financially as long as he got to make the film he wanted to. On *Clones* more than any other film of his career, Lucas's oft-repeated assertion that journalists write only to agree with one another seemed reflected in the unanimity of their verdicts.

In the *Chicago-Sun Times*, Roger Ebert, who has been far kinder than most to *The Phantom Menace*, wasn't happy. He complained that the characters talked 'more like lawyers than the heroes of a romantic fantasy' and called the film as a whole 'a technological exercise that lacks juice and delight', commenting pithily, 'the title is more appropriate than it should be'. Of some interest was Ebert's dissection of the movie's visuals, which he found to lack the urgency and immediacy that he expected from them having seen *The Phantom Menace*. He eventually concluded that it was the fault of the film transfer the digitally-shot film had gone through to be projected in ordinary theatres. Despite his disappointment he claimed to be anxiously looking forward to the DVD of the film.

In the *Guardian* the dialogue was again attacked ('clunky') and the acting pilloried (Natalie Portman was 'a fully formed flower of bad acting', and Hayden Christiansen like 'a wussy twelve-year-old girl'). Equally the visuals were again praised ('On this front, *Episode II* delivers in a very big way') and there was some praise for Lucas, 'whose attempt at complexity and ambiguity is engaging, even admirable'.

The *Los Angeles Times* praised the 'truly involving' visuals and the 'well done' action sequences, but labelled the dialogue 'pious' and 'flat' and the acting 'uniformly impassive'.

The cast of *Clones* has been much criticised. For this writer Hayden Christiansen works very hard with an exceptionally difficult role and achieves much, while Ewan McGregor appears to be enjoying himself tremendously, Obi-Wan indulging in sly looks and facial comedy of a kind not present in *The Phantom Menace*. Christopher Lee, Anthony Daniels and Frank Oz are all superb. There is something to be said for the argument (also applicable to *The Phantom Menace*) that a lot of the reason for dissatisfaction with the performances comes from the immense visual scale and invention. The actors *are* dwarfed by the production, not because their performances are lacking but because the environments they are standing in are so distracting. Further viewings of both films (of the kind necessary when writing a book like this) allow for greater appreciation of some of subtleties of performance on display.

The most interesting thing about *Clones* is that it is the first *Star Wars* film visibly made by the same George Lucas who made non-linear films in the 1960s and who shot *THX-1138*. It has a continually shifting visual style, something accompanied by frequent, almost Pythonesque, shifts in tone. It is often palpably absurd, yet just when it is about to wink at the audience, it runs off and creates moments of utter sincerity. While Lucas's films often mix the sweetly sentimental with mild horror, *Clones*, with its strange combination of slapstick and sadism, political melodrama and romantic comedy, resembles more than ever the work of Lucas's idol Akira Kurosawa. There is no sense in which this cannot be taken as a massive compliment.

TRIVIA: Lucas turned down approaches from fast-food companies for tie-ins to the picture. Some reports cited the precedent of Warner Bros' 1992 *Batman Returns*, where McDonalds pulled their sponsorship from Tim Burton's film after children were carried out of a preview screening crying. He also suggested in interviews that he felt the media blitz around *The Phantom Menace*, although largely not of his doing, had got far too large.

EXPERT WITNESS: '[Threepio] is the same suit as it was nineteen years ago in *Return of the Jedi* . . . I had to lose 10 lb in weight and build up my strength in the gym every morning. When filming . . . I was usually in the gym by 5.30 a.m. . . . you have to be fit to do this kind of work.' Actor Anthony Daniels (See-Threepio)

'The story and the characters are almost in the public domain . . . I was playing a character who was already defined by other films. It's almost like playing a real person.' Actor Hayden Christiansen (Anakin Skywalker)

'I think a lot of the questions about good and evil speak to people in a country [America] that's increasingly split between no religion and fundamentalist theory.' Actor Natalie Portman (Padmé Amidala)

LUCAS ON ATTACK OF THE CLONES: 'It's what I was always aspiring to but never quite got there . . . anything I can imagine I can do.'

Star Wars: Episode III (2005)

20th Century Fox
A Lucasfilm Ltd Production
Screenplay by George Lucas & Jonathan Hales
Story by George Lucas
Production Designer: Gavin Bouquet
Produced by Rick McCallum
Executive Producer: George Lucas
Music by John Williams
Directed by George Lucas

CONFIRMED CAST: Ewan McGregor (*Obi-Wan [Ben] Kenobi*), Natalie Portman (*Padmé Amidala Skywalker*), Hayden Christiansen (*Anakin Skywalker/Darth Vader*), James Earl Jones (*Voice of Darth Vader*), Samuel L Jackson (*Mace Windu*), Frank Oz (*Yoda*), Anthony Daniels (*See-Threepio [C-3PO]*), Kenny Baker (*Artoo-Detoo [R2-D2]*), Jimmy Smits (*Bail Organa*)

SUMMARY: The Clone Wars are fought. During them Obi-Wan Kenobi achieves the rank of general and serves under Bail Organa, senator for the planet Alderaan; Supreme Chancellor Palpatine is declared Emperor; Anakin Skywalker is seduced by the dark side of the force and becomes the Sith Lord Darth Vader. At the Emperor's instruction, he hunts down and destroys the Jedi Knights one by one.

A small group of Anakin's friends – including Obi-Wan Kenobi – conspire to hide his pregnant wife and unborn children from him, fearful of what may happen to them. Obi-Wan is forced to abandon even his name, becoming known as 'Ben'.

Ben believes that there is still good in Vader, and that his former pupil can be redeemed. He appeals to him, but instead master and pupil fight a desperate duel, during which Vader is hideously injured but somehow survives; surgery saves his life but he becomes more machine than man. Ben hides on Tatooine keeping watch on Vader's son, Luke, left with Anakin's stepbrother Owen Lars. Padmé and her daughter Leia go to Alderaan under the protection of Bail Organa. Leia is said to be Organa's child. Yoda begins his exile on Dagobah. The Republic becomes the Empire and a quarter-century rule of terror and tyranny begins.

The embattled survivors wait for a new hope.

PRODUCTION: Lucas and Jonathan Hales plan to have completed the shooting draft of the screenplay by the end of 2002, with set construction expected to begin in Spring 2003. At time of writing the movie is still expected to be shot at Fox studios, Australia, although rising costs combined with the sheer number of leaks on set have prompted press suggestions that a return to England is in order for the final *Star Wars* film.

Shooting, again on digital videotape, should begin in June 2003, mostly second-unit shooting on location and not involving the principal actors. Locations Lucasfilm have publicly talked about using include the Czech Republic and/or Scotland. If a final return to the planet Naboo is deemed necessary by Lucas, more shooting will be undertaken in Italy. There is no need to return to Tunisia since scenes set near the Lars homestead for *Episode III* were shot as part of *Episode II*. This does not mean that there will be no new Tatooine sequences shot, however; the scenes set around Jabba's palace in *Return of the Jedi* were shot in Yuma, Arizona, and a return to the Hutt's domain would necessitate a return to Arizona rather than Tunisia for Lucas and his team.

Pick-up shooting will be done for a few days between June and November 2004 depending on scheduling. Two trailers will be produced: one in Autumn 2004, the other in early 2005.

FORWARDS/BACKWARDS: A plot strand that will need much explanation in *Episode III* is that of 'the prophecy of one who will bring balance to the force' – this is explicitly Anakin, although the manner in which he will do this (and indeed when he will do it) is more of a mystery. An intriguing possibility is that the 'balance' the prophecy speaks of is the extermination of the Jedi. This would certainly explain Mace Windu and Yoda's constant worrying over Anakin. While they know that he is 'the chosen one' they also know that what he has been chosen to do is to their detriment. What is certain is that in the Republic trilogy, the force is somehow out of balance. In *Clones* Mace Windu speaks of how the Jedi's ability to utilise the force has diminished in recent years, and this too may be relevant. It is possible that the reason that the force is out of balance is that there are thousands of Jedi and only two Sith – perhaps the Jedi and the Sith are meant (like much in the *Star Wars* story) to live in balance, and the Jedi's dominance is what needs correcting. It is also possible that the Jedi did the Sith a great wrong at some distant time in the past. The Jedi appear convinced that the Sith have been 'extinct for millennia' and in *The Phantom Menace* Darth Maul speaks of 'revenge' on the Jedi. Were the Jedi in some sense responsible for the extermination of the Sith? Is the secret of the Republic that it is the paradise built on the corpses of its enemies, and that retribution is eventually inevitable?

If this is applied to the Imperial trilogy, a lot of circumstantial supporting evidence can seen. At the time of *Star Wars* there are only two Jedi (Kenobi/Yoda) and two Sith (Vader/the Emperor). When Kenobi is killed, Luke seems to inherit some of his abilities and Yoda trains him. Balance is maintained. Yoda dies, leaving Luke the solo Jedi faced against two Sith. Crucially, though, Luke himself seems to be in some sense 'balance': although a Jedi he dresses in a black jumpsuit and heavy grey robe reminiscent of a Sith Lord rather than the brown monkish garb of a Jedi, and his cloak even has a heavy metal chain fastener across the throat as the Emperor and Vader's do. The most obvious piece of symbolism is Luke's single artificial hand: he literally has one hand in the darkness and the other in the light.

In this interpretation the end of *Jedi* takes on a new context. By killing the Emperor and dying in the process Vader not only retrieves his status as Jedi Knight for a moment, but also ensures that there is only one Jedi left alive, his son, who genuinely appears to be a balance between the two rival kinds of knights.

This is all pure speculation.

RECURRING CONCERNS: One thing that will have to be dealt with in detail in *Episode III* is the process whereby Anakin Skywalker becomes Darth Vader. The details of this are going to be interesting insofar as they should increase the viewer's knowledge of what Lucas sees as succumbing to 'the dark side' of the force. In *The Imperial Trilogy* Yoda and Obi-Wan talk of the dark side and refer to it as 'the quick and easy path', allowing oneself to 'give in to hate'. They seem to understand the process only as the idea of using the force for selfish, rather than selfless ends. Yet Vader, who should obviously know more about the process than they do, speaks more than once of 'the power of the dark side' and even seems regretful when he talks of his own evil in *Jedi*. It may well be that the process resembles possession or is akin to becoming schizoid; that 'the dark side' is in some sense conscious and overwhelms those who seek to use it in the short term for personal reward. This is supported by the way Anakin, Palpatine and Count Dooku all have a second name for use as a Sith Lord. Is it an identifier to separate their previous self from their new one? Vader does say of the name Anakin Skywalker, 'That name no longer has any meaning for me'. Again this would make it a metaphor for, and a representation of, human corruption rather than an examination of it (not unlike the metaphorical but convincing corrupting power of the One Ring in Tolkien). Certainly in *Star Wars* Ben Kenobi reluctantly agrees when Luke asks him if the force 'controls your actions'.

RELEASE: *Star Wars: Episode III* will reach cinemas worldwide in May 2005, most likely at midnight on the Wednesday before the penultimate weekend in the month. Despite being described by its director as a story which is 'very small and personal' and too dark to really succeed as mainstream summer entertainment, it will in all likelihood break box office records.

TITLE TATTLE: The title for *Episode III* will be revealed exclusively on starwars.com in Summer 2004.

LUCAS ON EPISODE III: 'I will not do a 7, 8 and 9. This is it. This is all there is.'

Indiana Jones IV (2005)

Paramount
A Lucasfilm Limited Production
Screenplay by Frank Darabont
Story by George Lucas
Executive Producer: George Lucas
Music: John Williams
Editor: Michael Kahn
Directed by Steven Spielberg

CONFIRMED CAST: Harrison Ford (*Dr Henry 'Indiana' Jones Junior*), Kate Capshaw (*Willie Scott*)

SCREENPLAY: Rumoured on and off since shooting on *Indiana Jones and the Last Crusade* completed, *Indy IV* finally became a concrete project in 2002. After initially asking M Night Shyamalan, the writer/director of the acclaimed *The Sixth Sense* (1999), *Unbreakable* (2001) and *Signs* (2002), to write a screenplay based upon a 'haunted house' outline prepared by Lucas, the producer and director then asked Frank Darabont to handle scripting chores, working from another Lucas plotline of which little is known other than that Ford and Spielberg both approved it before Darabont began work. Darabont is the Oscar-nominated writer/director of *The Shawshank Redemption* (1994) and *The Green Mile* (2001), and has previously written several episodes of *Young Indiana Jones* with and for Lucas. His résumé, combined with his inarguable familiarity with the characters (including Indy's father, for whom he wrote with some skill in the episode 'Travels with Father', amongst others) is encouraging. 'That was a great call to get,' Darabont told cinescape.com in May 2002: 'George called and said, "Would you be interested in doing this?" . . . I said, "Yeah, George, I'm there." It's the only gig I've taken sight unseen.'

Returning director Steven Spielberg intends to shoot the movie in April and/or May 2004, and has publicly expressed his hope that Sean Connery will return to play Henry Jones Senior (see **Indiana Jones and the Last Crusade**). He has also confirmed that Kate Capshaw, the actress who played Willie Scott in *Indiana Jones and the Temple of Doom* – and now, incidentally, his wife – will be appearing. Whether this will be a cameo or as the film's leading lady has not been made clear. The film will be set in the 1950s (see the 'Young Indiana Jones and the Mystery of the Blues' section of **Young Indiana Jones**) in partial deference to Harrison Ford having aged since 1989, but Lucas and Spielberg insist that the action-packed nature of the films will remain unchanged. 'Harrison Ford can still kick the shit out of most people half his age,' replied Spielberg when it was suggested that his star might be getting too old to play an action hero. 'He's in great condition to put the hat and the leather jacket back on and crack the bullwhip a few more times.'

Something else that is certain is that Indy himself will be a father. 'Indiana will have a son,' Lucas has confirmed, but on the topic of casting he simply demurred, 'Yes, I know who. But I won't tell you yet.'

RELEASE: At the time of writing it is intended for *Indy IV* (as its creators are currently referring to it) to be released over the 4 July weekend 2005, a little under two months after *Star Wars: Episode III*, a double bill described by Steven Spielberg as 'a one two punch' for Lucasfilm.

Other Projects

Note: Any list of 'other projects' Lucas has been involved in depends, by necessity, on the criteria used to define 'involved'. It is neither possible nor desirable to list the many hundreds of video games, comics and novels based upon his characters. It is equally impossible and pointless to list every project produced by one of Lucas's subsidiary companies, such as LucasArts. They are no more worthy of discussion than the canned fruit factory Lucas once owned, or his brief interest in taking over the bankrupt Delorean car company. The list below is in chronological order and is as comprehensive as it can be with regard to film and television productions that George Lucas made a personal contribution to.

Wipeout (Paul Golding, 1965)

A montage of images depicting war and sports put together by Lucas's USC classmate Paul Golding (see **Herbie**). Lucas is credited as 'help'.

Glut (Basil Poledouris, 1966)

Lucas was sound recordist on this USC-produced mock documentary drama concerning and starring Don Glut, in reality as in fiction the school's most dissident student. Glut incidentally went on to pen the novelisation of *The Empire Strikes Back*.

Marcello, I'm Bored (John Milius, 1966)

Lucas acted as sound recordist and co-editor on fellow USC student (and later screenwriter of *Apocalypse Now*) John Milius's animated film.

Why Man Creates (Saul Bass, 1966)

A short film by Hitchcock's title designer Saul Bass, on which Lucas worked as a cameraman capturing images of cars moving at speed.

Grand Prix (John Frankenheimer, 1966)

The opening titles for this James Garner-starring picture were the responsibility of Saul Bass (see **Why Man Creates**) who allowed Lucas to assist him with second-unit shooting.

Journey to the Pacific (1967)

A documentary film about 36th US President Lyndon Johnson's tour of the Pacific Basin; Lucas co-edited it during his year teaching nights at USC. It was during this project that he met his future wife Marcia Griffin. (They later divorced.)

Gimme Shelter (Albert Maysles, David Maysles, Charlotte Zwerin, 1971)

Lucas was hired as a cameraman to shoot crowd scenes during the Rolling Stones free concert held in Northern California in December 1969 (just east of Oakland at Altamont Speedway). He is credited for cinematography on the finished film, which his USC compatriot Walter Murch also worked on in the sound department.

Urban myth repeatedly throws up the legend that Lucas's camera captured the controversial sequence in which festivalgoer Meredith Hunter is beaten to death by the Hell's Angels who had been place in charge of 'security' by festival organisers. Lucas himself has commented that he remembers little of his experiences on the film, but is confident that he would remember shooting such a horrific event.

The Godfather (Francis Ford Coppola, 1972)

Lucas shot inserts for his friend Francis Ford Coppola's Oscar-winning film; they include the shot of Al Pacino holding the newspaper that informs him that someone has attempted to assassinate his father, and other similar cutaways.

Apocalypse Now (Francis Ford Coppola, 1979)

One of American Zoetrope's initial batch of movie ideas from the late 60s, and it was certainly originally intended that Lucas would direct John Milius's Vietnam War-set screenplay based loosely on Joseph Conrad's novel *Heart of Darkness*. Coppola was then set to produce the film.

Details of the project's origin and gestation are hazy; all parties involved give markedly different accounts of both whose idea it was originally and of the sequence of events which led to it being directed by Coppola instead. Milius and Lucas disagree over the details of the shoot as originally planned. Lucas claims that it was to been shot on faked-up locations in America, using handheld 16mm film cameras, whereas Milius insists that the plan was to shoot in Vietnam itself with as much co-operation from US armed forces as possible.

Regardless of the technical details, Lucas certainly regarded the long-delayed project as his to direct whenever he wanted, and when – during the writing of *Star Wars* and shortly before the release of *American Graffiti* – he approached Coppola about making the film he was taken aback by the deal his old friend proposed for it; under its terms Coppola and Lucas would own 25% each of the resultant picture, but Lucas would have to pay Milius out of his share.

This was unacceptable to him, and it has been suggested that Coppola offered him such a deal knowing that Lucas would reject it, freeing him to direct the movie himself. Coppola was then at the very height of his power and fame, with Oscars for both *Godfather* pictures and *Patton*. The 1975 ceremony had seen him become the first writer/director in history to compete against himself for best picture and best screenplay, with both *The Conversation* and *The Godfather Part II* having been nominated for both awards. He looked to many, and perhaps considered himself, unstoppable creatively, critically and commercially. *Apocalypse Now* as he envisaged it, a vast sprawling epic filmed abroad, would be his most ambitious project yet.

Milius sided with Coppola, regarding the project as his own and by connection Francis's because of its days on the slate at Zoetrope. Lucas, as far as he was concerned, was attached as director because of his obvious talent and the fact that at that time he needed a break, but having rejected the deal he returned to the process of rewriting and prepping *Star Wars* and haggling with Universal over *American Graffiti*.

Or at least that's one account. Another has it that Lucas did some preparatory work on *Apocalypse* over this period, even coming close to a deal with Columbia for them to fund it and sending Gary Kurtz (whom he'd nominated as producer) to scout locations in the Philippines before Coppola's insistence on retaining his 25% and the urgent need to work on *Star Wars* caused Lucas to pull out. The facts remain uncertain. Coppola regarded Lucas's decision as foolish and then decided to direct the movie himself; as producer he wanted it released for the USA's bicentennial in 1976, a fitting release date for a movie that was, in a sense, about the concerns of contemporary America.

Harrison Ford's character, never identified by name in dialogue, wears a name tag which identifies him as Colonel G Lucas, an obvious nod to the project's original director. His role (it is he who sends Sheen's captain to eliminate Marlon Brando's twisted Colonel Kurtz) is perhaps an acknowledgement of Lucas's efforts in getting the project started.

Body Heat (Lawrence Kasdan, 1981)

Kasdan, the screenwriter of *Raiders of the Lost Ark*, *Empire* and *Jedi* wanted to direct as well as write features. Initially given a deal by Alan Ladd Jr when the producer was at Fox, Kasdan's mock 40s thriller idea was put into turnaround once Ladd left the studio. Taking the project again to Ladd who now headed his own company, Kasdan still found it hard to make a deal. On hearing of Kasdan's problems Lucas approached Ladd himself, and offered to executive produce the picture, without credit, if it would help with funding. Lucas was paid $250,000, which he stipulated should be used to fund overruns if the production ran into trouble. Lucas sat in on the editing of the picture, and contributed several ideas which Kasdan subsequently used.

Twice Upon a Time (John Korty, 1982)

An animated adventure on which Lucas is credited as Executive Producer – A Lucasfilm Limited Presentation.

Latino (Haskell Wexler, 1985)

A controversial anti-Reaganite pseudo-documentary about the US-backed contra guerrilla movement in Nicaragua. Again Lucas was executive producer for a distinctly non-commercial project being proposed by an old friend, and had some input into the editing. A Lucasfilm Limited Presentation.

Mishima (Paul Schrader, 1985) (aka Mishima: A Life in Four Acts)

A fictionalized account in four sections of the life and work of the Japanese writer, ideologue and suicide, starring Ken Ogata as Yukio Mishima. Three of the segments parallel events in Mishima's life with events in his own novels (*The Temple of the Golden Pavilion, Kyoko's House* and *Runaway Horses*), and the fourth depicts his death. Although very much Schrader's baby the picture was made by Lucasfilm, with Lucas executive producing and taking a keen interest in the project. He also had a hand in the preparation of the final cut.

Labyrinth (Jim Henson/Frank Oz, 1986)

Jennifer Connolly takes on David Bowie with help from Muppets in this bizarre semi-musical children's adventure. A Henson Associates and Lucasfilm Limited Presentation.

Howard the Duck (Willard Huyck, 1986) (aka Howard: A New Breed of Hero)

Created by Steve Gerber, the countercultural Marvel Comics series *Howard the Duck* ran for 31 issues, starting in January 1976. Admired at the time by Lucas and his *American Graffiti* creative partners, husband-and-wife writing team Willard Huyck and Gloria Katz, there was some consideration given by all three parties to the idea of making a film version together. The series concerned the titular hero, a Donald-like anthropomorphic duck from Duckworld, an other-dimensional version of Earth where ducks rather than monkeys had evolved as the dominant bipedal species. Howard came to the 'usual' Marvel Comics Earth (the one that, say, Spider-Man lives on) and was trapped there. The series was dominated by media parodies, hip post-modern referencing and satire and was a huge seller in its day, becoming one of the first 'hot' comic books. One of the films singled out for parody was *Star Wars* itself, given a severe kicking in #23. The Walt Disney Company, incidentally, did not take kindly to a character with obvious similarities to one of their most treasured properties being used subversively, and sued. The comic came to an end in May 1979.

The screen rights for the property were bought by Universal executive Christopher Price who, in the mid-1980s, offered to back Huyck and Katz to co-write, and direct and produce respectively, a film he hoped would be Universal's answer to Columbia's *Ghostbusters* (Harold Ramis, 1985), a production Price had supervised whilst at Columbia. One condition was that George Lucas should stand as financial guarantor – for his trouble he would receive a credit as Executive Producer, although he would have almost no direct involvement in the picture.

Although the film was largely produced in Marin County, a few miles from Skywalker Ranch, Lucas visited the set fewer than half a dozen times, leaving his old collaborators to work their project through on their own. The picture went roughly 20% over budget and failed to break even when it opened to disastrous reviews on 1 August 1986. The film's epic failure dented Lucas's image despite his lack of tangible involvement, which led to him publicly stating on more than one occasion that his level of participation in the project was 'far less than people assumed'.

The project was such a disaster that Christopher Price resigned from Universal Pictures shortly afterwards. The cast, however, largely went on to better things – Lea Thompson to the *Back to the Future* sequels and the lead role in popular sitcom *Caroline in the City*; Jeffrey Jones to a series of widely praised character roles and numerous fruitful collaborations with Tim Burton; and Tim Robbins to near canonisation via independent movie credibility. *Howard the Duck* was sufficiently damaged as a property by the event that the comic book did not return to regular publication (again written by Steve Gerber) until 2002, when, bizarrely, although the book had retained its full title Howard had ceased to be a duck. The film is a Lucasfilm Production.

Captain Eo (Francis Ford Coppola, 1986)

One of Lucas's (and indeed Coppola's) most bizarre projects ever, Captain Eo was part of a ride/theatrical experience/show that was screened exclusively at Disney-owned theme parks for several years before being replaced by *Honey I Shrunk The Audience* (Randall Kleiser, 1995). Michael Jackson stars as the eponymous captain who heads off to deliver a gift to a wicked queen (Anjelica Houston) and gets caught up in lots of special effects along the way. Written and executive produced by Lucas, the seventeen-minute film was only of minor interest *in situ*. Dated and unfunny now, it's less than a curio.

Droids

A cartoon series about *Star Wars'* R2-D2 and C-3PO having adventures (ostensibly set between *Star Wars: Episode III* and the original *Star Wars*). Anthony Daniels again voiced the golden droid. Well animated and far more sophisticated than most children's cartoons of the era, fifteen episodes were split into four multi-part stories. Some of the scripts were by Lucasfilm's Oscar-winning sound editor Ben Burtt. The series began on 7 September 1985 and concluded on 7 June 1986.

Ewoks

A more comedic cartoon about the Endor critters, which ran in parallel with *Droids* for its first season and then on its own for a second. 32 episodes were produced, one of which bore the in-joke title 'Blue Harvest'.

Tucker: The Man and His Dream (Francis Ford Coppola, 1988)

A biopic of Preston Tucker, a wannabe car manufacturer who designed a car now judged to have been 'ahead of its time' in terms of its safety features, but whose ambitions were thwarted by the organs of big business. Filming Tucker's life had long been an ambition of Coppola's, and Lucas – who was also fascinated by the peculiarly American maverick – encouraged Coppola to pursue it as a project (both men owned more than one of the fifty or so Tucker cars actually built).

Lucas put up the $24 million budget himself, and executive produced it, having input into the screenplay, costing and casting. Beautifully shot in Marin County, the picture contains a dynamic central performance from Jeff Bridges and an astounding, Oscar-nominated one from Martin Landau. One of the most emotionally satisfying projects of Lucas's career, it's also one of the most frequently forgotten. A Lucasfilm Ltd/Zoetrope Studios Production.

Postscript

Defining Star Wars

Discussions of George Lucas's work always return to the *Star Wars* project. It's inevitable. It remains the dominant part of his career, the vessel into which he's poured the bulk of his creative endeavours, both personal and technical. He's also spent a lifetime making it. He's called it 'my destiny' and his 'narrative symphony', a summary that reflects not only its dominance in his life and absorption of his creativity, but which also suggests his strangely musical approach to dramatic structure. This approach is one in which motifs such as lines of dialogue or images are picked up and reprised, repeated with different emphases to reflect upon thematic content: a process identified by critic Thomas Snyder as one of 'duplication and inversion' that he saw as in tune with anthropologist Arnold van Gennep's seminal *Rites of Passage* (1909).

What the original *Star Wars* does is combine Campbellian archetypes and extensive semiotic referencing with an unusual cinematic technique, Lucas's self-described 'documentary fantasy' approach. It places the kind of people who are easy to understand in a setting that's unreal yet compelling, then pushes simple, spiritually aware yet ultimately secular values forward via those characters: values as basic yet often overlooked as 'the importance of living a compassionate life, as opposed to a selfish one', as Lucas himself once put it, or 'the concepts of valour, dedication and honour', as *Variety* – the industry bible that usually assesses films based entirely on their commercial potential – felt moved to say shortly after the release of *Star Wars*.

It does so, moreover, in a sprawling, engrossing yet easily accessible plot, and in a form that is both mass-market and easily comprehensible, with jokes and monsters and explosions, and some of the most exciting set-pieces ever committed to celluloid.

Its sequels and prequels do much the same, adding Snyder's inversions and duplications, ironies and shadings, whilst maintaining that accessibility and a probably unmatched ability to inspire loyalty and enthusiasm in audiences.

In film historian Peter Biskind's view Lucas's achievement was to 'strip away the Marxist ideology of a master of editing like Eisenstein . . . or the critical irony of an *avant garde* filmmaker like Bruce Connor', and put their techniques solely to the service of the story. What Lucas then discovered – perhaps what he already knew – was that the story had an intrinsic value in and of itself.

During and after the film's initial release Lucas would only talk of it in terms of it being 'a fairy tale' and 'fun'; it was only in later years that he felt able to go into detail about what he felt fairy tales meant to western culture: 'someone has to tell young people what we think is a good person. "This is what a good person is; this is who we aspire to be." You need that in a society. It's the basic job of mythology'.

Whether Lucas set out to create a modern myth or whether it suddenly occurred to him that he was creating one is difficult to define. And if the latter, whether he realised it during the writing or the shooting or the rapturous public and critical reception it initially received is equally uncertain. What is certain is that he hit a nerve, and that he fulfilled Campbell's 1961 prediction in 'The Impact of Science on Myth' that the next story to enrapture a large portion of western culture would conform to his notions of mythic archetypes and take place on the one unknown frontier left to humanity's storytellers – outer space.

Star Wars' impact, not simply on its medium but also on the world outside it, is undeniable. The hysteria that greeted the opening of the first prequel movie has simply no equal in contemporary pop culture. Even the sheer ferocity of the attacks on *The Phantom Menace* by both critics and those who loved the original trilogy as children is an acknowledgment of a simple fact: *Star Wars* is huge; *Star Wars* is the most significant fiction of the childhoods of *millions*.

Whether the *Star Wars* series is its medium's first self-generated myth is not for the generations who witnessed its creation to decide. Whatever Lucas's most ardent fans wish, it is by no means yet the time to label it one of western culture's mythologies; to argue – as some already have – that it will acquire 'the cultural weight of an *Iliad* or *Odyssey*'. Lucas may very well turn out to be more Charlie Chaplin than Homer. Chaplin was fiercely creative, iconic in his time, loved and reviled in equal measure in his own age, yet a filmmaker whose appeal less than a quarter of a century after his death is incomprehensible to all but those with a interest in the technical side of motion picture production.

Star Wars has certainly been part of the daily common currency of pop culture for decades and there are no signs that this is about to end. It has gone beyond being simply a series of films – simply a pop-cultural artefact.

However it absolutely isn't a religion; Lucas has been both adamant and careful about that, even demystifying and redefining the force and the Jedi within the fiction itself in order to separate himself from those who see it that way. He curtly dismissed friend and former mentor Francis Ford Coppola's half-serious suggestion that he found a Jedi church ('forget it' was his response to the idea) in the manner of science fiction novelist Lafayette Ron Hubbard's Church of Scientology, and refused to make the force his own dianetics. He also publicly explained why he felt it would be wrong for him to do so. He's a filmmaker, or more simply a storyteller, not an ideologue, and one without 'any interest in power'.

What *Star Wars* truly is is not yet definable but it is, to borrow a phrase from one of Lucas's cast, 'more than just movies' now. For the time being at least, that, surely, is achievement enough?

Index of Quotations

In the interests of simplicity reviews are simply endnoted with the title of the periodical and the date of publication. Interviews with a single person are again simply identified as such. Long articles, joint interviews and news pieces that include quotations used are referenced in full with writer credits.

American Graffiti
30 'a uniquely . . .' Lucas quoted in 'The Making of American Graffiti' DVD
31 'the loss of . . .' Lucas quoted in 'The Making of American Graffiti' DVD
33 'enormous talent' Roos quoted in 'The Making of American Graffiti' DVD
33 'readings . . .' Dreyfuss quoted in The Making of American Graffiti DVD
40 'The car is . . .' Dublicay, Carl, 'George Lucas', *Film Reader*, no 1, Autumn 1975
43 'Get down . . .' Coppola quoted in 'The Making of American Graffiti' DVD
45 'monotonous . . .' *Modesto Bee*, 13 September 1973
45 'a most vivid . . .' *Variety*, 20 June 1973
45 'full of . . .' *New York Times*, 13 August 1973
45 'the funniest . . .' *New York Times*, 16 September 1973
45 'toughness . . .' *New York Times*, 6 January 1974
46 'Where were . . .' *New Statesman*, 5 April 1974
47 'endearing . . .' *Daily Telegraph*, 19 March 1974
47 'convincing . . .' *Spectator*, 6 April 1974
48 'George let us . . .' Charlie Martin Smith quoted in Stuart, Alexander, 'Sixties Slapstick', *Films and Filming*, vol 26, no 1, October 1979
48 'It all happened . . .' Lucas quoted in the *American Graffiti* Production Notes, 1978 re-release
48 'The film is . . .'Lucas quoted in Sturhahn, Larry, 'The Filming of American Graffiti', *Filmmaker's Newsletter*, vol 7, no 5, March 1974

Star Wars
52 'a good idea . . .' Lucas quoted in *American Cinematographer*, July 1977
53 'The book . . .' Lucas speaking at the National Arts Club, Campbell lecture, June 1985
53 'cohesive reality' Lucas quoted in *American Cinematographer*, July 1977
54 'I'm interested . . .' Lucas quoted on the *Star Wars* VHS, 1995
57 'I'm not . . .' Lucas quoted in *Filmmaker's Newsletter*, March 1974
62 'I just . . .' James Earl Jones quoted in *Starburst* Special, October 1994
63 'He was . . .' Anthony Daniels quoted in *Starburst* Special #53, August 2002
70 'wasn't satisfied . . .' Lucas quoted on the *Star Wars* Special Edition VHS, 1997
71 'At that point . . .' Lucas quoted in *Starburst* #223, March 1997
72 'One is . . .' Lucas quoted in *Starburst* #223, March 1997
72 'In terms . . .' Lucas quoted in *Starburst* #223, March 1997
80 'a witty critique . . .' *New York Times*, 26 May 1977
80 'a film . . .' *New York Times*, 7 June 1977
80 'a magnificent film . . .' *Variety*, 25 May 1977
81 'a wow of . . .' *Box Office* magazine, 6 June 1977
81 'delightful . . .' *Washington Post*, 27 May 1977
82 'How much . . .' Lucas quoted in Crawley, Tony, 'Lucas Talks!', *Starburst* #125, January 1989
83 'a subliminal . . .' *Time*, June 1977
83 'a knowing . . .' *New York Times*, 20 June 1981

86   'It's got . . .' Hamill quoted in *Starburst* Classic Sci-Fi Special #21, October 1994
86   'life sends . . .' Lucas quoted in *Mail on Sunday*, 28 April 2002

More American Graffiti
89   'took risks . . .' Lucas quoted in Stuart, Alexander, 'Sixties Slapstick', *Films and Filming*, vol 26, no 1, October 1979
90   'Editing . . .' Norton quoted in Stuart, Alexander, 'Sixties Slapstick', *Films and Filming*, vol 26, no 1, October 1979
91   'white-bread . . .' Norton quoted in Stuart, Alexander, 'Sixties Slapstick', *Films and Filming*, vol 26, no 1, October 1979
93   'daring but . . .' *Variety*, 25 June 1979
93   'trivialisation . . .' *New York Times*, 17 August 1979
93   'all the coherence . . .' *Empire*, no 132, June 2000
96   'The idea . . .' Norton quoted in Stuart, Alexander, 'Sixties Slapstick', *Films and Filming*, vol 26, no 1, October 1979
96   'I did . . .' Lucas quoted on the *Star Wars: Episode I – The Phantom Menace* DVD

Star Wars: Episode V – The Empire Strikes Back
100   'I get . . .' Kasdan quoted in *Film Comment*, vol 17, no 5, September–October 1985
102   'I don't know . . .' Kasdan quoted in *Creative Screenwriting* #42, Nov–Dec 1998
103   'the perfect . . .' Kershner quoted in *Starburst* Classic Sci-Fi Special #21, October 1994
105   'When I . . .' Lucas quoted on *The Empire Strikes Back* VHS, 1995
105   'Don't be . . .' Kershner quoted in *Starburst* Classic Sci-Fi Special #21, October 1994
107   'consider it . . .' Kershner quoted in *Starburst* Classic Sci-Fi Special #21, October 1994
114   'Grainier . . .' *New York Times*, 21 May 1980
115   'I like . . .' Carrie Fisher quoted in *Starburst* #66, February 1984
115   'It's the second . . .' Kershner quoted in *Starburst* Classic Sci-Fi Special #21, October 1994
115   'It's the middle . . .' Lucas quoted on *The Empire Strikes Back* VHS, 1995

Raiders of the Lost Ark
118   'serial . . .' Lucas quoted on the *Indiana Jones and the Raiders of the Lost Ark* VHS, 2000
119   '*Raiders*, you can . . .' Kasdan quoted in *Film Comment*, vol 17, no 5, September–October 1981
119   'I wanted . . .' Lucas quoted on the *Indiana Jones and the Raiders of the Lost Ark* VHS, 2000
119   'the fact . . .' Ford quoted on the *Indiana Jones and the Raiders of the Lost Ark* VHS, 2000
120   'I try . . .' Ford quoted on the *Indiana Jones and the Raiders of the Lost Ark* VHS, 2000

149   'Yes. [It's] . . .' *Starburst* #74, September 1984
149   'sore bum . . .' *Guardian*, May 1984
150   'Old-time . . .' *New York Times*, 23 May 1984

The Ewok Adventure
155   'Burl Ives . . .' 'The Ewok Adventure', *Starlog* #89, December 1984
155   'Worst George . . .' 'It's Only A Movie!' *Starburst* #79, March 1985
155   'Passable . . .' *Films and Filming*, no 364, January 1985
156   'Hansel . . .' *Cinefantastique*, vol 15, no 2, May 1985
156   'enchanting' *Hollywood Reporter*, 21 November 1984
156   'an evergreen . . .' *Variety*, 4 December 1985
156   'George said . . .' John Korty quoted in *Cinefantastique*, vol 15, no 2, May
       1985
157   'Warwick . . .' Thomas G Smith quoted in the contemporary *The Ewok
       Adventure* press kit.
157   'There are lots . . .' Lucas quoted in *Rolling Stone*, 24 July–4 August 1984

Ewoks – The Battle for Endor
159   'more intense . . .' *Hollywood Reporter*, 22 November 1985
160   'a worthy . . .' *Variety*, 4 December 1985
162   'You wear . . .' Davis quoted in *Starlog* #101, December 1985

Willow
164   'I remember . . .' George Lucas quoted in Crawley, Tony, 'Lucas Talks!',
       Starburst #125, January 1989
164   'The three . . .' Ron Howard quoted in the *Willow* Production Notes
167   'I think . . .' Warwick Davis quoted on the *Willow* DVD
167   'very, very . . .' Warwick Davis quoted on the *Willow* DVD
168   'They grow . . .' Ron Howard quoted in Crawley, Tony, 'Lucas Talks!',
       Starburst #125, January 1989
168   'The actual . . .' Ron Howard quoted in Crawley, Tony, 'Lucas Talks!',
       Starburst #125, January 1989
168   'I'm not . . .' George Lucas quoted in Crawley, Tony, 'Lucas Talks!',
       Starburst #126, February 1989
168   'an unbelievable . . .' Ron Howard quoted in *Willow: The Making of an
       Adventure* TV documentary
168   'very respectful . . .' Ron Howard quoted in *Willow: The Making of an
       Adventure* TV documentary
168   'Lucas was . . .' Warwick Davis quoted on the *Willow* DVD
168   'George Lucas . . .' Val Kilmer quoted in the *Willow* Production Notes
169   'Sometimes I . . .' Ron Howard quoted in *Willow: The Making of an
       Adventure* TV documentary
169   'really, really . . .' Warwick Davis quoted on the *Willow* DVD
171   'I happen . . .' George Lucas quoted in Crawley, Tony, 'Lucas Talks!',
       Starburst #125, January 1989
172   'first time . . .' Dennis Muren quoted in 'From MORF to Morphing' on the
       Willow DVD

227 'You have . . .' McGregor quoted in *Starburst* #253, September 1999
227 'I wanted to . . .' McGregor quoted in *Sunday Times Magazine*, 16 May 1999
228 'becoming him . . .' McGregor quoted in *Starburst* #253, September 1999
228 'sometimes . . .' *Film Review* #584, August 1999
230 'a wonderful ease . . .' Neeson quoted in *Starburst* #253, September 1999
231 'Scotch tape . . .' Hamill quoted on *Star Wars* Special Edition VHS, 1997
234 'seamlessly . . .' *Chicago Sun-Times*, 18 May 1999
238 'a happy surprise . . .' *New York Times*, 17 May 1999
239 'be hailed . . .' *Chicago Sun-Times*, 18 May 1999
242 'George knows . . .' Neeson quoted in *Starburst* #253, September 1999
242 'There were . . .' McGregor quoted in *Starburst* #253, September 1999
242 'I made this . . .' Lucas quoted in *Starburst* #252, August 1999

Star Wars: Episode II – Attack of the Clones
248 'a wonderful . . .' Daniels quoted in *Starburst* Special #53, August 2002
248 'it's like . . .' Christiansen quoted in *The A–Z of* Star Wars: Episode II – Attack of the Clones, ITV1, 25 May 2002
248 'get out there . . .' Jackson quoted in *The A–Z of* Star Wars: Episode II – Attack of the Clones, ITV1, 25 May 2002
249 'my own ship . . .' McGregor quoted in *The A–Z of* Star Wars: Episode II – Attack of the Clones, ITV1, 25 May 2002
250 'a chase . . .' Lucas quoted on starwars.com
261 '[Threepio] . . .' Daniels quoted in *Starburst* Special #53, August 2002
261 'The story . . .' Christiansen quoted in the *Mail on Sunday*, 28 April 2002
261 'I think a . . .' Portman quoted in *Esquire*, vol 12, no 6, June 2002
261 'It's what . . .' Lucas quoted in *The A–Z of* Star Wars: Episode II – Attack of the Clones, ITV1, 25 May 2002

Star Wars Episode III
264 'very small . . .' Lucas quoted in *DreamWatch*, August 2002
265 'I will not . . .' Lucas quoted in *Starburst* #252, August 1999

Indiana Jones IV
265 'That was . . .' Darabont quoted on Cinescape.com
266 'Harrison Ford . . .' Spielberg quoted in *Cinescape* #62, July 2002
266 'Indiana will . . .' Lucas quoted in *DreamWatch*, August 2002
266 'one two . . .' Spielberg quoted in *Cinescape* #62, July 2002

Postscript
275 'duplication and . . .' from 'The *Star Wars* Saga' in *Films*, 4th edition, 2000
275 'the importance . . .' Lucas quoted in Crawley, Tony, 'Lucas Talks!', *Starburst* #126, February 1989
275 'the concepts of . . .' *Variety*, 25 May 1977
275 'strip away . . .' from Biskind, Peter, *Easy Riders, Raging Bulls*, Bloomsbury, London, 1998
276 'This is what . . .' from Crawley, Tony, 'Lucas Talks!', *Starburst* #125, January 1989

277 'forget it' Lucas in Massa, Maria, 'Hyperspace Cadet', *Big Issue*, 24–30 May 1999

277 'more than just . . .' Ewan McGregor quoted in *Starburst* #253, September 1999

Select Bibliography

Books
Arnold, Alan, *Once Upon a Galaxy: A Journal of the Making of The Empire Strikes Back*, Ballantine Books, New York, 1980
Baxter, John, *George Lucas – A Biography*, HarperCollins, London, 1999
Biskind, Peter, *Easy Riders, Raging Bulls*, Bloomsbury, London, 1998
Caesar, *The Gallic Wars*
Freer, Ian, *The Complete Spielberg*, Virgin Publishing, London, 2001
Guinness, Alec, *My Name Escapes Me*, Hamish Hamilton, London, 1996
Guinness, Alec, *A Positively Final Appearance*, Hamish Hamilton, London, 2000
Kasdan, Lawrence and Lucas, George, *Star Wars: Episode VI – Return of the Jedi* (screenplay), Faber & Faber, London, 1996
Lucas, George, *Star Wars: Episode IV – A New Hope* (screenplay), Faber & Faber, London, 1996
Lucas, George (and Foster, Alan Dean), *Star Wars* (novelisation), Comet, 1977
Pollock, Dale, *Skywalking: The Life and Films of George Lucas*, Da Capo Press, New York, 1999
Sangster, Jim and Condon, Paul, *The Complete Hitchcock*, Virgin Publishing, London, 1999
Sarris, Andrew, *You Ain't Heard Nothing Yet*, Oxford University Press, Oxford, 1998
Smith, Thomas G, *Industrial Light & Magic: The Art of Special Effects*, Ballantine Books, New York, 1986
Walker, John (ed), *Halliwell's Film & Video Guide*, HarperCollins, London, 2000
Walker, John (ed), *Halliwell's Who's Who in the Movies*, HarperCollins, London, 2000

Articles (see also endnotes)
Lancashire, Anne, 'Complex Design in *The Empire Strikes Back*', *Film Criticism*, Spring, 1981
Rosenbaum, Jonathan, 'The Solitary Pleasures of *Star Wars*', *Sight and Sound*, Autumn, 1977
Roth, L, 'Bergsonian Comedy and the Human Machine in *Star Wars*', *Film Criticism*, Winter, 1979
Wood, Denis, 'The Stars in Our Hearts – A critical commentary on George Lucas's *Star Wars*', *Journal of Popular Film*, no 3, 1978
Zito, S, 'George Lucas Goes Far Out', *American Film*, April 1977

Acknowledgment is also given to the following online resources:
www.imdb.com, www.starwars.com, www.thenumbers.com, www.lucasfan.com, www.shinyshelf.com as well as the LucasArts CD Rom '*Star Wars* Behind the Myth' (1997) and the DVD and VHS editions of all of the films given chapters within the main text of the book.

Index